Pope John Paul II

A Reader

EDITED BY
Gerald O'Collins, SJ,
Daniel Kendall, SJ, and
Jeffrey LaBelle, SJ

PAULIST PRESS
New York/Mahwah, NJ

The text of the papal documents © *Libreria Editrice Vaticana.* Used with permission.

Cover design by Cynthia Dunne
Book design by Lynn Else

Library of Congress Cataloging-in-Publication Data

John Paul II, Pope, 1920–2005.
 [Selections. English. 2007]
 Pope John Paul II : a reader / edited by Gerald O'Collins, Daniel Kendall, and Jeffrey LaBelle.
  p. cm.
 Includes bibliographical references and index.
 ISBN 978-0-8091-4479-2 (alk. paper)
 1. Catholic Church—Doctrines. I. O'Collins, Gerald. II. Kendall, Daniel. III. LaBelle, Jeffrey. IV. Title.
 BX1751.3.J642 2007
 230'.2—dc22

2007006267

Published by Paulist Press
997 Macarthur Boulevard
Mahwah, New Jersey 07430

www.paulistpress.com

Printed and bound in the
United States of America

Contents

To John Paul II (pope 1978–2005)
with admiration and gratitude

Abbreviations

AAS   *Acta Apostolicae Sedis,* Rome, 1909– .

ApExMiller   J. Michael Miller (ed.), *The Post-Synodal Apostolic Exhortations of John Paul II* (Huntington, IN: Our Sunday Visitor, 1998).

EB   *Enchiridion Biblicum* (Bologna: Dehoniane, 1991).

EncMiller   J. Michael Miller (ed.), *The Encyclicals of John Paul II* (Huntington, IN: Our Sunday Visitor, 2001).

ND   J. Neuner and J. Dupuis (eds.), *The Christian Faith,* 7th ed. (New York: Alba House, 2001).

OR   *L'Osservatore Romano,* Rome, 1861– .

OREnglish   *L'Osservatore Romano,* English Edition, Rome, 1968– .

Origins   *Origins* (Washington, DC: Catholic News Service, 1971–).

Pope Speaks   *The Pope Speaks* (Huntington, IN: Our Sunday Visitor, 1954–2005).

Introduction

In a papacy that lasted for over twenty-six years (1978–2005), Pope John Paul II has left behind an enormous legacy. It includes well over seventy thousand pages of teaching, found in encyclicals, apostolic exhortations and letters, homilies, addresses, letters, and other published texts. His teaching took up a very wide range of themes—from the self-revelation of God, through the sacramental life of the church, relations with other Christians and the followers of other religions, to questions of social and sexual morality, and on to basic elements in the Christian spiritual life.

We want to ensure that the highlights of this teaching, especially its fresh developments, remain available to a wide audience. To make things more accessible, we have arranged what John Paul II wrote and said according to themes: from the divine self-revelation to the Christian spiritual life. Within each of our twelve chapters (or, in some cases, sections of chapters) we follow, where possible and appropriate, the chronological order in which the documents on which we draw were published.

This reader cites only the official teaching of John Paul II. Hence it does not include any extracts from his poetry and such personal writings as *Crossing the Threshold of Hope* (New York: Knopf, 1994) and *Gift and Mystery* (New York: Doubleday, 1996). Nor do we draw from any documents published during his papacy by offices of the Roman Curia such as *An Instruction on the Study of the Fathers* (published in 1989 by the Congregation for Catholic Education), *Dialogue and Proclamation* (published in 1991 by the Pontifical Council for Interreligious Dialogue and the Congregation for the Evangelization of Peoples), and the *Directory for the Application of Principles and*

Norms on Ecumenism (published in 1993 by the Pontifical Council for Promoting Christian Unity).

During his papacy, John Paul II promulgated two codes of canon law, the *Code of Canon Law* in 1983 and the *Code of Canons of the Eastern Churches* in 1990. In earlier centuries, general councils of the church, right from the First Council of Nicaea in 325, had often adopted various "canons" or rulings about Christian practice and ecclesial order. But the 1990 code was the first complete book ever published for Eastern Catholic Churches, and the 1983 code brought up to date, especially in the light of the Second Vatican Council, the first complete book of canon law for the entire Western Church that was published in 1917. John Paul II also promulgated (in 1992) the *Catechism of the Catholic Church* as an official summary and expansion of the teaching coming from Vatican II. The Council of Trent (1545–64) was the only other general council to be followed by a catechism. But this reader does not include any passages from either the *Catechism* of 1992 or the two codes of canon law. We already had an enormous amount of material to draw upon, even when we limited ourselves to the official teaching coming from John Paul himself during a papacy of more than a quarter of a century.

The texts we cite from John Paul II's teaching on Christian and Catholic "faith and morals" obviously have different levels of authority and command different kinds of assent from faithful Catholics.[1] One should ask: (1) *What* was he speaking or writing about? Matters that clearly belong to the foundational revelation communicated through Jesus Christ and the coming of the Holy Spirit? Or matters necessarily connected with that revelation? Or matters that concern Christian life and to which Christian principles should be applied? (2) *What degree of authority* was he invoking? His local authority as bishop of Rome or his universal authority as pope of the Catholic Church? (3) This second question is closely connected with two more questions: *To whom* was he speaking and *in what context* was he writing? Was he speaking, for instance, to a group of bishops from one country? Or was he speaking to a synod representing the bishops and local churches of the whole world?

From a formal point of view, we can to some extent gauge the authority of a particular teaching from the status of the document in which we find it. Thus the fourteen encyclical letters that John Paul

Introduction

II published from 1979, *Redemptor hominis* (The Redeemer of the Human Person), to 2003, *Ecclesia de Eucharistia* (The Church from the Eucharist), enjoy as such a higher level of authority than the numerous addresses he made every Wednesday to the general audiences of pilgrims (estimated at 17,600,000 persons), to other visitors in Rome, to the communities of over 300 Roman parishes, to other groups of Italians, or during the 104 journeys he made outside Italy. Nevertheless, some of these "occasional" addresses and homilies contain gems that deserve retrieval. In making our choices we have been guided above all by the question: What texts illuminate and nourish most vividly belief and behavior for the lives of Catholics and other Christians—and sometimes, indeed, for the lives of followers of other religions? Our joint attempt to answer that question has guided the choices we have made from the legacy of John Paul II's teaching.

We indicate where to find the full texts of the documents from which we draw. Whenever possible, we also indicate where the extracts that we print from these documents are to be found in the seventh edition (2001) of J. Neuner and J. Dupuis (eds.), *The Christian Faith*. That volume, by arranging in thematic sections the teaching coming from councils, popes, and other sources, sets the teaching of John Paul II within the broad context of official teaching.

In working with this reader, we have been much encouraged by some remarks made by Pope Benedict XVI for a program on Polish national television that was aired on October 16, 2005, the anniversary of the election of John Paul II in 1978: "I consider it my essential and personal mission not so much to produce many new documents, but to see to it that [John Paul's] documents are assimilated, because they are a very rich treasure, the authentic interpretation of Vatican II." We too have found in those documents a very rich treasure. If our joint work helps toward their assimilation, we will be thoroughly satisfied.

With deep gratitude, we wish to thank a number of people who read at least part of the manuscript, offered valuable suggestions, or in other ways gave us real help in our joint work: Chris Bellitto, Jim Bretzke, Lois Lorentzen, and Tom Massaro. With gratitude and admiration, we dedicate this book to the memory of Pope John Paul II.

Gerald O'Collins, SJ, Daniel Kendall, SJ,
and Jeffrey LaBelle, SJ, July 31, 2006

NOTE

1. For a full account of the authority vested in various categories of official teaching, see F. A. Sullivan, *Creative Fidelity: Weighing and Interpreting Documents of the Magisterium* (New York: Paulist Press, 1996).

CHAPTER ONE

Revelation, Faith, Tradition, and Scripture

1.1 Divine revelation aims at arousing or strengthening the faith of human beings. The Second Vatican Council's Constitution on Divine Revelation, *Dei Verbum* (The Word of God), understood revelation to be *primarily* the *self*-revelation of God, to which human beings respond not merely with an intellectual assent but with the commitment of their whole person (no. 5). In the history of revelation/salvation, this divine self-communication reached its fullness in the incarnation, life, death, and resurrection of Jesus Christ, followed by the outpouring of the Holy Spirit (no. 4).

Through personally encountering the Son of God and receiving the Spirit, the first Christians came to know more truth (for example, that God is tripersonal). These revealed truths make up the "deposit of faith" or "treasure of revelation" (nos. 10, 26), transmitted through tradition and the inspired scriptures. But revelation remains primarily an encounter with the "Mystery" or deep truth of God manifested in the person of Jesus Christ.

The dense opening chapter of *Dei Verbum* uses the terms *revelation* and *salvation* more or less interchangeably. The *economy* or *history of revelation* is inseparably the history of salvation and vice versa. The text of the constitution shuttles back and forth between the two terms (for example, no. 2).

Dei Verbum speaks of the divine self-disclosure not only in the past tense, as something already completed with the story of Christ and the gift of the Spirit (no. 4), but also in the present and future tenses. Revelation is a dynamic present event that invites

1

human faith: "The obedience of faith...must be given to God as he reveals himself" (no. 5). The constitution associates revelation as it happened then and as it happens now in the church: "God, who spoke in the past, continues to converse with the spouse of his beloved Son" (no. 8). But there is also a "not yet" of revelation, which the New Testament highlights. Drawing on 1 Timothy 6:14 and Titus 2:13, *Dei Verbum* points to what is still to come at the end of all history: the definitive "glorious manifestation of our Lord, Jesus Christ" (no. 4).

John Paul II likewise understood revelation to be, in the first place, the *self*-revelation of God through the whole Christ-event, which comprises everything from his incarnation to the resurrection and the gift of the Holy Spirit. He followed the lead of Vatican II by respecting the precedence of the revealed Mystery or Truth (in upper case and in the singular) over the particular revealed mysteries or truths (in lower case and in the plural). Thus his first encyclical, *Redemptor hominis* (The Redeemer of the Human Person) of 1979, spoke sixty-five times of the "Mystery of Redemption," the "Paschal Mystery," and so forth, never of the (revealed) "mysteries," and only once of "the truths [plural] revealed by God" (no. 6).

Right from that first encyclical, John Paul II also indicated that the divine revelation and the "Mystery of Redemption" are inseparable (for instance, no. 9). By a clear margin, his favorite biblical source was John's Gospel, which he quotes or to which he refers forty-eight times. (Paul's Letter to the Romans comes in second, with twenty-four references or quotations.) John Paul II appreciated how, in John's Gospel, Christ is inseparably the Light of the world (revelation) and the Life of the world (redemption). John Paul II also presented the divine self-revelation (and redemptive activity) not only as completed in the past but also as a dynamic present reality and as something to be definitively consummated in the future. *Redemptor hominis* also shows how ready John Paul II was to recognize the human *experience* of the divine self-revelation. Here he went beyond *Dei Verbum,* which introduced the language of "experience" only twice (nos. 8, 14) and still reflected a certain unease about "experience." John Paul II rightly had no problems with such language: In *Redemptor hominis* he used the noun *experience* four times and the verb *experience* twice. In *Dives in misericordia* (Rich in Mercy), he used *experience* as a noun twelve times and as a verb five times. If the divine self-revelation does not enter our experience (to arouse or strengthen our faith), it simply does not happen as far as we are concerned. Non-experienced revelation makes no sense.

Of all the texts that John Paul II left us on revelation, easily the fullest is his second encyclical, *Dives in misericordia* of 1980, which took as its theme "the revelation of the mystery of the Father and his love" (no. 1). The language of the entire document repeatedly recalls the central theme. Over eighty times it uses the verb *reveal* or the noun *revelation*. Other revelational terms like *manifest, make known,* and *proclaim* turn up constantly. If *Redemptor hominis* focuses on the human condition, *Dives in misericordia* highlights the revelation of the divine mercy that "responds" to our primordial needs. No other document published by John Paul II has more to say on the theme of revelation, the living Word of God who spoke to us in the past (Heb 1:2) and who continues to address us in the present.

Revelation reaches its goal when it arouses the human response of faith. In his 1979 apostolic exhortation, *Catechesi tradendae* (Handing on Catechesis), John Paul II presented faith as based on God's word and engaged in a journey toward "things not yet in our possession."

The Revelation of Love

The Cross on Calvary, through which Jesus Christ—a Man, the Son of the Virgin Mary, thought to be the son of Joseph of Nazareth—"leaves" this world, is also a fresh manifestation of the eternal fatherhood of God, who in him draws near again to humanity, to each human being, giving him the thrice holy "Spirit of truth" (cf. John 16:13).

This revelation of the Father and outpouring of the Holy Spirit, which stamp an indelible seal on the mystery of the Redemption, explain the meaning of the Cross and death of Christ. The God of creation is revealed as the God of redemption, as the God who is "faithful to himself" (cf. 1 Thess 5:24) and faithful to his love for human beings and the world, which he revealed on the day of creation. His is a love that does not draw back before anything that justice requires in him. Therefore "for our sake (God) made him (the Son) to be sin who knew no sin" (2 Cor 5:21; cf. Gal 3:13). If he "made to be sin" him who was without any sin whatever, it was to reveal the love that is always greater than the whole of creation, the love that is he himself, since "God is love" (1 John 4:8, 16). Above all, love is greater than sin, than weakness, than the "futility of creation" (cf. Rom 8:20), it is stronger than death; it is a love always ready to raise up and forgive, always ready to go to meet the prodigal son (cf. Luke 15:11–32), always looking for "the revealing of the sons of God" (Rom 8:19), who are called to the glory "that is to be revealed" (cf. Rom 8:18). This revelation of love is also described as mercy; and in human history this revelation of love and mercy (cf. St. Thomas, *Summa Theol.*, III, q. 46, a. 1, ad 3) has taken a form and a name: that of Jesus Christ.[1]

Christ Revealed Continually

The opening made by the Second Vatican Council has enabled the Church and all Christians to reach a more complete awareness of the mystery of Christ, "the mystery hidden for ages" (Col 1:26) in God, to be revealed in time in the man Jesus Christ, and to be revealed continually in every time. In Christ and through Christ, God has revealed himself fully to humankind and has definitively drawn close to it; at the same time, in Christ and through Christ human beings have acquired full awareness of their dignity, of the heights to which they are raised, of the surpassing worth of their own humanity, and of the meaning of their existence....

We can and must immediately reach and display to the world our unity in proclaiming the mystery of Christ, in revealing the divine dimension and also the human dimension of the Redemption, and in struggling with unwearying perseverance for the dignity that each human being has reached and can continually reach in Christ, namely the dignity of both the grace of divine adoption and the inner truth of humanity, a truth which—if in the common awareness of the modern world it has been given such fundamental importance—for us is still clearer in the light of the reality that is Jesus Christ.[2]

Revelation, Past and Present

Authentic catechesis is always an orderly and systematic initiation into the revelation that God has given of himself to humanity in Christ Jesus, a revelation stored in the depths of the Church's memory and in Sacred Scripture, and constantly communicated from one generation to the next by a living, active *traditio*....

In our pastoral care we ask ourselves: How are we to reveal Jesus Christ, God made man, to this multitude of children and young people, reveal him not just in the fascination of a first fleeting encounter but through an acquaintance, growing deeper and clearer daily, with him, his message, the plan of God that he has revealed, the call he addresses to each person, and the kingdom that he wishes to establish in this world.[3]

The Journey of Faith

A more subtle challenge occasionally comes from the very way of conceiving faith. Certain contemporary philosophical schools, which seem to be exercising a strong influence on some theological currents and, through them, on pastoral practice, like to emphasize that the fundamental human attitude is that of seeking the infinite, a seeking that never attains its object. In theology, this view of things will state very categorically that faith is not certainty but questioning, not clarity but a leap in the dark.

These currents of thought certainly have the advantage of reminding us that faith concerns things not yet in our possession, since they are hoped for; that as yet we see only "in a mirror dimly" (1 Cor 13:12); and that God dwells always in inaccessible light (cf. 1 Tim 6:16). They help us to make the Christian faith not the attitude of one who has already arrived, but a journey forward as with

Abraham. For all the more reason one must avoid presenting as certain things which are not.

However, we must not fall into the opposite extreme, as too often happens. The Letter to the Hebrews says that "faith is the assurance of things hoped for, the conviction of things not seen" (Heb 11:1). Although we are not in full possession, we do have an assurance and a conviction. When educating children, adolescents and young people, let us not give them too negative an idea of faith—as if it were absolute non-knowing, a kind of blindness, a world of darkness—but let us show them that the humble yet courageous seeking of the believer, far from having its starting point in nothingness, in plain self-deception, in fallible opinions or in uncertainty, is based on the Word of God who cannot deceive or be deceived, and is unceasingly built on the immovable rock of this Word.[4]

The Past and Present Revelation of the Divine Mercy

It is "God, who is rich in mercy" (Eph 2:4) whom Jesus Christ has revealed to us as Father: it is his very Son who, in himself, has manifested him and made him known to us.... I devoted the encyclical *Redemptor hominis* to the truth about human beings, a truth that is revealed to us in its fullness and depth in Christ. A no less important need in these critical and difficult times impels me to draw attention once again in Christ to the countenance of the "Father of mercies and God of all comfort." We read in the Constitution *Gaudium et spes*: "Christ the new Adam...fully reveals human beings to themselves and brings to light his lofty calling," and does it "in the very revelation of the mystery of the Father and of his love" (no. 22).[5]

What else, then, does the cross of Christ say to us, the cross that in a sense is the final word of his messianic message and mission? And yet this is not yet the word of the God of the covenant: that will be pronounced at the dawn when first the women and then the Apostles come to the tomb of the crucified Christ, see the tomb empty and for the first time hear the message "He is risen." They will repeat this message to the others and will be witnesses to the risen

Christ. Yet, even in this glorification of the Son of God, the cross remains, that cross which—through all the messianic testimony of the man [who is] the Son, who suffered death upon it—speaks and never ceases to speak of God the Father, who is absolutely faithful to his eternal love for humans, since he "so loved the world"—therefore persons in the world—that "he gave his only Son, that whoever believes in him should not perish but have eternal life."[6]

In the name of Jesus Christ crucified and risen, in the spirit of his messianic mission, enduring in the history of humanity, we raise our voices and pray that the love which is in the Father may once again be revealed at this stage of history, and that, through the work of the Son and Holy Spirit, it may be shown to be present in our modern world and to be more powerful than evil: more powerful than sin and death.[7]

1.2 After an opening chapter on revelation, *Dei Verbum* dedicates its second chapter to the living transmission of revelation or tradition. This takes place, under the guidance of the Holy Spirit and in the "doctrine, life and worship" through which the church hands on "to every generation all that she herself is, all that she believes" (no. 8). Within that broad reality of tradition, the scriptures, which are inspired by the Spirit, have a special and inseparable role. The scriptures are united with tradition in their origin (in divine revelation), function (the salvation and sanctification of human beings), and goal (the final revelation and redemption to come in heavenly life) (no. 9). Then the constitution dedicates four chapters to the inspired scriptures: "Sacred Scripture: Its Divine Inspiration and Its Interpretation," "The Old Testament," "The New Testament," and "Sacred Scripture in the Life of the Church."

In April 1993, in the presence of cardinals, the diplomatic corps accredited to the Holy See, and others, and on the occasion of the presentation of a document of the Biblical Commission, "The Interpretation of the Bible in the Church," John Paul II dedicated a remarkable address to biblical interpretation. We quote it in full.

Your Eminences, Your Excellencies, the Heads of Diplomatic Missions, Members of the Pontifical Biblical Commission, Professors of the Pontifical Biblical Institute:

1. I wholeheartedly thank Cardinal Ratzinger for the sentiments he expressed a few moments ago in presenting the document prepared by the Pontifical Biblical Commission on the Interpretation of the Bible in the Church. I joyfully accept this document, the fruit of a collegial work undertaken on Your Eminence's initiative, and perseveringly continued over several years. It responds to a heartfelt concern of mine, for the interpretation of Sacred Scripture is of capital importance for the Christian faith and the Church's life.

As the Council well reminded us: "In the sacred books the Father who is in heaven comes lovingly to meet his children, and talks with them. And such is the force and power of the word of God that it can serve the Church as her support and vigor, and the children of the Church as strength for their faith, food for the soul, and a pure and lasting source of spiritual life" (*Dei Verbum*, n. 21). For men and women today the manner in which biblical texts are interpreted has immediate consequences for their personal and community relationship with God, and it is also closely connected with the Church's mission. A vital problem is at issue and deserves all your attention.

2. Your work is finishing at a very opportune moment, for it provides me with the opportunity to celebrate with you two richly significant anniversaries: the centenary of the Encyclical *Providentissimus Deus,* and the 50th anniversary of the Encyclical *Divino afflante Spiritu,* both concerned with biblical questions. On November 18, 1893, Pope Leo XIII, very attentive to intellectual problems, published his encyclical on scriptural studies with the goal, he wrote, "of encouraging and recommending them" as well as "orienting them in a way that better corresponds to the needs of the time" (*EB,* 82).

Fifty years later, Pope Pius XII gave Catholic exegetes further encouragement and new directives in his encyclical *Divino afflante Spiritu.* Meanwhile, the papal Magisterium showed its constant concern for scriptural problems through numerous interventions. In 1902 Leo XIII established the Biblical Commission; in 1909 Pius X founded the Biblical Institute. In 1920 Benedict XV celebrated the 1500th anniversary of St. Jerome's death with an encyclical on the interpretation of the Bible. The strong impetus thus given to biblical studies was fully confirmed at the Second Vatican Council so that the whole Church benefited from it. The Dogmatic Constitution *Dei Verbum* explains the work of Catholic exegetes and invites pastors and the faithful to take greater nourishment from the word of God contained in the Scriptures.

Today I want to highlight some aspects of the teaching of these two encyclicals and the permanent validity of their orientation through changing circumstances, in order to profit more from their contribution.

I. From *Providentissimus Deus* to *Divino afflante Spiritu*

3. First, one notes an important difference in these two documents, namely, the polemical, or to be more exact, the apologetic part of the two encyclicals. In fact, both appear concerned to answer attacks on the Catholic interpretation of the Bible, but these attacks did not follow the same direction. On the one hand, *Providentissimus Deus* wanted especially to protect Catholic interpretation of the Bible from the attacks of rationalistic science; on the other hand, *Divino afflante Spiritu* was primarily concerned with defending Catholic interpretation from attacks that opposed the use of science by exegetes and that wanted to impose a non-scientific, so-called "spiritual interpretation" of Sacred Scripture.

This radical change of perspective was obviously due to the circumstances. *Providentissimus Deus* appeared in a period marked by vicious polemics against the Church's faith. Liberal exegesis gave important support to these polemics, for it made use of all the scientific resources, from textual criticism to geology, including philology, literary criticism, history of religions, archaeology and other disciplines besides. On the other hand, *Divino afflante Spiritu* was published shortly after an entirely different polemic arose, particularly in Italy, against the scientific study of the Bible. An anonymous pamphlet was widely circulated to warn against what it described as "a very serious danger for the Church and souls: the critico-scientific system in the study and interpretation of Sacred Scripture, its disastrous deviations and aberrations."

4. In both cases the reaction of the Magisterium was significant, for instead of giving a purely defensive response, it went to the heart of the problem and thus showed (let us note this at once) the Church's faith in the mystery of the Incarnation. Against the offensive of liberal exegesis, which presented its allegations as conclusions based on the achievements of science, one could have reacted by anathematizing the use of science in biblical interpretation and ordering Catholic exegetes to hold to a "spiritual" explanation of the texts.

Providentissimus Deus did not take this route. On the contrary, the encyclical earnestly invites Catholic exegetes to acquire genuine scientific expertise so that they may surpass their adversaries in their own field. "The first means of defense," it said, "is found in studying the ancient languages of the East as well as the practice of scientific criticism" (*EB*, 18). The Church is not afraid of scientific criticism. She distrusts only preconceived opinions that claim to be based on science, but which in reality surreptitiously cause science to depart from its domain.

Fifty years later in *Divino afflante Spiritu*, Pope Pius XII could note the fruitfulness of the directives given by *Providentissimus Deus:* "Due to a better knowledge of the biblical languages and of everything regarding the East,...a good number of the questions raised at the time of Leo XIII against the authenticity, antiquity, integrity and historical value of the Sacred Books...have now been sorted out and resolved" (*EB*, 546). The work of Catholic exegetes "who correctly use the intellectual weapons employed by their adversaries" (ibid., 562) has borne its fruit. It is for this very reason that *Divino afflante Spiritu* seems less concerned than *Providentissimus Deus* to fight against the positions of rationalistic exegesis.

5. However, it became necessary to respond to attacks coming from the supporters of a so-called "mystical" exegesis (*EB*, 552), who sought to have the Magisterium condemn the efforts of scientific exegesis. How did the encyclical respond? It could have limited itself to stressing the usefulness and even the necessity of these efforts for defending the faith, which would have favored a kind of dichotomy between scientific exegesis, intended for external use, and spiritual interpretation, reserved for internal use.

In *Divino afflante Spiritu*, Pius XII deliberately avoided this approach. On the contrary, he vindicated the close unity of the two approaches, on the one hand emphasizing the "theological" significance of the literal sense, methodically defined (EB, 551), and on the other, asserting that, to be recognized as the sense of a biblical text, the spiritual sense must offer proof of its authenticity. A merely subjective inspiration is insufficient. One must be able to show that it is a sense "willed by God himself," a spiritual meaning "given by God" to the inspired text (*EB*, 552–53). Determining the spiritual sense, then, belongs itself to the realm of exegetical science.

Thus we note that, despite the great difference in the difficulties they had to face, the two encyclicals are in complete agreement at the deepest level. Both of them reject a split between the human and the divine, between scientific research and respect for the faith, between the literal sense and the spiritual sense. They thus appear to be in perfect harmony with the mystery of the Incarnation.

II. The Harmony between Catholic Exegesis and the Mystery of the Incarnation

6. The strict relationship uniting the inspired biblical texts with the mystery of the incarnation was expressed by the Encyclical *Divino afflante Spiritu* in the following terms: "Just as the substantial Word of God became like men in every respect except sin, so too the words of God, expressed in human languages, became like human language in every respect except error" (*EB*, 559). Repeated almost literally by the conciliar Constitution *Dei Verbum* (13), this statement sheds light on a parallelism rich in meaning.

It is true that putting God's words into writing, through the charism of scriptural inspiration, was the first step toward the incarnation of the Word of God. These written words, in fact, were an abiding means of communication and communion between the chosen people and their one Lord. On the other hand, it is because of the prophetic aspect of these words that it was possible to recognize the fulfillment of God's plan when "the Word became flesh and made his dwelling among us" (see John 1:14).

After the heavenly glorification of the humanity of the Word made flesh, it is again due to written words that his stay among us is attested to in an abiding way. Joined to the inspired writings of the first covenant, the inspired writings of the new covenant are a verifiable means of communication and communion between the believing people and God, the Father, Son and Holy Spirit. This means certainly can never be separated from the stream of spiritual life that flows from the heart of Jesus crucified and which spreads through the Church's sacraments. It has nevertheless its own consistency precisely as a written text which verifies it.

7. Consequently, the two encyclicals require that Catholic exegetes remain in full harmony with the mystery of the Incarnation, a mystery of the union of the divine and the human in a determinate historical life. The earthly life of Jesus is not defined only by the places and dates at the beginning of the 1st century in Judea and Galilee, but also by his deep roots in the long history of a small nation of the ancient Near East, with its weaknesses and its greatness, with its men of God and its sinners, with its slow cultural evolution and its political misadventures, with its defeats and its victories, with its longing for peace and the kingdom of God.

The Church of Christ takes the realism of the incarnation seriously, and this is why she attaches great importance to the "historico-critical" study of the Bible. Far from condemning it, as those who support "mystical" exegesis would want, my predecessors vigorously approved. "With my vehement approval," Leo XIII wrote, "let our exegetes (namely the Catholic ones) cultivate the discipline of a critical skill that is most useful for understanding deeply the meaning of the sacred writer" (Apostolic Letter *Vigilantiae,* establishing the Biblical Commission, October 30, 1902: *EB,* 142). The same "vehemence" in the approval and the same adverb *(vehementer)* are found in *Divino afflante Spiritu* regarding research in textual criticism (cf. *EB,* 548).

8. *Divino afflante Spiritu,* we know, particularly recommended that exegetes study the literary genres used in the Sacred Books, going so far as to say that Catholic exegesis must "be convinced that this part of its task cannot be neglected without serious harm to

Catholic exegesis" (*EB*, 560). This recommendation starts from the concern to understand the meaning of the texts with all the accuracy and precision possible and, thus, in their historical, cultural context.

A false idea of God and the incarnation presses a certain number of Christians to take the opposite approach. They tend to believe that, since God is the absolute Being, each of his words has an absolute value, independent of all the conditions of human language. Thus, according to them, there is no room for studying these conditions in order to make distinctions that would relativize the significance of the words. However, that is where the illusion occurs and the mysteries of scriptural inspiration and the incarnation are really rejected, by clinging to a false notion of the Absolute.

The God of the Bible is not an absolute Being who, crushing everything he touches, would suppress all differences and all nuances. On the contrary, he is God the Creator, who created the astonishing variety of beings "each according to its kind," as the Genesis account says repeatedly (see Gen 1). Far from destroying differences, God respects them and makes use of them (see 1 Cor 12:18, 24, 28). Although he expresses himself in human language, he does not give each expression a uniform value, but uses its possible nuances with extreme flexibility and likewise accepts its limitations.

That is what makes the task of exegetes so complex, so necessary and so fascinating! None of the human aspects of language can be neglected. The recent progress in linguistic, literary and hermeneutical research have led biblical exegesis to add many other points of view (rhetorical, narrative, structuralist) to the study of literary genres; other human sciences, such as psychology and sociology, have likewise been employed. To all this one can apply the charge which Leo XIII gave the members of the Biblical Commission: "Let them consider nothing that the diligent research of modern scholars will have newly found as foreign to their realm; quite the contrary, let them be alert to adopt without delay anything useful that each period brings to biblical exegesis" (*Vigilantiae: EB,*140). Studying the human circumstances of the word of God should be pursued with ever renewed interest.

9. Nevertheless, this study is not enough. In order to respect the coherence of the Church's faith and of scriptural inspiration, Catholic exegesis must be careful not to limit itself to the human

aspects of the biblical texts. First and foremost, it must help the Christian people more clearly perceive the word of God in these texts so that they can better accept them in order to live in full communion with God. To this end it is obviously necessary that the exegete himself perceive the divine word in the texts. He can do this only if his intellectual work is sustained by a vigorous spiritual life.

Without this support, exegetical research remains incomplete; it loses sight of its main purpose and is confined to secondary tasks. It can even become a sort of escape. Scientific study of the merely human aspects of the texts can make the exegete forget that the word of God invites each person to come out of himself to live in faith and love.

On this point the Encyclical *Providentissimus Deus* recalls the special nature of the Sacred Books and their consequent need for interpretation: "The Sacred Books," it said, "cannot be likened to ordinary writings, but, since they have been dictated by the Holy Spirit himself and have extremely serious contents, mysterious and difficult in many respects, we always need, in order to understand and explain them, the coming of the same Holy Spirit, that is, his light and grace, which must certainly be sought in humble prayer and preserved by a life of holiness" (*EB*, 89). In a shorter formula, borrowed from St. Augustine, *Divino afflante Spiritu* expressed the same requirement: "*Orent ut intelligent* (let them pray that they may understand)!" (*EB*, 569).

Indeed, to arrive at a completely valid interpretation of words inspired by the Holy Spirit, one must first be guided by the Holy Spirit and it is necessary to pray for that, to pray much, to ask in prayer for the interior light of the Spirit and docilely accept that light, to ask for the love that alone enables one to understand the language of God, who "is love" (see 1 John 4:8, 16). While engaged in the very work of interpretation, one must remain in the presence of God as much as possible.

10. Docility to the Holy Spirit produces and reinforces another attitude needed for the correct orientation of exegesis: fidelity to the Church. The Catholic exegete does not entertain the individualist illusion leading to the belief that one can better understand the biblical texts outside the community of believers. The contrary is true, for these texts have not been given to individual researchers "to sat-

isfy their curiosity or provide them with subjects for study and research" (*Divino afflante Spiritu: EB*, 566); they have been entrusted to the community of believers, to the Church of Christ, in order to nourish faith and guide the life of charity.

Respect for this purpose conditions the validity of the interpretation. *Providentissimus Deus* recalled this basic truth and observed that, far from hampering biblical research, respect for this fact fosters its authentic progress (cf. *EB*, 108–9). It is comforting to note that recent studies in hermeneutical philosophy have confirmed this point of view and that exegetes of various confessions have worked from similar perspectives by stressing, for example, the need to interpret each biblical text a part of the scriptural canon recognized by the Church, or by being more attentive to the contributions of patristic exegesis.

Being faithful to the Church, in fact, means resolutely finding one's place in the mainstream of the great Tradition that, under the guidance of the Magisterium, assured of the Holy Spirit's special assistance, has recognized the canonical writings as the word addressed by God to his people and has never ceased meditating on them and discovering their inexhaustible riches. The Second Vatican Council asserted this again: "All that has been said about the manner of interpreting Scripture is ultimately subject to the judgment of the Church, which exercises the divinely conferred commission and ministry of watching over and interpreting the word of God" (*Dei Verbum*, 12).

It is nevertheless true—the Council also states this, repeating an assertion of *Providentissimus Deus*—that it "is the task of exegetes to work, according to these rules, toward a better understanding and explanation of the meaning of Sacred Scripture in order that their research may help the Church to form a firmer judgment" (*Dei Verbum*, 12; cf. *Providentissimus Deus: EB*, 109).

11. In order to carry out this very important ecclesial task better, exegetes will be keen to remain close to the preaching of God's word, both by devoting part of their time to this ministry and by maintaining relations with those who exercise it and helping them with publications of pastoral exegesis (cf. *Divino afflante Spiritu: EB*, 551). Thus they will avoid becoming lost in the complexities of abstract scientific research which distances them from the true

meaning of the Scriptures. Indeed, this meaning is inseparable from their goal, which is to put believers into a personal relationship with God.

III. The New Document of the Biblical Commission

12. In these perspectives, *Providentissimus Deus* stated, "a vast field of research is open to the personal work of each exegete" (*EB*, 109). Fifty years later, *Divino afflante Spiritu* again made the same encouraging observation: "There are still many points, some very important, in the discussion and explanation of which the intellectual penetration and talent of Catholic exegetes can and should be freely exercised" (*EB*, 565).

What was true in 1943 remains so even in our day, for advances in research have produced solutions to certain problems and, at the same time, new questions to be studied. In exegesis as in other sciences, the more one pushes back the limits of the unknown, the more one enlarges the area to be explored. Less than five years after the publication of *Divino afflante Spiritu,* the discovery of the Qumran scrolls shed the light of a new day on a great number of biblical problems and opened up other fields of research. Since then, many discoveries have been made and new methods of investigation and analysis have been perfected.

13. It is this changed situation that has made a new examination of the problems necessary. The Pontifical Biblical Commission has worked on this task and today presents the fruit of its work, entitled *The Interpretation of the Bible in the Church.*

What is striking on first reading this document is the spirit of openness in which it was conceived. The methods, approaches and interpretations practiced today in exegesis have been examined and, despite occasionally serious reservations which must be stated, one acknowledges in almost every case, the presence of valid elements for an integral interpretation of the biblical text. For Catholic exegesis does not have its own exclusive method of interpretation, but starting with the historico-critical basis freed from its philosophical presuppositions or those contrary to the truth of our faith, it makes the most of all the current methods by seeking in each of them the "seeds of the Word."

14. Another characteristic feature of this synthesis is its balance and moderation. In its interpretation of the Bible, it knows how to harmonize the diachronic and the synchronic by recognizing that the two are mutually complementary and indispensable for bringing out all the truth of the text and for satisfying the legitimate demands of the modern reader.

Even more importantly, Catholic exegesis does not focus its attention on only the human aspects of biblical Revelation, which is sometimes the mistake of the historico-critical method, or on only the divine aspects, as fundamentalism would have it; it strives to highlight both of them as they are united in the divine "condescension" (*Dei Verbum,* 13), which is the basis of all Scripture.

15. Lastly, one will perceive the document's stress on the fact that the biblical Word is at work speaking universally, in time and space, to all humanity. If "the words of God...are like human language" (*Dei Verbum,* 13), it is so that they may be understood by all. They must not remain distant, "too mysterious and remote for you.... For the word is very near to you, already in your mouths and in your hearts; you have only to carry it out (see Deut 30:11, 14).

This is the aim of biblical interpretation. If the first task of exegesis is to arrive at the authentic sense of the sacred text or even at its different senses, it must then communicate this meaning to the recipient of Sacred Scripture, who is every human person, if possible. The Bible exercises its influence down the centuries. A constant process of actualization adapts the interpretation to the contemporary mentality and language. The concrete, immediate nature of biblical language greatly facilitates this adaptation, but its origin in an ancient culture causes not a few difficulties. Therefore, biblical thought must always be translated anew into contemporary language so that it may be expressed in ways suited to its listeners. This translation, however, should be faithful to the original and cannot force the texts in order to accommodate an interpretation or an approach fashionable at a given time. The word of God must appear in all its splendor, even if it is "expressed in human words" (*Dei Verbum,* 13).

Today the Bible has spread to every continent and every nation. However, in order for it to have a profound effect, there must be inculturation according to the genius proper to each people. Perhaps nations less marked by the deviances of modern Western civilization will understand the biblical message more easily than those who are already insensitive as it were to the action of God's word because of secularization and the excesses of demythologization.

In our day, a great effort is necessary, not only on the part of scholars and preachers, but also those who popularize biblical thought: they should use every means possible—and there are many today—so that the universal significance of the biblical message may be widely acknowledged and its saving efficacy may be seen everywhere.

Thanks to this document, the interpretation of the Bible in the Church will be able to obtain new vigor for the good of the whole world, so that the truth may shine forth and stir up charity on the threshold of the third millennium.

IV. Conclusion

16. Finally, I have the joy as my predecessors, Leo XIII and Pius XII, had of being able to offer to Catholic exegetes, and in particular, to you, the members of the Pontifical Biblical Commission, both my thanks and encouragement.

I cordially thank you for the excellent work you have accomplished in service to the word of God and the People of God: a work of research, teaching and publication; an aid to theology, to the liturgy of the word and to the ministry of preaching; initiatives fostering ecumenism and good relations between Christians and Jews; involvement in the Church's efforts to respond to the aspirations and difficulties of the modern world.

To this I add my warm encouragement for the next step to be taken. The increasing complexity of the task requires everyone's effort and a broad interdisciplinary cooperation. In a world where scientific research is taking on greater importance in many domains, it is indispensable for exegetical science to find its place at a comparable level. It is one of the aspects of inculturating the faith which is part of the Church's mission in connection with accepting the mystery of the Incarnation.

May you be guided in your research by Jesus Christ, the incarnate Word of God, who opened the minds of his disciples to the understanding of the Scriptures (see Luke 24:45). May the Virgin Mary serve as a model for you not only by her generous docility to the word of God, but also and especially by her way of accepting what was said to her! St. Luke tells us that Mary reflected in her heart on the divine words and the events that took place (see Luke 2:19). By welcoming the Word she is the model and mother of disciples (see John 19:27). Therefore, may she teach you fully to accept the word of God, not only in intellectual research but also with your whole life!

In order that your work and your activity may make the light of the Scriptures shine ever more brightly, I wholeheartedly give you my Apostolic Blessing.[8]

1.3   In his penultimate encyclical, *Fides et ratio* (Faith and Reason) of 1998, John Paul II returned to the theme of revelation and necessarily so. Since faith is triggered and fed by the divine self-revelation, one cannot present faith without dealing also with revelation.

The Full Truth in the Final Revelation

The Church is no stranger to this journey of discovery, nor could she ever be. From the moment when, through the Paschal Mystery, she received the gift of the ultimate truth about human life, the Church has made her pilgrim way along the paths of the world to proclaim that Jesus Christ is "the way, and the truth, and the life" (John 14:6). It is her duty to serve humanity in different ways, but one way in particular imposes a responsibility of a quite special kind: the *diakonia* [service] *of the truth*. This mission on the one hand makes the believing community a partner in humanity's shared struggle to arrive at truth (cf. *Gaudium et spes*, 16); and on the other hand it obliges the believing community to proclaim the certitudes arrived at, albeit with a sense that every truth attained is but a step towards that fullness of truth which will appear with the final revelation of God: "For now we see in a mirror dimly, but then face to face. Now I know in part; then I shall understand fully" (1 Cor 13:12).[9]

Jesus the Revealer

In the incarnation of the Son of God we see forged the enduring and definitive synthesis which the human mind of itself could not even have imagined: the Eternal enters time, the Whole lies hidden in the part, God takes on a human face. The truth communicated in Christ's revelation is therefore no longer confined to a particular place or culture, but is offered to every man and woman who would welcome it as the word which is the absolutely valid source of meaning for human life. Now, in Christ, all have access to the Father, since by his death and resurrection Christ has bestowed the divine life which the first Adam had refused (cf. Rom 5:12–15). Through this revelation, men and women are offered the ultimate truth about their own life and about the goal of history. As the Constitution *Gaudium et spes* puts it (no. 22), "only in the mystery of the incarnate Word does the mystery of human beings take on light." Seen in any other terms, the mystery of personal existence remains an insoluble riddle. Where might the human being seek the answer to dramatic questions such as pain, the suffering of the innocent and death, if not in the light streaming from the mystery of Christ's passion, death and resurrection?

It should nonetheless be kept in mind that revelation remains charged with mystery. It is true that Jesus, with his entire life, revealed the countenance of the Father, for he came to teach the secret things of God (*Dei Verbum*, 4). But our vision of the face of God is always fragmentary and impaired by the limits of our understanding. Faith alone makes it possible to penetrate the mystery in a way that allows us to understand it coherently.[10]

Revelation through Nature

The Book of Wisdom contains several important texts which cast further light on this theme. There the sacred author speaks of God who reveals himself in nature. For the ancients, the study of the natural sciences coincided in large part with philosophical learning. Having affirmed that with their intelligence human beings can "know the structure of the world and the activity of the elements...the cycles of the year and the constellations of the stars, the natures of animals and the tempers of wild beasts" (Wis 7:17, 19–20)—in a word, that they philosophize—the sacred text takes a significant step forward. Making his own the thought of Greek philosophy, to which he seems to refer in the context, the author affirms that, in reasoning about nature, the human being can rise to God: "From the greatness and beauty of created things comes a corresponding perception of their Creator" (Wis 13:5). This is to recognize as a first stage of divine revelation the marvelous "book of nature," which, when read with the proper tools of human reason, can lead to knowledge of the Creator. If human beings with their intelligence fail to recognize God as Creator of all, it is not because they lack the means to do so, but because their free will and their sinfulness place an impediment in the way.[11]

NOTES

1. *Redemptor hominis,* 9, in *AAS* 71 (1979), 273–74; *EncMiller,* 58; *Origins* 8:40 (1979), 631; *Pope Speaks* 24:2 (1979), 109.

2. Ibid., 11, in *AAS* 71 (1979), 277; *EncMiller,* 60; *Origins* 8:40 (1979), 632; *Pope Speaks* 24:2 (1979), 112.

3. *Catechesi tradendae,* 22, 35, in *AAS* 71 (1979), 1296, 1307–8; *ApExMiller,* 82, 92; *Origins* 9:21 (1979), 335, 338; *Pope Speaks* 25:1 (1980), 49–50, 59.

4. Ibid., 60, in *AAS* 71 (1979), 1325–26; *ApExMiller,* 106–7; *ND,* 163a; *Origins* 9:21 (1979), 343; *Pope Speaks* 25:1 (1980), 74–75.

5. *Dives in misericordia,* 1, in *AAS* 72 (1980), 1177–78; *EncMiller,* 104–5; *Origins* 10:26 (1980), 401-3; *Pope Speaks* 26:1 (1981), 20–21.

6. Ibid., 7, in *AAS* 72 (1980), 1202–3; *EncMiller,* 120; *Origins* 10:26 (1980), 408–9; *Pope Speaks* 26:1 (1981), 38.

7. Ibid., 15, in *AAS* 72 (1980), 1231; *EncMiller,* 137; *Origins* 10:26 (1980), 416; *Pope Speaks* 26:1 (1981), 58.

8. *Address to the Pontifical Biblical Commission (April 23, 1993),* in *AAS* 86 (1994), 232–43; *OREnglish* 17 (April 28, 1993), 3, 4, 6.

9. *Fides et ratio,* 2, in *AAS* 91 (1999), 6–7; *EncMiller* 850–51; *Origins* 28:19 (1998), 319; *Pope Speaks* 44:1 (1999), 2.

10. Ibid., 12-13, in *AAS* 91 (1999), 14–15; *EncMiller,* 856–57; *Origins* 28:19 (1998), 322; *Pope Speaks* 44:1 (1999), 8.

11. Ibid., 19, in *AAS* 91 (1999), 21; *EncMiller,* 861–62; *ND,* 441; *Origins* 28:19 (1998), 324; *Pope Speaks* 44:1 (1999), 12–13.

CHAPTER TWO

Faith and Reason

In its last and longest document, *Gaudium et spes* (Joy and Hope), the Pastoral Constitution on the Church in the Modern World, Vatican II explored and expounded the relations between Christian faith (that responds to the divine self-revelation) and reason in its theological, philosophical, and scientific forms (no. 36). John Paul II knew this constitution well, since he not only attended the council but also worked on one of the drafting committees for *Gaudium et spes*. From the start of his pontificate, he developed further such themes from *Gaudium et spes* as the relations between faith and the natural sciences and the larger issue of faith and reason.

2.1 An address by John Paul II to scientists in the Cologne Cathedral (November 1980) described the role of science and the appropriate relation to faith in our time.

The Truth of Science and Faith

The claim to truth of a science based on rationality is recognized; in fact it is accepted in its contents, completed, corrected and developed in its independent rationality. And precisely in this way it becomes the property of the Christian world. In this way the latter sees its own understanding of the world enormously enriched without having to give up any essential element of its tradition, far less the foundation of its faith. For there can be no fundamental conflict between (1) a reason which, in conformity with its own nature that comes from God, is geared to truth and is qualified to know truth and (2) a faith which refers to the same divine source of all truth.[1]

Past Conflicts between Science and Faith

Many people see the core of these questions in the relationship between the Church and modern natural sciences, and they still feel the weight of those notorious conflicts which arose from the interference of religious authorities in the process of the development of scientific knowledge. The Church remembers this with regret, for today we realize the errors and shortcomings of these ways of proceeding. We can say today that they have been overcome: thanks to the power of persuasion of science, and thanks above all to the work of a scientific theology, which has deepened understanding of faith and freed it from the conditions of time.[2]

The Crisis of Merely Functional Science

Our culture, in all its areas, is imbued with a science which proceeds in a way that is largely functionalistic. This applies also to the area of values and norms, of spiritual orientation in general. Precisely here science comes up against its own limits. There is talk of a crisis of legitimation of science, nay more, of a crisis of orientation of our whole scientific culture. What is its essence? Science alone is not able to give a complete answer to the question of meanings, which is raised in the crisis. Scientific affirmations are always particular. They are justified only in consideration of a given starting point, they are set in a process of development, and they can be corrected and left behind in this process. But above all: how could something constitute the result of a scientific starting point and therefore already be presupposed by it? Science alone is not capable of answering the question of meanings, in fact it cannot even set it in the framework of its starting point.

24

And yet this question of meanings cannot tolerate indefinite postponement of its answer. If widespread confidence in science is disappointed, then the state of mind easily changes into hostility of science. In this space that has remained empty, ideologies suddenly break in. They sometimes behave as if they were "scientific" but they owe their power of persuasion to the urgent need for an answer to the question of meanings and to interest in social and political change. Science that is purely functional, without values and alienated from truth, can enter the service of these ideologies; a reason that is only instrumental runs the risk of losing its freedom.[3]

Human Dignity and the Right Use of Science

There is no reason to consider technico-scientific culture as opposed to the world of God's creation. It is clear beyond all doubt that technical knowledge can be used for good as well as for evil. Anyone who studies the effects of poisons can use this knowledge to cure as well as to kill. But there can be no doubt in what direction we must look to distinguish good from evil. Technical science, aimed at the transformation of the world, is justified on the basis of the service it renders the human person and humanity.

It cannot be said that progress has gone too far as long as many people, in fact whole peoples, still live in distressing conditions, unworthy of human beings, which could be improved with the help of technico-scientific knowledge. Enormous tasks still lie before us, which we cannot shirk. To carry them out represents a brotherly service for our neighbor, to whom we owe [as] those in need the work of charity, which helps [them in] their necessity.

We render our neighbor a fraternal service because we recognize in our brothers and sisters that dignity characteristic of a moral being; we are speaking of a personal dignity, Faith teaches us that the fundamental prerogative of humans consists in being the image of God. Christian tradition adds that humans are of value for their own sakes, and are not a means for any other end. Therefore the personal

dignity of humans represents the criterion by which all cultural application of technico-scientific knowledge must be judged.[4]

Science Must Promote
Human Freedom

The human and social sciences, but also the sciences of culture,
not least of all philosophy and theology, have stimulated in multiple
ways the reflection of modern persons about themselves and their
existence in a world dominated by science and technology. The spirit
of modern consciousness, which accelerates the development of the
modern natural sciences, has also set for itself as its purpose the scientific analysis of human beings and of the world in which they live,
at the social and cultural level. An absolutely incalculable mass of
knowledge has thereby come to light, which has repercussions on
both public and private life. The social system of modern states, the
health and educational system, economic processes and cultural
activities are all marked in many ways by the influence of these sciences. But it is important that science should not keep humans under
its thumb. Also in the culture of technology, humans, in conformity
with their dignity, must remain free; in fact, it must be the meaning
of this culture to give them greater freedom.[5]

Science Is Bound to Truth

To be able to influence praxis, it [science] must first be determined by truth, and therefore be free for truth. A free science, bound
only to truth, does not let itself be reduced to the model of function-
alism or any other [model], which limits understanding of scientific
rationality. Science must be open, in fact it must also be multiform,
and we need not fear the loss of a unified approach. This is given by
the trinomial of personal reason, freedom and truth, in which the
multiplicity of concrete realizations is founded and confirmed.

I do not hesitate at all to see also the science of faith on the
horizon of rationality understood in this way. The Church wants

26

independent theological research, which is not identified with the ecclesiastical Magisterium, but which knows it is committed with regard to it in common service of the truth of faith and the people of God. It cannot be ignored that tensions and even conflicts may arise. But this cannot be ignored either as regards the relationship between Church and science. The reason is to be sought in the finiteness of our reason, limited in its extension and therefore exposed to error. Nevertheless, we can always hope for a solution of reconciliation, if we take our stand on the ability of this same reason to attain truth.[6]

Science Needs Faith

In the past, protagonists of modern science fought against the Church with the slogans: reason, freedom and progress. Today, in view of the crisis with regard to the meaning of science, the multiple threats to its freedom and the doubt about progress, the battlefronts have been inverted. Today it is the Church that takes up the defense:

—for reason and science, which she recognizes as having the ability to attain truth, which legitimizes it as a human realization;

—for the freedom of science, through which the latter possesses its dignity as a human and personal good;

—for progress in the service of humanity which needs it to safeguard its life and dignity.

With this task, the Church and all Christians are at the center of the debate in these times of ours. An adequate solution of the pressing questions about the meaning of human existence, norms of action, and the prospects of a more far-reaching hope, is possible only in the renewed connection between scientific thought and the power of faith in human beings in search of truth. The pursuit of a new humanism, on which the future of the third millennium can be based, will be successful only on condition that scientific knowledge again enters upon a living relationship with the truth revealed to human beings as God's gift. Human reason is a grand instrument for knowledge and structuring of the world. It needs, however, in order to realize the whole wealth of human possibilities, to open [itself] to the Word of Eternal Truth, which became human in Christ.[7]

2.2 In September 1987, a study week was held at Castel Gandolfo, the pope's summer residence, on the multiform relationships among theology, philosophy, and the natural sciences. On the occasion of the publication of the papers in 1988, John Paul II wrote to Father George V. Coyne, the director of the Vatican Observatory, on the proper and enriching dialogue that should be promoted between theology and science.

Science Supports Faith's Perception of Unity in the Universe

The scientific disciplines too, as is obvious, are endowing us with an understanding and appreciation of our universe as a whole and of the incredibly rich variety of intricately related processes and structures which constitute its animate and inanimate components. This knowledge has given us a more thorough understanding of ourselves and of our humble yet unique role within creation. Through technology it also has given us the capacity to travel, to communicate, to build, to cure and to probe in ways which would have been almost unimaginable to our ancestors. Such knowledge and power, as we have discovered, can be used greatly to enhance and improve our lives or they can be exploited to diminish and destroy human life and the environment even on a global scale.

The unity we perceive in creation on the basis of our faith in Jesus Christ as Lord of the universe, and the correlative unity for which we strive in our human communities, seems to be reflected and even reinforced in what contemporary science is revealing to us. As we behold the incredible development of scientific research, we detect an underlying movement toward the discovery of levels of law and process which unify created reality and which at the same time have given rise to the vast diversity of structures and organisms that constitute the physical and biological, and even the psychological and sociological worlds.[8]

Science and Religion in Dialogue

By encouraging openness between the Church and the scientific communities, we are not envisioning a disciplinary unity between theology and science like that which exists within a given scientific field or within theology proper. As dialogue and common searching continue, there will be growth toward mutual understanding and a gradual uncovering of common concerns which will provide the basis for further research and discussion. Exactly what form that will take must be left to the future. What is important, as we have already stressed, is that the dialogue should continue and grow in depth and scope. In the process we must overcome every regressive tendency to a unilateral reductionism, to fear and to self-imposed isolation. What is critically important is that each discipline should continue to enrich, nourish and challenge the other to be more fully what it can be and to contribute to our vision of who we are and who we are becoming.

We might ask whether or not we are ready for this crucial endeavor. Is the community of world religions, including the Church, ready to enter into a more thoroughgoing dialogue with the scientific community, a dialogue in which the integrity of both religion and science is supported and the advance of each is fostered? Is the scientific community now prepared to open itself to Christianity and indeed to all the great world religions, working with us all to build a culture that is more humane and in that way more divine? Do we dare to risk the honesty and the courage that this task demands? We must ask ourselves whether both science and religion will contribute to the integration of human culture or to its fragmentation. It is a single choice, and it confronts us all.

For a simple neutrality is no longer acceptable. If they are to grow and mature, peoples cannot continue to live in separate compartments, pursuing totally divergent interests from which they evaluate and judge their world. A divided community fosters a fragmented vision of the world; a community of interchange encourages its members to expand their partial perspectives and form a new unified vision.

Yet the unity that we seek, as we have already stressed, is not identity. The Church does not propose that science should become religion or religion [become] science. On the contrary, unity always

29

presupposes the diversity and the integrity of its elements. Each of these members should become not less itself but more itself in a dynamic interchange, for a unity in which one of the elements is reduced to the other is destructive, false in its promises of harmony and ruinous of the integrity of its components. We are asked to become one. We are not asked to become each other.[9]

Theology Should Weigh Scientific Findings

Theology has been defined as an effort of faith to achieve understanding, as *fides quaerens intellectum*. As such, it must be in vital interchange today with science just as it always has been with philosophy and other forms of learning. Theology will have to call on the findings of science to one degree or another as it pursues its primary concern for the human person, the reaches of freedom, the possibilities of Christian community, the nature of belief, and the intelligibility of nature and history. The vitality and significance of theology for humanity will in a profound way be reflected in its ability to incorporate these findings.

Now this is a point of delicate importance, and it has to be carefully qualified. Theology is not to incorporate indifferently each new philosophical or scientific theory. As these findings become part of the intellectual culture of the time, however, theologians must understand them and test their value in bringing out from Christian belief some of the possibilities which have not yet been realized. The hylomorphism of Aristotelian natural philosophy, for example, was adopted by the medieval theologians to help them explore the nature of the sacraments and the hypostatic union. This did not mean that the Church adjudicated the truth or falsity of the Aristotelian insight, since that is not her concern. It did mean that this was one of the rich insights offered by Greek culture, that it needed to be understood and taken seriously and tested for its value in illuminating various areas of theology. Theologians might well ask, with respect to contemporary science, philosophy and the other areas of human knowing, if they have accomplished this extraordinarily difficult process as well as did these medieval masters.

If the cosmologies of the ancient Near Eastern world could be purified and assimilated into the first chapters of Genesis, might contemporary cosmology have something to offer to our reflections upon creation? Does an evolutionary perspective bring any light to bear upon theological anthropology, the meaning of the human person as the *imago Dei*, the problem of Christology—and even upon the development of doctrine itself? What, if any, are the eschatological implications of contemporary cosmology, especially in light of the vast future of our universe? Can theological method fruitfully appropriate insights from scientific methodology and the philosophy of science?

Questions of this kind can be suggested in abundance. Pursuing them further would require the sort of intense dialogue with contemporary science that has, on the whole, been lacking among those engaged in theological research and teaching. It would entail that some theologians, at least, should be sufficiently well versed in the sciences to make authentic and creative use of the resources that the best-established theories may offer them.[10]

2.3 In 1981 John Paul II appointed a papal commission to study the censuring by the church of Galileo Galilei (in 1633). At a meeting of the Pontifical Academy of Sciences in October 1992, the pope received the findings of the commission and commented on them in an address.

The Need to Distinguish Faith and Science

If contemporary culture is marked by a tendency to scientism, the cultural horizon of Galileo's age was uniform and carried the imprint of a particular philosophical formation. This unitary character of culture, which in itself is positive and desirable even in our own day, was one of the reasons for Galileo's condemnation. The majority of theologians did not recognize the formal distinction between Sacred Scripture and its interpretation, and this led them unduly to transpose into the realm of the doctrine of the faith a question which in fact pertained to scientific investigation.[11]

Our Transformed Understanding of the Universe

From the Galileo affair we can learn a lesson which remains valid in relation to similar situations which occur today and which may occur in the future.

In Galileo's time, to depict the world as lacking an absolute physical reference point was, so to speak, inconceivable. And since the cosmos, as it was then known, was contained within the solar system alone, this reference point could only be situated in the earth or in the sun. Today, after Einstein and within the perspective of contemporary cosmology neither of these two reference points has the importance they once had. This observation, it goes without saying, is not directed against the validity of Galileo's position in the debate; it is only meant to show that often, beyond two partial and contrasting perceptions, there exists a wider perception which includes them and goes beyond both of them.[12]

Knowledge through Revelation and Reason

Another lesson which we can draw is that the different branches of knowledge call for different methods. Thanks to his intuition as a brilliant physicist and by relying on different arguments, Galileo, who practically invented the experimental method, understood why only the sun could function as the center of the world, as it was then known, that is to say, as a planetary system. The error of the theologians of the time, when they maintained the centrality of the earth, was to think that our understanding of the physical world's structure was, in some way, imposed by the literal sense of Sacred Scripture. Let us recall the celebrated saying attributed to Cardinal Cesare Baronius [d. 1607]: "Spiritui Sancto mentem fuisse nos docere quomodo ad coelum eatur, non quomodo coelum gradiatur" (it was the intention of the Holy Spirit to teach us how to go to heaven, not how the heaven goes round)! In fact, the Bible does not concern itself with the details of the physical world, the understanding of which is the competence of human experience and reasoning. There exist two realms of knowledge, one which has its source in revelation and one which reason can discover by its own power. To the latter belong especially the experimental sciences and philosophy. The distinction between the two realms of knowledge ought not to be understood as opposition. The two realms are not altogether foreign to each other; they have points of contact. The methodologies proper to each make it possible to bring out different aspects of reality.[13]

Science and Faith: Two Modes of Development and Growth

Humanity has before it two modes of development. The first involves culture, scientific research and technology, that is to say, whatever falls within the horizontal aspect of human beings and creation which is growing at an impressive rate. In order that this progress should not remain completely external to human beings, it presupposes a simultaneous raising of conscience, as well as its actuation. The second mode of development involves what is deepest in human beings, when transcending the world and transcending themselves, they turn to the One who is the Creator of all. It is only this vertical direction which can give full meaning to their being and action, because it situates them in relation to their origin and their end. In this twofold direction, horizontal and vertical, they realize themselves fully as spiritual beings and as *homo sapiens*. But we see that development is not uniform and linear, and that progress is not always well ordered. This reveals the disorder which affects the human condition. The scientist who is conscious of this twofold

33

development and takes it into account contributes to the restoration of harmony.

Those who engage in scientific and technological research admit as the premise of its progress, that the world is not a chaos but a "cosmos"—that is to say, that there exist order and natural laws which can be grasped and examined, and which, for this reason, have a certain affinity with the spirit. Einstein used to say: "What is eternally incomprehensible in the world is that it is comprehensible" (*The Journal of the Franklin Institute*, 221:3 [March 1936]). This intelligibility, attested to by the marvelous discoveries of science and technology, leads us, in the last analysis, to the transcendent and primordial thought imprinted on all things.[14]

2.4 The 1998 encyclical letter *Fides et ratio* (Faith and Reason), when clarifying the right relation of faith and reason, examined, among other things, the relation of philosophy to revelation and faith.

Revelation Stimulates
Rational Inquiry

From the teaching of the two Vatican Councils there also emerges a genuinely novel consideration for philosophical learning. Revelation has set within history a point of reference which cannot be ignored if the mystery of human life is to be known. Yet this knowledge refers back constantly to the mystery of God which the human mind cannot exhaust but can only receive and embrace in faith. Between these two poles, reason has its own specific field in which it can enquire and understand, restricted only by its finiteness before the infinite mystery of God.

Revelation therefore introduces into our history a universal and ultimate truth which stirs the human mind to ceaseless effort; indeed, it impels reason continually to extend the range of its knowledge until it senses that it has done all in its power, leaving no stone unturned. To assist our reflection on this point we have one of the most fruitful and important minds in human history, a point of reference for both philosophy and theology: Saint Anselm [d. 1109]. In his *Proslogion*, the Archbishop of Canterbury puts it this way: "Thinking of this problem frequently and intently, at times it seemed I was ready to grasp what I was seeking; at other times it eluded my thought completely, until finally, despairing of being able to find it, I wanted to abandon the search for something which was impossible to find. I wanted to rid myself of that thought because, by filling my mind, it distracted me from other problems from which I could gain some profit; but it would then present itself with ever greater insistence....Woe is me, one of the poor children of Eve, far from God, what did I set out to do and what have I accomplished? What was I aiming for and how far have I got? What did I aspire to and what did I long for?...O Lord, you are not only that than which nothing greater can be conceived (*non solum es quo maius cogitari nequit*), but you are greater than all that can be conceived (*quiddam maius quam cogitari possit*)....If you were not such, something greater than you could be thought, but this is impossible" (*Proemium* and nos. 1, 15).

The truth of Christian Revelation, found in Jesus of Nazareth, enables all men and women to embrace the "mystery" of their own life. As absolute truth, it summons human beings to be open to the transcendent, whilst respecting both their autonomy as creatures and their freedom. At this point the relationship between freedom and truth is complete, and we understand the full meaning of the Lord's words: "You will know the truth, and the truth will make you free" (John 8:32).

Christian Revelation is the true lodestar of men and women as they strive to make their way amid the pressures of an immanentist habit of mind and the constrictions of a technocratic logic. It is the ultimate possibility offered by God for the human being to know in all its fullness the seminal plan of love which began with creation. To those wishing to know the truth, if they can look beyond themselves and their own concerns, there is given the possibility of taking full and harmonious possession of their lives, precisely by following the path of truth. Here the words of the Book of Deuteronomy are pertinent: "This commandment which I command you is not too hard for you, neither is it far off. It is not in heaven that you should say, 'Who will go up for us to heaven, and bring it to us, that we may hear it and do it?'

Neither is it beyond the sea, that you should say, 'Who will go over the sea for us, and bring it to us, that we may hear and do it?' But the word is very near you; it is in your mouth and in your heart, that you can do it" (30:11–14). This text finds an echo in the famous dictum of the holy philosopher and theologian Augustine [d. 430]: "Do not wander far and wide but return into yourself. Deep within the human being there dwells the truth" (*Noli foras ire, in te ipsum redi. In interiore homine habitat veritas*, in *De Vera Religione*, 39, 72).

These considerations prompt a first conclusion: the truth made known to us by revelation is neither the product nor the consummation of an argument devised by human reason. It appears instead as something gratuitous, which itself stirs thought and seeks acceptance as an expression of love. This revealed truth is set within our history as an anticipation of that ultimate and definitive vision of God which is reserved for those who believe in him and seek him with a sincere heart. The ultimate purpose of personal existence, then, is the theme of philosophy and theology alike. For all their difference of method and content, both disciplines point to that "path of life" (Ps 16:11) which, as faith tells us, leads in the end to the full and lasting joy of the contemplation of the Triune God.[15]

Faith and Philosophical Reason Need Each Other

The history of philosophy, then, reveals a growing separation between faith and philosophical reason. Yet closer scrutiny shows that even in the philosophical thinking of those who helped drive faith and reason further apart there are found at times precious and seminal insights which, if pursued and developed with mind and heart rightly tuned, can lead to the discovery of truth's way. Such insights are found, for instance, in penetrating analyses of perception and experience, of the imaginary and the unconscious, of personhood and intersubjectivity, of freedom and values, of time and history. The theme of death as well can become for all thinkers an incisive appeal to seek within themselves the true meaning of their own life. But this does not mean that the link between faith and reason as it now stands does not need to be carefully examined, because each without the other is impoverished and enfeebled. Deprived of what revelation offers, reason has taken sidetracks which expose it to the danger of losing sight of its final goal. Deprived of reason, faith has stressed feeling and experience, and so has run the risk of no longer being a universal proposition. It is an illusion to think that faith, tied to weak reasoning, might be more penetrating; on the contrary, faith then runs the grave risk of withering into myth or superstition. By the same token, reason which is unrelated to an adult faith is not prompted to turn its gaze to the newness and radicality of being.

This is why I make this strong and insistent appeal—not, I trust, untimely—that faith and philosophy recover the profound unity which allows them to stand in harmony with their nature without compromising their mutual autonomy. The *parrhesia* (boldness) of faith must be matched by the boldness of reason.[16]

Unified Vision of Knowledge

The importance of metaphysics becomes still more evident if we consider current developments in hermeneutics and the analysis of language. The results of such studies can be very helpful for the understanding of faith, since they bring to light the structure of our thought and speech and the meaning which language bears. However, some scholars working in these fields tend to stop short at the question of how reality is understood and expressed, without going further to see whether reason can discover its essence. How can we fail to see in such a frame of mind the confirmation of our present crisis of confidence in the powers of reason? When, on the basis of preconceived assumptions, these positions tend to obscure the contents of faith or to deny their universal validity, then not only do they abase reason but in so doing they also disqualify themselves. Faith clearly presupposes that human language is capable of expressing divine and transcendent reality in a universal way—analogically, it is true, but no less meaningfully for that (cf. Fourth Lateran Ecumenical Council, *De Errore Abbatis Ioachim*, II). Were this not so, the word of God, which is always a divine word in human language, would not be capable of saying anything about God. The interpretation of this word cannot merely keep referring us to one interpretation after another, without ever leading us to a statement which is simply true; otherwise there would be no revelation of God, but only the expression of human notions about God, and about what God presumably thinks of us.

I am well aware that these requirements which the word of God imposes upon philosophy may seem daunting to many people involved in philosophical research today. Yet this is why, taking up what has been taught repeatedly by the popes for several generations and reaffirmed by the Second Vatican Council itself, I wish to reaffirm strongly the conviction that the human being can come to a unified and organic vision of knowledge. This is one of the tasks which Christian thought will have to take up through the next millennium of the Christian era. The segmentation of knowledge, with its splintered approach to truth and consequent fragmentation of meaning, keeps people today from coming to an interior unity. How could the Church not be concerned by this? It is the Gospel which imposes this sapiential task directly upon her pastors, and they cannot shrink from their duty to undertake it.[17]

Meaning and Truth

An initial problem is that of the relationship between meaning and truth. Like every other text, the sources which the theologian interprets primarily transmit a meaning which needs to be grasped and explained. This meaning presents itself as the truth about God which God himself communicates through the sacred text. Human language thus embodies the language of God, who communicates his own truth with that wonderful "condescension" which mirrors the logic of the incarnation (cf. *Dei Verbum*, 13). In interpreting the sources of revelation, then, the theologian needs to ask what is the deep and authentic truth which the texts wish to communicate, even within the limits of language.

The truth of the biblical texts, and of the Gospels in particular, is certainly not restricted to the narration of simple historical events or the statement of neutral facts, as historicist positivism would claim (cf. Pontifical Biblical Commission, *Instruction on the Historical*

Truth of the Gospels [21 April 1964]). Beyond simple historical occurrence, the truth of the events which these texts relate lies rather in the meaning they have in and for the history of salvation. This truth is elaborated fully in the Church's constant reading of these texts over the centuries, a reading which preserves intact their original meaning. There is a pressing need, therefore, that the relationship between fact and meaning, a relationship which constitutes the specific sense of history, be examined also from the philosophical point of view.[18]

Formulas Conditioned by History

The word of God is not addressed to any one people or to any one period of history. Similarly, dogmatic statements, while reflecting at times the culture of the period in which they were defined, formulate an unchanging and ultimate truth. This prompts the question of how one can reconcile the absoluteness and the universality of truth with the unavoidable historical and cultural conditioning of the formulas which express that truth. The claims of historicism, I noted earlier, are untenable; but the use of a hermeneutic open to the appeal of metaphysics can show how it is possible to move from the historical and contingent circumstances in which the texts developed to the truth which they express, a truth transcending those circumstances. Human language may be conditioned by history and constricted in other ways, but the human being can still express truths which surpass the phenomenon of language. Truth can never be confined to time and culture; in history it is known, but it also reaches beyond history.

To see this is to glimpse the solution of another problem: the problem of the enduring validity of the conceptual language used in conciliar definitions. This is a question which my revered predecessor Pius XII addressed in his encyclical letter *Humani generis*.

This is a complex theme to ponder, since one must reckon seriously with the meaning which words assume in different times and cultures. Nonetheless, the history of thought shows that across the range of cultures, and their development, certain basic concepts retain their universal epistemological value and thus retain the truth of the propositions in which they are expressed. Were this not the case, philosophy and the sciences could not communicate with each other, nor could they find a place in cultures different from those in which they were conceived and developed. The hermeneutical problem exists, to be sure; but it is not insoluble. Moreover, the objective value of many concepts does not exclude that their meaning is often imperfect. This is where philosophical speculation can be very helpful. We may hope, then, that philosophy will be especially concerned to deepen the understanding of the relationship between conceptual language and truth, and to propose ways which will lead to a right understanding of that relationship.[19]

NOTES

1. *Address to Scientists, Cologne (1980)*, 2, in *AAS* 73 (1981), 50; *ND*, 164; *OREnglish*, 47 (November 24, 1980), 6, 7, 12; *Origins* 10:25 (1980), 395.

2. Ibid., 3, in *AAS* 73 (1981), 51; *OREnglish* 47 (November 24, 1980), 6, 7, 12; *Origins* 10:25 (1980), 396.

3. Ibid., 3, in *AAS* 73 (1981), 52–53; *OREnglish* 47 (November 24, 1980), 6, 7, 12; *Origins* 10:25 (1980), 396.

4. Ibid., 4, in *AAS* 73 (1981), 53–54; *OREnglish* 47 (November 24, 1980), 6, 7, 12; *Origins* 10:25 (1980), 396–97.

5. Ibid., 4, in *AAS* 73 (1981), 55; *OREnglish* 47 (November 24, 1980), 6, 7, 12; *Origins* 10:25 (1980), 397.

6. Ibid., 5, in *AAS* 73 (1981), 56–57; *OREnglish* 47 (November 24, 1980), 6, 7, 12; *Origins* 10:25 (1980), 397.

7. Ibid., 5, in *AAS* 73 (1981), 57; *OREnglish* 47 (November 24, 1980), 6, 7, 12; *Origins* 10:25 (1980), 397.

8. *Letter to Father George V. Coyne, S.J. (1988)*, in *AAS* 81 (1989), 277; *ND*, 176a; *OREnglish* 46 (November 14, 1988); *Origins*, 18 (1988–89), 375; *Pope Speaks* 34:1 (1989), 4.

9. Ibid., in *AAS* 81 (1989), 278–79; *ND*, 176b; *OREnglish* 46 (November 14, 1988); *Origins*, 18 (1988–89), 375; *Pope Speaks* 34:1 (1989), 5.

10. Ibid., in *AAS* 81 (1989), 280–81; *ND*, 176c; *OREnglish* 46 (November 14, 1988); *Origins*, 18 (1988–89), 375; *Pope Speaks* 34:1 (1989), 6–7.

11. *Address to the Pontifical Academy of Science (1992)*, 9, in *AAS* 85 (1993), 768; *ND*, 184a; *OREnglish* 44 (November 4, 1992), 1–2; *Origins* 22:22 (1992), 372.

12. Ibid., 11, in *AAS* 85 (1993) 769–70; *OREnglish* 44 (November 4, 1992), 1–2; *Origins* 22:22 (1992), 373.

13. Ibid., 12, in *AAS* 85 (1993), 770; *OREnglish* 44 (November 4, 1992), 1–2; *Origins* 22:22 (1992), 373.

14. Ibid., 14, in *AAS* 85 (1993), 373; *ND*, 434b; *OREnglish* 44 (November 4, 1992), 1–2; *Origins* 22:22 (1992), 373.

15. *Fides et ratio*, 14–15, in *AAS* 91 (1999), 16–18; *EncMiller*, 858–59; *ND*, 190a; *Origins* 28:19 (1998), 322–23; *Pope Speaks* 44:1 (1999), 9–10.

16. Ibid., 48, in *AAS* 91 (1999), 43; *EncMiller*, 878–79; *ND*, 190b; *Origins* 28:19 (1998), 331; *Pope Speaks* 44:1 (1999), 28–29.

17. Ibid., 84–85, in *AAS* 91 (1999), 71–72; *EncMiller*, 900; *Origins* 28:19 (1998), 340; *Pope Speaks* 44:1 (1999), 47–48.

18. Ibid., 94, in *AAS* 91 (1999), 94–95; *EncMiller*, 905–6; *Origins* 28:19 (1998), 342; *Pope Speaks* 44:1 (1999), 52–53.

19. Ibid., 95–96, in *AAS* 91 (1999), 79–80; *EncMiller*, 906–7; *Origins* 28:19 (1998), 342; *Pope Speaks* 44:1 (1999), 53.

CHAPTER THREE

The Triune God
and Jesus Christ

3.1 John Paul II dedicated three of his early encyclicals to the Trinity: in 1979 to the Son (*Redemptor hominis*, The Redeemer of the Human Person), in 1980 to the Father (*Dives in misericordia*, Rich in Mercy), and in 1986 to the Holy Spirit (*Dominum et vivificantem*, The Lord and Giver of Life). In all three encyclicals he stressed the loving and saving initiatives of God toward human beings and their world: The triune God is "God for us." *Dives in misericordia* highlighted a parable that is usually called the parable of the prodigal son (Luke 15:11–32) but that would be more accurately called the parable of the merciful father. *Dominum et vivificantem*, the first encyclical to be devoted to the Holy Spirit since Leo XIII's *Divinum illud* (That Divine [Office]) of 1897, introduced a fresh terminology into official teaching by twelve times calling the Holy Spirit "the Self-communication of God." In a remarkable address to the aboriginal peoples of Australia, John Paul II added to the teaching of *Dominum et vivificantem* by developing the theme of the mysterious presence and activity of the divine Spirit in the culture and religions of those peoples. Even before he issued *Redemptor hominis*, John Paul II had important things to say about Jesus Christ in his address to the Third General Assembly of Latin American Bishops in January 1979: for instance, about the kingdom of God that Jesus proclaimed—a theme to which the Pope returned in his 1990 encyclical *Redemptoris missio* (The Mission of the Redeemer).

The Truth concerning Jesus Christ

From you, pastors, the faithful of your countries expect and demand first and foremost a careful and zealous transmission of the truth about Jesus Christ. This truth is at the core of evangelization and constitutes its essential content: "There is no authentic evangelization so long as one does not announce the name, the teaching, the life, the promises, the kingdom, the mystery of Jesus of Nazareth, the Son of God" (*Evangelium nuntiandi*, 22).

The vigor of the faith of millions of people will depend on a lively knowledge of this truth. On such knowledge will also depend the strength of their adhesion to the Church and their active presence as Christians in the world. From it will flow options, values, attitudes, and behavior patterns that can give direction and definition to our Christian living, that can create new human beings and then a new humanity through the conversion of the individual and social conscience (cf. *Evangelium nuntiandi*, 18). It is from a solid Christology that light must be shed on so many of the doctrinal and pastoral themes and questions that you propose to examine in the coming days.

So we must profess Christ before history and the world, displaying the same deeply felt and deeply lived conviction that Peter did in his profession: "You are the Messiah,...the Son of the living God" (Matt 16:16).

This is the Good News, unique in a real sense. The Church lives by it and for it, even as the Church draws from it all that it has to offer to all human beings, regardless of nation, culture, race, epoch, age, or condition. Hence "on the basis of that profession [Peter's], the history of sacred salvation and of the People of God should take on a new dimension" (John Paul II, *Inaugural homily of his pontificate*, October 22, 1978). This is the one and only Gospel. And as the Apostle wrote so pointedly, "Even if we, or an angel from heaven, should preach to you a Gospel not in accord with the one we delivered to you, let a curse be upon him" (Gal 1:8).[1]

Re-readings of the Gospel

Now today we find in many places a phenomenon that is not new. We find "re-readings" of the Gospel that are the product of theoretical speculations rather than of authentic meditation on the word of God and a genuine evangelical commitment. They cause confusion insofar as they depart from the central criteria of the Church's faith, and people have the temerity to pass them on as catechesis to Christian communities. In some cases people are silent about Christ's divinity, or else they indulge in types of interpretation that are at variance with the Church's faith. Christ is alleged to be only a "prophet," a proclaimer of God's Kingdom and love, but not the true Son of God. Hence he allegedly is not the center and object of the Gospel message itself.

In other cases people purport to depict Jesus as a political activist, as a fighter against Roman domination and the authorities, and even as someone involved in the class struggle. This conception of Christ as a political figure, a revolutionary, as the subversive of Nazareth, does not tally with the Church's catechesis. Confusing the insidious pretext of Jesus' accusers with the attitude of Jesus himself —which was very different—people claim that the cause of his death was the result of a political conflict; they say nothing about the Lord's willing self-surrender or even his awareness of his redemptive mission. The Gospels show clearly that for Jesus anything that would alter his mission as the Servant of Yahweh was a temptation (Matt 4:8; Luke 4:5). He does not accept the position of those who mixed the things of God with merely political attitudes (Matt 22:21; Mark 12:17; John 18:36). He unequivocally rejects recourse to violence; he opens his message of conversion to all, and he does not exclude even the publicans. The perspective of his mission goes much deeper. It has to do with complete and integral salvation through a love that brings transformation, peace, pardon, and reconciliation. And there can be no doubt that all this imposes exacting demands on the attitude of any Christians who truly wish to serve the least of their brothers and sisters, the poor, the needy, the marginalized: i.e., all those whose lives reflect the suffering countenance of the Lord (cf. *Lumen gentium*, 8).

Against such "re-readings," therefore, and against the perhaps brilliant but fragile and inconsistent hypotheses flowing from them, "evangelization in Latin America's present and future" cannot cease to affirm the Church's faith: Jesus Christ, the Word and Son of God, becomes human to draw close to human beings and to offer them, through the power of his mystery, the great gift of God that is salvation (cf. *Evangelium nuntiandi*, 19, 27).[2]

The Redeemer and Human Beings

Human beings cannot live without love. They remain beings that are incomprehensible for themselves; their lives are senseless, if love is not revealed to them, if they do not encounter love, if they do not experience it and make it their own, if they do not participate intimately in it. This, as has already been said, is why Christ the Redeemer "fully reveals human beings to themselves." If we may use the expression, this is the human dimension of the mystery of the Redemption. In this dimension people find again the greatness, dignity and value that belong to their humanity. In the mystery of the redemption people become newly "expressed" and, in a way, are newly created. Created anew! "There is neither Jew nor Greek, there is neither slave nor free, there is neither male nor female; for you are all one in Christ Jesus" (Gal 3:28). Those who wish to understand themselves thoroughly—and not just in accordance with immediate, partial, often superficial, and even illusory standards and measures of their being—must with their unrest, uncertainty, and even their weakness and sinfulness, with their lives and deaths, draw near to Christ. Humans must, so to speak, enter into him with their entire selves; they must "appropriate" and assimilate the whole of the reality of the incarnation and redemption in order to find themselves.[3]

The God of Merciful Love

The Paschal Mystery is Christ at the summit of the revelation of the inscrutable mystery of God. It is precisely then that the words pronounced in the Upper Room are completely fulfilled: "He who has seen me has seen the Father" (John 14:9). In fact, Christ, whom the

Father "did not spare" (Rom 8:32) for the sake of humans and who in his passion and in the torment of the cross did not obtain human mercy, has revealed in his resurrection the fullness of the love that the Father has for him and, in him, for all people. "He is not God of the dead, but of the living" (Mark 12:27). In his resurrection Christ has revealed the God of merciful love, precisely because he accepted the cross as the way to the resurrection. And it is for this reason that, when we recall the cross of Christ, his passion and death, our faith and hope are centered on the Risen One: on that Christ who "on the evening of that day, the first day of the week,...stood among them" in the upper room, "where the disciples were,...breathed on them, and said to them: 'Receive the Holy Spirit. If you forgive the sins of any, they are forgiven; if you retain the sins of any, they are retained'" (John 20:19–23).

Here is the Son of God, who in his resurrection experienced in a radical way mercy shown to himself, that is to say, the love of the Father which is more powerful than death. And it is also the same Christ, the Son of God, who at the end of his messianic mission—and, in a certain sense, even beyond the end—reveals himself as the inexhaustible source of mercy, of the same love that, in a subsequent perspective of the history of salvation in the Church, is to be ever-lastingly confirmed as more powerful than sin. The paschal Christ is the definitive incarnation of mercy, its living sign in salvation history and eschatology.[4]

The Holy Spirit within the Eternal Life of God

In his intimate life, God "is love" (cf. 1 John 4:8, 16), the essential love shared by the three divine persons: personal love is the Holy Spirit as the Spirit of the Father and the Son. Therefore he "searches even the depths of God" (cf. 1 Cor 2:10) as uncreated Love-Gift. It can be said that in the Holy Spirit the intimate life of the Triune God becomes totally gift, an exchange of mutual love between the divine persons and that through the Holy Spirit God exists in the mode of gift. It is the Holy Spirit who is the personal expression of this self-giving, of this being-love (cf. St. Thomas Aquinas, *Summa Theologiae*, I, 37–38). He is Person-Love. He is Person-Gift. Here we have an inexhaustible treasure of the reality and an inexpressible deepening of the concept of person in God, which only divine revelation makes known to us.[5]

The Self-Communication of God

Describing his "departure" as a condition for the "coming" of the Counselor, Christ links the new beginning of God's salvific self-communication in the Holy Spirit with the mystery of the redemption. It is a new beginning, first of all because between the first beginning and the whole of human history—from the original fall onwards—sin has intervened, sin which is in contradiction to the presence of the Spirit of God in creation, and which is above all in contradiction to God's salvific self-communication to man. St. Paul writes that, precisely because of sin, "creation...was subjected to futility,...has been groaning in travail together until now" and "waits with eager longing for the revealing of the sons of God" (Rom 8:19-22).

Therefore Jesus Christ says in the upper room, "It is to your advantage I go away;...if I go, I will send him to you" (John 16:7). The "departure" of Christ through the cross has the power of the redemption, and this also means a new presence of the Spirit of God in creation: the new beginning of God's self-communication to human beings in the Holy Spirit. "And that you are children is proven by the fact that God has sent into our hearts the Spirit of his Son who cries: Abba, Father!"—as the Apostle Paul writes in the Letter to the Galatians (Gal 4:6; cf. Rom 8:15). The Holy Spirit is the Spirit of the Father, as the words of the farewell discourse in the upper room bear witness. At the same time he is the Spirit of the Son: he is the Spirit of Jesus Christ, as the apostles and particularly Paul of Tarsus will testify (cf. Gal 4:6; Phil 1:19; Rom 8:11). With the sending of this Spirit "into our hearts," there begins the fulfillment of that for which "creation waits with eager longing," as we read in the Letter to the Romans.

The Holy Spirit comes at the price of Christ's "departure." While this "departure" caused the apostles to be sorrowful (cf. John

16:6), and this sorrow was to reach its culmination in the passion and death on Good Friday: "this sorrow will turn into joy" (cf. John 16:20). For Christ will add to this redemptive "departure" the glory of his resurrection and ascension to the Father. Thus the sorrow with its underlying joy is, for the apostles in the context of their Master's "departure," an "advantageous" departure, for thanks to it another "Counselor" will come (cf. John 16:7). At the price of the cross which brings about the redemption, in the power of the whole Paschal Mystery of Jesus Christ, the Holy Spirit comes in order to remain from the day of Pentecost onwards with the apostles, to remain with the Church and in the Church, and through her in the world.[6]

The Mystery of God's Spirit

At the beginning of time, as God's Spirit moved over the waters, he began to communicate something of his goodness and beauty to all creation. When God then created man and woman, he gave them the good things of the earth for their use and benefit; and he put into their hearts abilities and powers, which were his gifts. And to all human beings throughout the ages God has given a desire for himself, a desire which different cultures have tried to express in their own ways.

As the human family spread over the face of the earth, your people settled and lived in this big country that stood apart from all the others. Other people did not even know this land was here; they only knew that somewhere in the southern oceans of the world there was "The Great South Land of the Holy Spirit." But for thousands of years you have lived in this land and fashioned a culture that endures to this day. And during all this time, the Spirit of God has been with you. Your "Dreaming," which influences your lives so strongly that, no matter what happens, you remain for ever people of your culture, is your only way of touching the mystery of God's Spirit in you and in creation. You must keep striving for God and hold on to it in your lives.

The rock paintings and the discovered evidence of your ancient tools and implements indicate the presence of your age-old culture and prove your ancient occupancy of this land. Your culture, which shows the lasting genius and dignity of your race, must not be allowed to disappear. Do not think that your gifts are worth so little that you should no longer bother to maintain them. Share them with each other and teach them to your children. Your songs, your stories, your paintings, your dances, your languages, must never be lost. Do you perhaps remember those words that Paul VI spoke to the Aboriginal people during his visit to them in 1970? On that occasion he said: "We know that you have a life style proper to your own ethnic genius or culture, a culture which the Church respects and which she does not in any way ask you to renounce....Society itself is enriched by the presence of different cultural and ethnic elements. For us, you and the values you represent are precious. We deeply respect your dignity and reiterate our deep affection for you" (*Address to Aboriginals in Sydney*, December 2, 1970).

For thousands of years this culture of yours was free to grow without interference by people from other places. You lived your lives in spiritual closeness to the land, with its animals, birds, fishes, waterholes, rivers, hills and mountains. Through your closeness to the land you touched the sacredness of humanity's relationship with God, for the land was the proof of a power in life greater than yourselves. You did not spoil the land, use it up, exhaust it, and then walk away from it. You realized that your land was related to the source of life. The silence of the Bush taught you a quietness of soul that put you in touch with another world, the world of God's Spirit. Your careful attention to the details of kinship spoke of your reverence for birth, life and human generation. You knew that children need to be loved, to be full of joy. They need a time to grow in laughter and to play, secure in the knowledge that they belong to their people. You had a great respect for the need which people have for law, as a guide to living fairly with each other. So you created a legal system—very strict it is true—but closely adapted to the country in which you lived your lives. It made your society orderly. It was one of the reasons why you survived in this land. You marked the growth of your young men and women with ceremonies of discipline that taught them responsibility as they came to maturity. These achievements are indications of human strivings. And in these strivings you showed a dignity open to the message of God's revealed wisdom to all men and women, which is the great truth of the Gospel of Jesus Christ.

Some of the stories from your Dreamtime legends speak powerfully of the great mysteries of human life, its frailty, its need for help, its closeness to spiritual powers and the value of the human person. They are not unlike some of the great inspired lessons from the people among whom Jesus himself was born. It is wonderful to see how people, as they accept the Gospel of Jesus, find points of agreement between their own traditions and those of Jesus and his people.[7]

Jesus Reveals the Kingdom

The kingdom which Jesus inaugurates is the kingdom of God. Jesus himself reveals who this God is, the One whom he addresses by the intimate term "Abba," Father (cf. Mark 14:36). God, as revealed above all in the parables (cf. Luke 15:3–32; Matt 20:1–16), is sensitive to the needs and sufferings of every human being: he is a Father filled with love and compassion, who grants forgiveness and freely bestows the favors asked of him. St. John tells us that "God is love" (1 John 4:8, 16). Every person therefore is invited to "repent" and to "believe" in God's merciful love. The kingdom will grow insofar as every person learns to turn to God in the intimacy of prayer as to a father (cf. Luke 11:2; Matt 23:9) and strive to do his will (cf. Matt 7:21).

Jesus gradually reveals the characteristics and demands of the kingdom through his words, his actions and his own person. The kingdom of God is meant for all humankind, and all people are called to become members of it.[8]

3.2 John Paul II's teaching on Christ and the Trinity included three texts that aimed at union of doctrine with separated churches. First, in November 1994 he signed a joint declaration with Mar Dinkha IV, patriarch of the Assyrian Church of the East. The declaration echoed the language of the Council of Chalcedon of 451 (for example, the two natures in the one person of Christ, as well as the famous four adverbs, here translated as "without confusion or change, without division or separation"). The declaration respected the sensibilities of the followers of Patriarch Nestorius of Constantinople (d. after 451) by not insisting on the mariological title "Mother of God" as strictly necessary.

Second, in a homily given in St. Peter's Basilica on June 29, 1995, in the presence of the Ecumenical Patriarch Bartholomew I, the spiritual head of Orthodox Christians, John Paul II asked that a text be prepared for him to clarify the "traditional doctrine for the *Filioque*" (from the Son), which the Latin version of the Creed uses in its liturgy, and to show how this addition is in harmony with what the Creed of Constantinople I (381) confesses: the Father as the source of the whole Trinity and the one origin of the Son and of the Holy Spirit. The Pontifical Council for Promoting Christian Unity prepared and published three months later such a clarification.

Third, in December 1996 John Paul II signed a joint declaration with Catholicos Karekin I, the Supreme Patriarch and Catholicos of all Armenians, which repeats the four famous adverbs from Chalcedon (here translated as "without confusion, without alteration, without division, without any form of separation"). When confessing the unity of perfect divinity and perfect humanity in the one person of the Son of God, the declaration uses language from Chalcedon. However, out of respect for the Armenians, it does not include that council's terminology of *consubstantial* and *two natures*.

The One Christ Is True God and True Man

Therefore our Lord Jesus Christ is true God and true man, perfect in his divinity and perfect in his humanity, consubstantial with the Father and consubstantial with us in all things but sin. His divinity and his humanity are united in one person, without confusion or change, without division or separation. In him has been preserved the difference of the natures of divinity and humanity, with all their properties, faculties and operations. But far from constituting "one and another," the divinity and humanity are united in the person of the same and unique Son of God and Lord Jesus Christ who is the object of a single adoration.

Christ therefore is not an "ordinary man" whom God adopted in order to reside in him and inspire him, as in the righteous ones and the prophets. But the same God the Word, begotten of his Father

51

before all worlds without beginning according to his divinity, was born of a mother without a father in the last times according to his humanity. The humanity to which the Blessed Virgin Mary gave birth always was that of the Son of God himself. That is why the Assyrian Church of the East is praying [to] the Virgin Mary as "the Mother of Christ our God and Savior." In the light of this same faith the Catholic tradition addresses the Virgin Mary as "the Mother of God" and also as "the Mother of Christ." We both recognize the legitimacy and rightness of these expressions of the same faith and we both respect the preference of each Church in her liturgical life and piety.[9]

The Father, the Sole Source

The Catholic Church acknowledges the conciliar, ecumenical, normative, and irrevocable value, as expression of the one common faith of the Church and of all Christians, of the Symbol professed in Greek at Constantinople in 381 by the Second Ecumenical Council. No profession of faith peculiar to a particular liturgical tradition can contradict this expression of the faith taught by the undivided Church....

The Father alone is the principle without principle (*arche anarchos*) of the two other persons of the Trinity, the sole source (*peghe*) of the Son and of the Holy Spirit. The Holy Spirit, therefore, takes his origin from the Father alone (*ek monou tou Patros*) in a principal, proper, and immediate manner.... The doctrine of the *Filioque* must be understood and presented by the Catholic Church in such a way that it cannot appear to contradict the Monarchy of the Father nor the fact that he is the sole origin (*arche, aitia*) of the *ekporeusis* of the Spirit....

Being aware of this, the Catholic Church has refused the addition of *kai tou Uiou* to the formula *ek tou Patros ekporeuomenon* of the Symbol of Nicaea-Constantinople in the churches, even of Latin rite, which use it in Greek. The liturgical use of this original text remains always legitimate in the Catholic Church.[10]

Christ, Perfect God and Perfect Man

Pope John Paul II and Catholicos Karekin I recognize the deep spiritual communion which already unites them and the bishops, clergy and lay faithful of their Churches. It is a communion which finds its roots in the common faith in the Holy and Life-giving Trinity proclaimed by the Apostles and transmitted down the centuries by the many fathers and doctors of the Church and the bishops, priests, and martyrs who have followed them. They rejoice in the fact that recent developments of ecumenical relations and theological discussions carried out in the spirit of Christian love and fellowship have dispelled many misunderstandings inherited from the controversies and dissensions of the past. Such dialogues and encounters have prepared a healthy situation of mutual understanding and recovery of the deeper spiritual communion based on the common faith in the Holy Trinity that they have been given through the Gospel of Christ and in the Holy Tradition of the Church.

They particularly welcome the great advance that their Churches have registered in their common search for unity in Christ, the Word of God made flesh. Perfect God as to his divinity, perfect man as to his humanity, his divinity is united to his humanity in the Person of the Only-begotten Son of God, in a union which is real, perfect, without confusion, without alteration, without division, without any form of separation.[11]

NOTES

1. *Address at Puebla (January 1979)*, 1.2–3, in *AAS* 72 (1979), 189–90; *ND*, 674; *Origins* 8:34 (1979), 531–32; *Pope Speaks* 24 (1979), 52.

2. Ibid., 1.4–5, in *AAS* 72 (1979), 190–91; *ND*, 675, 676; *Origins* 8:34 (1979), 532; *Pope Speaks* 24:1 (1979), 52–54.

3. *Redemptor hominis*, 10, in *AAS* 71 (1979), 274–75; *EncMiller*, 58–59; *ND*, 678; *Origins* 8:40 (1979), 631; *Pope Speaks* 24:2 (1979), 110.

4. *Dives in misericordia*, 8, in *AAS* 72 (1980), 1206–7; *EncMiller*, 122; *ND*, 68; *Origins* 10:26 (1980), 409–10; *Pope Speaks* 26:1 (1981), 40–41.

5. *Dominum et vivificantem*, 13–14, in *AAS* 78 (1986), 820–22; *EncMiller*, 251–52; *Origins* 16:4 (1986), 81; *Pope Speaks* 31:2 (1986), 205–6.

6. Ibid., 13–14, in *AAS* 78 (1986), 820–22; *EncMiller*, 251–52; *Origins* 16:4 (1986), 81; *Pope Speaks* 31:2 (1986), 207–8.

7. *Address to Aborigines and Torres Strait Islanders of Australia, November 29, 1986*, in *AAS* 79 (1987), 973–75; *Origins*, 16:26 (1986), 473–75.

8. *Redemptoris missio*, 13–14, in *AAS* 81 (1991), 262; *EncMiller*, 445; *Origins* 20:34 (1991), 546; *Pope Speaks* 36:3 (1991), 145.

9. *Common Christological Declaration between the Catholic Church and the Assyrian Church of the East (November 11, 1994)*, in *AAS* 87 (1995), 685–87; *ND*, 683; *OREnglish* 46 (November 26, 1994), 1, 4; *Pope Speaks* 40:2 (1995), 114–15.

10. *The Father as the Source of the Whole Trinity: The Procession of the Holy Spirit in Greek and Latin Traditions (September 13, 1995)*, in *ND*, 339, 938; *OREnglish* 38 (September 20, 1995), 3, 6.

11. *Common Declaration of John Paul II and Catholicos Karekin I (December 13, 1996)*, in *AAS* 89 (1997), 96; *Pope Speaks* 42:3 (1997), 180–81.

CHAPTER FOUR

The Human Condition

4.1 Right from his address to the Third General Assembly of Latin American Bishops in January 1979 and the encyclical that followed just over a month later, *Redemptor hominis* (The Redeemer of the Human Person), John Paul II expounded Christian teaching on the human person, or "theological anthropology." The divine image in which all human beings are made creates the basis for their dignity and rights. Every human being is united with Christ, who brings the answers to our fundamental questions. Sin has deformed human life, but Christ, the last Adam, has restored and renewed our divine image.

The Human Person Is God's Image

Thanks to the Gospel, the Church possesses the truth about the human being. It is found in an anthropology that the Church never ceases to explore more deeply and to share. The primordial assertion of this anthropology is that the human being is the image of God and cannot be reduced to a mere fragment of nature or to an anonymous element in the human city (*Gaudium et spes*, 12, 14). This is the sense intended by St. Irenaeus when he wrote: "The glory of the human being is God; but the receptacle of all God's activity, wisdom, and power is the human being" (*Adversus haereses*, III, 20. 2–3).[1]

Basic Human Rights

This dignity [of the human person] is crushed underfoot when due regard is not maintained for such values as freedom, the right to profess one's religion, physical and psychic integrity, the right to life's necessities, and the right to life itself. On the social and political level it is crushed when human beings cannot exercise their right to participate, when they are subjected to unjust and illegitimate forms of coercion, when they are subjected to physical and psychic torture, and so forth....

In the light of what has been said above, the Church is profoundly grieved to see "the sometimes massive increase in violations of human rights in many parts of the world....Who can deny that today there are individual persons and civil authorities who are violating fundamental rights of the human person with impunity? I refer to such rights as the right to be born; the right to life; the right to responsible procreation; the right to work; the right to peace, freedom, and social justice; and the right to participate in making decisions that affect peoples and nations. And what are we to say when we run up against various forms of collective violence, such as racial discrimination against individuals and groups and the physical and psychological torturing of prisoners and political dissidents? The list grows when we add examples of abduction and of kidnapping for the sake of material gain, which represent such a traumatic attack on family life and the social fabric" (John Paul II, *Message to the United Nations*, December 2, 1978). We cry out once more: Respect the human being, who is the image of God! Evangelize so that this may become a reality, so that the Lord may transform hearts and humanize political and economic systems, with the responsible commitment of human beings as the starting point.[2]

Christ the New Adam

Christ, the Redeemer of the world, is the one who penetrated in a unique unrepeatable way into the mystery of human beings and entered their "heart." Rightly therefore does the Second Vatican Council teach: "The truth is that only in the mystery of the Incarnate

Word does the mystery of human beings become clear. For Adam, the first man, was a type of him who was to come (Rom 5:14), Christ the Lord. Christ the new Adam, in the very revelation of the mystery of the Father and of his love, *fully reveals human beings to themselves* and brings to light their most high calling." And the Council continues: "He who is the 'image of the invisible God' (Col 1:15), is himself the perfect man who has restored in the children of Adam that likeness to God which had been disfigured ever since the first sin. Human nature by that very fact was assumed, not absorbed, in him, [and] has been raised in us also an incomparable dignity. For, by his incarnation, he, the Son of God, *in a certain way united himself with each human person.* He worked with human hands, he thought with a human mind. He acted with a human will, and with a human heart he loved. Born of the Virgin Mary, he has truly been made one of us, like to us in all things except sin" (*Gaudium et spes*, 22), he, the Redeemer of human beings.[3]

All Human Beings Share in the Mystery of Christ

What is in question here are humans in all their truth, in their full magnitude. We are not dealing with the "abstract" person, but the real, "concrete," "historical" person. We are dealing with "each" person, for each one is included in the mystery of the redemption and with each one Christ has united himself for ever through this mystery. All come into the world through being conceived in their mothers' wombs and being born of their mothers, and precisely on account of the mystery of the redemption are entrusted to the care of the Church. Her care is about the whole person and is focused on them in an altogether special manner. The objects of her care are human beings in their unique, unrepeatable human reality, which keeps intact the image and likeness of God himself (cf. Gen 1:26). The Council points out this very fact when, speaking of that likeness, it recalls that the human being "is the only creature on earth that God willed for itself" (*Gaudium et spes*, 24). Human beings as "willed" by God, as "chosen" by him from eternity and called, destined for grace and glory: this is "each" person, "the most concrete" person, "the most real"; these are the human persons in all the fullness of the mystery in which they have become sharers in Jesus Christ, the mystery in which each one of the four thousand million human beings living on our planet has become a sharer from the moment they are conceived beneath the heart of their mothers.[4]

Personal History of Human Beings

The Church cannot abandon human beings, for their "destiny," that is to say their election, calling, birth and death, salvation or perdition, is so closely and unbreakably linked with Christ. We are speaking precisely of each person on this planet, this earth that the Creator gave to the first parents, saying to the man and the woman: "subdue it and have dominion" (Gen 1:28); of each person in all the unrepeatable reality of what one is and what one does, of intellect, will, conscience and heart. Human persons who in their singular reality, because they are "persons," have a history of their life that is their own and, most importantly, a history of their soul that is their own. In keeping with the openness of their spirit within and also with the many diverse needs of their body and their existence in time, they write this personal history of theirs through numerous bonds, contacts, situations, and social structures linking them with others, beginning to do so from the first moment of their existence on earth, from the moment of conception and birth. Each one in the full truth of existence, of one's personal being, one's community and social being—in the sphere of one's own family, in the sphere of society and very diverse contexts, in the sphere of one's own nation or people (perhaps still only that of one's clan or tribe), and in the sphere of the whole of humankind—this person is the primary route that the Church must travel in fulfilling her mission: the person is the primary and fundamental way for the Church, the way traced out by Christ himself, the way that leads invariably through the mystery of the incarnation and the redemption.

It was precisely this person in all the truth of one's life, with one's conscience, one's continual inclination to sin and at the same time in one's continual aspiration to truth, the good, the beautiful, justice and love that the Second Vatican Council had before its eyes when, in outlining our situation in the modern world, it always passed from the external elements of this situation to the truth within humanity (cf. *Gaudium et spes*, 10).[5]

Freedom as Self-Giving

Mature humanity means full use of the gift of freedom received from the Creator when he called into existence the human person made "in his image, after his likeness."...Nowadays it is sometimes held, though wrongly, that freedom is an end in itself, that each human being is free when one makes use of freedom as one wishes, and that this must be our aim in the lives of individuals and societies. In reality, freedom is a great gift only when we know how to use it consciously for everything that is our true good. Christ teaches us that the best use of freedom is charity, which takes concrete form in self-giving and in service. For this "freedom Christ has set us free" (Gal 5:1; cf. 5:13) and ever continues to set us free. The Church draws from this source the unceasing inspiration, the call and the drive for her mission and her service among all humankind. The full truth about human freedom is indelibly inscribed on the mystery of the redemption.[6]

4.2 During the 1980s and 1990s, John Paul II filled out his teaching on the human condition through the 1988 apostolic letter *Mulieris dignitatem* (The Dignity of a Woman), a message for the Twenty-third World Day of Peace (January 1, 1990), the 1991 encyclical *Centesimus annus* (The Hundredth Year), the 1993 encyclical *Veritatis splendor* (The Splendor of Truth), the 1995 encyclical *Evangelium vitae* (The Gospel of Life), and other texts. The message of January 1990, entitled "Peace with God the Creator, Peace with All of Creation," proved to be the pope's most powerful message on the ecological crisis.

Dignity and Equality of Men and Women

The revealed truth concerning the human person as "the image and likeness" of God constitutes the immutable *basis of all Christian anthropology*. "God created humanity in his own image, in the image of God he created it; male and female he created them" (Gen 1:27). This concise passage contains the fundamental anthropological truths: the human being is the highpoint of the whole order of creation in the visible world; the human race, which takes its origin from the calling into existence of man and woman, crowns the whole work of creation; *both man and woman are human beings to an equal degree*, both are created *in God's image*. This image and likeness of God, which is essential for the human being, is passed on by the man and woman, as spouses and parents, to their descendants: "Be fruitful and multiply, and fill the earth and subdue it" (Gen 1:28). The Creator entrusts dominion over earth to the human race, to all persons, to all men and women, who derive their dignity and vocation from the common beginning"…

The biblical text provides sufficient bases for recognizing the essential equality of man and woman from the point of view of their humanity. From the very beginning, both are persons, unlike the other living beings in the world about them. *The woman is another "I" in a common humanity*. From the very beginning they appear as a "unity of the two," and this signifies that the original solitude is overcome, the solitude in which man does not find "a helper fit for him" (Gen 2:20). Is it only a question here of a "helper," in activity, in "subduing the earth" (cf. Gen 1:28)? Certainly it is a matter of a life's companion, with whom, as a wife, the man can unite himself, becoming with her "one flesh" and for this reason leaving "his father and his mother" (cf. Gen. 2: 24). Thus in the same context as the creation of man and woman, the biblical account speaks of God's *instituting marriage* as an indispensable condition for the transmission of life to new generations, the transmission of life to which marriage and conjugal love are by their nature ordered: "Be fruitful and multiply, and fill the earth and subdue it" (Gen. 1:28).[7]

Love and Women's Dignity

A woman's dignity is closely connected with the love which she receives by the very reason of her femininity; it is likewise connected *with the love which she gives in return*. The truth about the person and about love is thus confirmed. With regard to the truth about the person, we must turn again to the Second Vatican Council: "The human person, who is the only creature on earth that God willed for its own sake, cannot fully find itself except through a sincere gift of self" (*Gaudium et spes*, 24). This applies to every human being, as a person created in God's image, whether man or woman. This ontological affirmation also indicates the ethical dimension of a person's vocation. *Woman can only find herself by giving love to others.*[8]

Creation Disturbed by Sin

Adam and Eve's call to share in the unfolding of God's plan of creation brought into play those abilities and gifts which distinguish the human being from all other creatures. At the same time, their call established a fixed relationship between humankind and the rest of creation. Made in the image and likeness of God, Adam and Eve were to have exercised their dominion over the earth (Gen 1:28) with wisdom and love. Instead, they destroyed the existing harmony *by deliberately going against the Creator's plan*, that is, by choosing to sin. This resulted not only in humanity's alienation from itself, in death and fratricide, but also in the earth's "rebellion" against humankind (cf. Gen 3:17–19; 4:12). All of creation became subject to futility, waiting in a mysterious way to be set free and to obtain a glorious liberty together with all the children of God (cf. Rom 8:20–21)....

These biblical considerations help us to understand better *the relationship between human activity and the whole of creation*. When a person turns his or her back on the Creator's plan, that individual provokes a disorder which has inevitable repercussions on the rest of the created order. If humanity is not at peace with God, then earth itself cannot be at peace: "Therefore the land mourns and all who dwell in it languish, and also the beasts of the field and the birds of the air and even the fish of the sea are taken away" (Hos 4:3).[9]

Original Sin and Politics

Human beings, who are created for freedom, bear within themselves the wound of original sin, which constantly draws them towards evil and puts them in need of redemption. Not only is this doctrine an integral part of Christian revelation; it also has great hermeneutical value insofar as it helps one to understand human reality. They tend towards good, but they are also capable of evil. They can transcend their immediate interest and still remain bound to it. The social order will be all the more stable, the more it takes this fact into account and does not place in opposition personal interest and the interests of society as a whole, but rather seeks ways to bring them into fruitful harmony. In fact, where self-interest is violently suppressed, it is replaced by a burdensome system of bureaucratic control which dries up the wellsprings of initiative and creativity. When people think they possess the secret of a perfect social organization which makes evil impossible, they also think that they can use any means, including violence and deceit, in order to bring that organization into being. Politics then becomes a "secular religion" which operates under the illusion of creating paradise in this world. But no political society, which possesses its own autonomy and laws (cf. *Gaudium et spes*, 36 and 39), can ever be confused with the Kingdom of God.[10]

Dignity of the Human Person

The spiritual and immortal soul is the principle of unity of the human being, whereby it exists as a whole...as a person. Such definitions not only point out that the body, which has been promised the resurrection, will also share in glory. They also remind us that reason and free will are linked with all the bodily and sense faculties. *The person, including the body, is completely entrusted to himself or herself, and it is in the unity of body and soul that the person is the subject of his or her own moral acts.* The person, by the light of reason and the support of virtue, discovers in the body the anticipatory signs, the expression and the promise of the gift of self, in conformity with the wise plan of the Creator. It is in the light of the dignity of the human person, a dignity which must be affirmed for its own sake, that reason grasps the specific moral value of certain goods towards which the person is naturally inclined. And since the human person cannot be reduced to a freedom which is self-designing, but entails a particular spiritual and bodily structure, the primordial moral requirement of loving and respecting the person as an end and never as a mere means also implies, by its very nature, respect for certain fundamental goods, without which one would fall into relativism and arbitrariness.[11]

Sin Deforms the Image of God

Unfortunately, God's marvelous plan was marred by the appearance of sin in history. Through sin, human beings rebel against their Creator and end up by worshipping creatures: "They exchanged the truth about God for a lie and worshipped and served the creature rather than the Creator" (Rom 1:25). As a result they not only deform the image of God in their own person, but are tempted to offenses against it in others as well, replacing relationships of communion by attitudes of distrust, indifference, hostility and even murderous hatred. When God is not acknowledged as God, the profound meaning of the human person is betrayed and communion between people is compromised.

In the life of each person, God's image shines forth anew and is again revealed in all its fullness at the coming of the Son of God in human flesh. "Christ is the image of the invisible God" (Col 1:15); he "reflects the glory of God and bears the very stamp of his nature" (Heb 1:3). He is the perfect image of the Father.

The plan of life given to the first Adam finds at last its fulfillment in Christ. Whereas the disobedience of Adam ruined and marred God's plan for human life and introduced death into the world, the redemptive obedience of Christ is the source of grace poured out upon the human race, opening wide to everyone the gates of the kingdom of life (cf. Rom 5:12–21). As the Apostle Paul states: "The first man Adam became a living being; the last Adam became a life-giving spirit" (1 Cor 15:45).

All who commit themselves to following Christ are given the fullness of life: the divine image is restored, renewed and brought to perfection in them. God's plan for human beings is this, that they should "be conformed to the image of his Son" (Rom 8:29). Only thus, in the splendor of this image, can they be freed from the slavery of idolatry, rebuild lost fellowship and rediscover their true identity.[12]

Evolution and the Origin of the Human Soul

Taking into account the scientific research of the era, and also the proper requirements of theology, the encyclical *Humani generis* [1950] treated the doctrine of "evolutionism" as a serious hypothesis, worthy of investigation and serious study, alongside the opposite hypothesis. Pius XII added two methodological conditions for this study: one could not adopt this opinion as if it were a certain and demonstrable doctrine, and one could not totally set aside the teaching of revelation on the relevant questions. He also set out the conditions on which this opinion would be compatible with the Christian faith, a point to which I shall return.

Today, almost a half-century after the appearance of that encyclical, some new findings lead us toward the recognition of evolution as more than an hypothesis. In fact it is remarkable that this theory has had progressively greater influence on the spirit of researchers, following a series of discoveries in different scholarly disciplines. The convergence in the results of these independent studies, which was neither planned nor sought, constitutes in itself a significant argument in favor of the theory.

What is the significance of a theory such as this one? To open this question is to enter into the field of epistemology. A theory is a meta-scientific elaboration, which is distinct from, but in harmony with, the results of observation. With the help of such a theory a group of data and independent facts can be related to one another and interpreted in one comprehensive explanation. The theory proves its validity by the measure to which it can be verified. It is constantly being tested against the facts; when it can no longer explain these facts, it shows its limits and its lack of usefulness, and it must be revised.

Moreover, the elaboration of a theory such as that of evolution, while obedient to the need for consistency with the observed data, must also involve importing some ideas from the philosophy of nature.

And to tell the truth, rather than speaking about the theory of evolution, it is more accurate to speak of the theories of evolution. The use of the plural is required here, in part because of the diversity of explanations regarding the mechanism of evolution, and in part because of the diversity of philosophies involved. There are materialist and reductionist theories, as well as spiritualist theories. Here the final judgment is within the competence of philosophy and, beyond that, of theology.

The Magisterium of the Church takes a direct interest in the question of evolution, because it touches on the conception of the human being, whom revelation tells us is created in the image and likeness of God. The conciliar constitution *Gaudium et spes* [no. 24] has given us a magnificent exposition of this doctrine, which is one of the essential elements of Christian thought. The Council recalled that the "human person is the only creature on earth that God wanted for its own sake." In other words, the human person cannot be subordinated as a means or a pure instrument of either the species or the society; one has a value *per se*. One is a person. With one's intellect and one's will, one is capable of entering into relationship, of communion, of solidarity, of the gift of oneself to others like himself or herself.

St. Thomas observed that the individual's resemblance to God resides especially in one's speculative intellect, for the person's relationship with the object of one's knowledge resembles God's relationship with his creation (*Summa Theologica* I–II, q 3, a 5, ad 1). But even beyond that, the person is called to enter into a loving relationship with God himself, a relationship which will find its full expression at the end of time, in eternity. Within the mystery of the risen Christ the full grandeur of this vocation is revealed to us (*Gaudium et spes*, 22). It is by virtue of one's eternal soul that the whole person possesses such great dignity, even in one's body. Pius XII underlined the essential point: if the origin of the human body comes through living matter which existed previously, the spiritual soul is created directly by God (*Humani generis*, 36).

As a result, the theories of evolution which, because of the philosophies which inspire them, regard the spirit either as emerging from the forces of living matter, or as a simple epiphenomenon of that matter, are incompatible with the truth about the human individual. They are therefore unable to serve as the basis for the dignity of the human person.[13]

NOTES

1. *Address at Puebla (January 1979)*, 1.9, in *AAS* 71 (1979), 195–96; *ND*, 425; *Origins* 8:34 (1979), 534; *Pope Speaks* 24:1 (1979), 58.

2. Ibid., 3.1, 3.5, in *AAS* 71 (1979), 198, 201–2; *ND*, 426; *Origins* 8:34 (1979), 536, 637; *Pope Speaks* 24:1(1979), 60–61, 63–64.

3. *Redemptor hominis*, 8, in *AAS* 71 (1979), 271–72; *EncMiller*, 57; *Origins* 8:40 (1979), 630–31; *Pope Speaks* 24:2 (1979), 108.

4. Ibid., 13, in *AAS* 71 (1979), 283–84; *EncMiller*, 64; *ND*, 427; *Origins* 8:40 (1979), 633; *Pope Speaks* 24:2 (1979), 116–17.

5. Ibid., 14, in *AAS* 71 (1979), 284–85; *EncMiller*, 64–65; *ND*, 428; *Origins* 8:40 (1979), 633–34; *Pope Speaks* 24:2 (1979), 117–18.

6. Ibid., 21, in *AAS* 71 (1979), 319–20; *EncMiller*, 86–87; *ND*, 430; *Origins* 8:40 (1979), 642; *Pope Speaks* 24:2 (1979), 143–44.

7. *Mulieris dignitatem*, 6, in *AAS* 80 (1988), 1662, 1664; *ND*, 431, 432; *Origins* 18:17 (1988), 265–66; *Pope Speaks* 34:1 (1989), 15–16.

8. Ibid., 30, in *AAS* 80 (1988), 1724; *ND*, 433; *Origins* 18:17 (1988), 280; *Pope Speaks* 34:1 (1989), 44–45.

9. *Message on the World Day of Peace (January 1, 1990)*, in *AAS* 82 (1990), 148–49; *ND*, 518, 519; *Origins* 19:28 (1989), 465–58; *Pope Speaks* 35:3 (1990), 201.

10. *Centesimus annus*, 25, in *AAS* 83 (1991), 823–24; *EncMiller*, 531–32; *ND*, 2194a; *Origins* 21:1 (1991), 10; *Pope Speaks* 36:5 (1991), 288.

11. *Veritatis splendor*, 48, in *AAS* 85 (1993), 1172; *EncMiller*, 616; *ND*, 435; *Origins* 23:18 (1993), 312–13; *Pope Speaks* 39:1 (1994), 29.

12. *Evangelium vitae*, 36, in *AAS* 87 (1995), 441–42; *EncMiller*, 708–9; *ND*, 524; *Origins* 24:42 (1995), 702; *Pope Speaks* 40:4 (1995), 226.

13. *Address to the Pontifical Academy of Sciences (October 22, 1996)*, 4–5, in *AAS* 89 (1997), 187–88; *ND*, 437, 438, *Origins* 26:25 (1996), 415; *Pope Speaks* 42:2 (1997), 119–20.

CHAPTER FIVE

Present Grace and Future Glory

5.1 Some of the best statements from John Paul II on the new life of grace, with which human beings are blessed through the power of the Holy Spirit, are to be found in such later texts as the 1994 apostolic letter *Tertio millennio adveniente* (The Arrival of the Third Millennium) and the 1995 encyclical *Evangelium vitae* (The Gospel of Life). God goes in search of sinful human beings. Through the life, death, and resurrection of Jesus Christ, they are enabled to overcome evil, become sons and daughters "in the Son," and so share the inmost life of God. This dynamic understanding of grace as a process of "deification" has flourished in the churches of the East. Not surprisingly, John Paul II cited an outstanding Eastern mystic, St. Simeon the New Theologian (d. 1022), to illustrate the luminous life conveyed by the Holy Spirit.

God Searches for Human Beings

In Jesus Christ God not only speaks to humans but also *seeks them out*. The Incarnation of the Son of God attests that God goes in search of humans. Jesus speaks of this search as the finding of a lost sheep (cf. Luke 15:1–7). It is a search which *begins in the heart of God* and culminates in the incarnation of the Word. If God goes in search of human beings, created in his own image and likeness, he does so because he loves them eternally in the Word, and wishes to raise them in Christ to the dignity of adopted sons or daughters. God therefore goes in search of human beings who *are his special possession* in a way unlike any other creature. Human beings are God's possession by virtue of a choice made in love. God seeks humans out, moved by his fatherly heart.

Why does God seek human beings out? Because they have turned away from him, hiding themselves as Adam did among the trees of the Garden of Eden (cf. Gen 3:8–10). Humans allowed themselves to be led astray by the enemy of God (cf. Gen 3:13). Satan deceived human beings, persuading them that they too were gods, that they, like God, were capable of knowing good and evil, ruling the world according to their own will without having to take into account the divine will (cf. Gen 3:5). Going in search of humans through his Son, God wishes to persuade human beings to abandon the paths of evil which lead them farther and farther afield. "Making them abandon" those paths means making them understand that they are taking the wrong path; it means *overcoming the evil* which is everywhere found in human history. *Overcoming evil: this is the meaning of the Redemption*. This is brought about in the sacrifice of Christ, by which humankind redeems the debt of sin and is reconciled to God. The Son of God became human, taking a body and soul in the womb of the Virgin, precisely for this reason: to become the perfect redeeming sacrifice. The religion of the Incarnation is the *religion* of the world's *Redemption* through the sacrifice of Christ, wherein lies victory over evil, over sin and over death itself. Accepting death on the Cross, Christ at the same time reveals and gives life, because he rises again and death no longer has power over him.[1]

Grace Means Dwelling in the Heart of God

The religion which originates in the mystery of the redemptive incarnation is the religion of *"dwelling in the heart of God,"* of sharing in God's very life. Saint Paul speaks of this in the passage already quoted: "God has sent the Spirit of his Son into our hearts, crying,

'Abba! Father!'" (Gal 4:6). Humanity cries out like Christ himself, who turned to God "with loud cries and tears" (Heb 5:7), especially in Gethsemane and on the Cross. Human beings cry out to God just as Christ cried out to him, and thus they bear witness that they share in Christ's sonship through the power of the Holy Spirit. The Holy Spirit, whom the Father has sent in the name of the Son, enables human beings to share in the inmost life of God. He also enables them *to be sons and daughters, in the likeness of Christ*, and heirs of all that belongs to the Son (cf. Gal 4:7). In this consists the religion of "dwelling in the inmost life of God," which begins with the Incarnation of the Son of God. The Holy Spirit, who searches the depths of God (cf. 1 Cor 2:10), leads us, all humanity, into these depths by virtue of the sacrifice of Christ.[2]

The New Life in Christ Initiates Eternal Life

The life which the Son of God came to give to human beings cannot be reduced to mere existence in time. The life which was always "in him" and which is the "light of humanity" (John 1:4) consists in being begotten of God and sharing in the fullness of his love: "To all who received him, who believed in his name, he gave power to become children of God; who were born, not of blood nor of the will of the flesh nor of the will of humankind, but of God" (John 1:12–13).

Sometimes Jesus refers to this life which he came to give simply as "life," and he presents being born of God as a necessary condition if human beings are to attain the end for which God has created them: "Unless one is born anew, one cannot see the kingdom of God" (John 3:3). To give this life is the real object of Jesus' mission: he is the one who "comes down from heaven, and gives life to the world" (John 6:33). Thus can he truly say: "Those who follow me...will have the light of life" (John 8:12).

At other times, Jesus speaks of "eternal life." Here the adjective does more than merely evoke a perspective which is beyond time. The life which Jesus promises and gives is "eternal" because it is a full participation in the life of the "Eternal One." Whoever believes in

Jesus and enters into communion with him has eternal life (cf. John 3:15; 6:40); because of that they hear from Jesus the only words which reveal and communicate to their existence the fullness of life. These are the "words of eternal life" which Peter acknowledges in his confession of faith: "Lord, to whom shall we go? You have the words of eternal life; and we have believed, and have come to know, that you are the Holy One of God" (John 6:68–69). Jesus himself, addressing the Father in the great priestly prayer, declares what eternal life consists in: "This is eternal life, that they may know you the only true God, and Jesus Christ whom you have sent" (John 17:3). To know God and his Son is to accept the mystery of the loving communion of the Father, the Son and the Holy Spirit into one's own life, which even now is open to eternal life because it shares in the life of God.

Eternal life is therefore the life of God himself and at the same time the life of the children of God. As they ponder this unexpected and inexpressible truth which comes to us from God in Christ, believers cannot fail to be filled with ever new wonder and unbounded gratitude. They can say in the words of the Apostle John: "See what love the Father has given us, that we should be called children of God; and so we are....Beloved, we are God's children now; it does not yet appear what he shall be, but we know that when he appears we shall be like him, for we shall see him as he is" (1 John 3:1–2).

Here the Christian truth about life becomes most sublime. The dignity of this life is linked not only to its beginning, to the fact that it comes from God, but also to its final end, to its destiny of fellowship with God in knowledge and love of him. In the light of this truth Saint Irenaeus qualifies and completes his praise of humanity: "the glory of God" is indeed "human beings, living human beings," but "the life of human persons consists in the vision of God" (*Adversus haereses*, 4.20.7).

Immediate consequences arise from this for human life in its earthly state, in which, for that matter, eternal life already springs forth and begins to grow. Although human beings instinctively love life because it is a good, this love will find further inspiration and strength, and new breadth and depth, in the divine dimensions of this good. Similarly, the love which every human being has for life cannot be reduced simply to a desire to have sufficient space for self-expression and for entering into relationships with others; rather, it develops in a joyous awareness that life can become the "place" where God manifests himself, where we meet him and enter into communion with him. The life which Jesus gives in no way lessens the value of our existence in time; it takes it and directs it to its final destiny: "I am the resurrection and the life...whoever lives and believes in me shall never die" (John 11:25–26).[3]

The Christian Is Inspired by the Spirit

I see the beauty of your grace, I contemplate its radiance, I reflect its light; I am caught up in its ineffable splendor; I am taken outside myself as I think of myself; I see how I was and what I have become. O wonder! I am vigilant, I am full of respect for myself, of reverence and of fear, as I would be were I before you; I do not know what to do, I am seized by fear, I do not know where to sit, where to go, where to put these members which are yours; in what deeds, in what works shall I use them, these amazing divine marvels![4]

5.2 Through canonizing 482 saints and declaring 1,338 heroic men and women "blessed," John Paul II witnessed in a dramatic way to the Christian hope for the full and final happiness of eternal life with God. In *Tertio millennio adveniente* (The Arrival of the Third Millennium) and the apostolic letter *Dies Domini* (The Day of the Lord), he also reflected on how the time we experience in human history will be fulfilled in the eternity of God.

The Fulfillment of Time

Speaking of the birth of the Son of God, Saint Paul places this event in the "fullness of time" (cf. Gal 4:4). Time is indeed fulfilled by the very fact that God, in the Incarnation, came down into human history. Eternity entered into time: what "fulfillment" could be greater than this? What other "fulfillment" would be possible? Some have thought in terms of certain mysterious cosmic cycles in which the history of the universe and of humankind in particular, would constantly repeat itself. True, human beings rise from the earth and return to it (cf. Gen 3:19): this is an immediately evident fact. Yet in humanity there is an irrepressible longing to live forever. How are we to imagine a life beyond death? Some have considered various forms of *reincarnation*: depending on one's previous life, one would receive a new life in either a higher or lower form, until full purification is attained. This belief, deeply rooted in some Eastern religions, itself indicates that human beings rebel against the finality of death. They are convinced that their nature is essentially spiritual and immortal.

Christian revelation excludes reincarnation, and speaks of a fulfillment which humanity is called to achieve in the course of a single earthly existence. Human beings achieve this fulfillment of their destiny through the sincere gift of self, a gift which is made possible only through their encounter with God. It is in God that humanity finds full self-realization: *this is the truth revealed by Christ*. Human beings fulfill themselves in God, who comes to meet them through his Eternal Son. Thanks to God's coming on earth, human time, which began at Creation, has reached its fullness. "The fullness of time" is in fact eternity, indeed, it is *the One who is eternal*, God himself. Thus, to enter into "the fullness of time" means to reach the end of time and to transcend its limits, in order to find time's fulfillment in the eternity of God.

In Christianity time has a fundamental importance. Within the dimension of time the world was created; within it the history of salvation unfolds, finding its culmination in the "fullness of time" of the incarnation, and its goal in the glorious return of the Son of God at the end of time. In Jesus Christ, the Word made flesh, time becomes a dimension of God, who is himself eternal. With the coming of Christ there begin "the last days" (cf. Heb 1:2), the "last hour" (cf. 1 John 2:18), and the time of the Church, which will last until the Parousia.

From this relationship of God with time there arises *the duty to sanctify time*. This is done, for example, when individual times, days or weeks, are dedicated to God, as once happened in the religion of the Old Covenant, and as happens still, though in a new way, in Christianity. In the liturgy of the Easter Vigil the celebrant, as he blesses the candle which symbolizes the Risen Christ, pro-claims: "Christ yesterday and today, the beginning and the end, Alpha and Omega, all time belongs to him, and all the ages, to him be glory and power through every age for ever." He says these words as he inscribes on the candle the numerals of the current year. The meaning of this rite is clear: it emphasizes the fact that *Christ is the Lord of time*; he is its beginning and its end; every year, every day and every moment are embraced by his Incarnation and Resurrection, and thus become part of the "fullness of time." For this reason, the Church too lives and celebrates the liturgy in the span of a year. The solar year is thus permeated by the liturgical year, which in a certain way reproduces the whole mystery of the Incarnation and Redemption, beginning from the First Sunday of Advent and ending on the Solemnity of Christ the King, Lord of the Universe and Lord of History. Every Sunday commemorates the day of the Lord's Resurrection.[5]

The Pilgrimage to the Lord's Day

As the Church journeys through time, the reference to Christ's Resurrection and the weekly recurrence of this solemn memorial help to remind us of *the pilgrim and eschatological character of the People of God*. Sunday after Sunday the Church moves towards the final "Lord's Day," that Sunday which knows no end. The expectation of Christ's coming is inscribed in the very mystery of the Church (*Lumen gentium*, 48–51), and is evidenced in every Eucharistic celebration. But, with its specific remembrance of the glory of the Risen Christ, the Lord's Day recalls with greater intensity the future glory of his "return." This makes Sunday the day on which the Church, showing forth more clearly her identity as "bride," anticipates in some sense the eschatological reality of the heavenly Jerusalem. Gathering her children into the Eucharistic assembly and teaching them to wait for the "divine bridegroom," she engages in a kind of "exercise of desire" (cf. St. Augustine, In *prima Ioan. tract.* 4.6), receiving a foretaste of the joy of the new heavens and new earth, when the holy city, the new Jerusalem, will come down from God, "prepared as a bride adorned for her husband" (Rev 21:2).[6]

The Coming of the Lord

Sustaining Christian life as it does, Sunday has the additional value of being a testimony and a proclamation. As a day of prayer, communion and joy, Sunday resounds throughout society, emanating vital energies and reasons for hope. Sunday is the proclamation that time, in which he who is the Risen Lord of history makes his home, is not the grave of our illusions but the cradle of an ever new future, an opportunity given to us to turn the fleeting moments of this life into seeds of eternity. Sunday is an invitation to look ahead; it is the day on which the Christian community cries out to Christ, "*Marana tha*: Come, O Lord!" (1 Cor 16:22). With this cry of hope and expectation, the Church is the companion and support of human hope. From Sunday to Sunday, enlightened by Christ, she goes forward towards the unending Sunday of the heavenly Jerusalem, which "has no need of the sun or moon to shine upon it, for the glory of God is its light and its lamp is the Lamb" (Rev 21.23).[7]

NOTES

1. *Tertio millennio adveniente*, 7, in *AAS* 87 (1995), 9–10; *ND*, 2000g; *Origins* 24:24 (1995), 404; *Pope Speaks* 40:2 (1995), 88–89.
2. Ibid., 8, in *AAS* 87 (1995), 10; *ND*, 2000h; *Origins* 24:24 (1995), 404–5; *Pope Speaks* 40:2 (1995), 49.
3. *Evangelium vitae*, 37–38, in *AAS* 87 (1995), 442–44; *ND*, 2000j; *EncMiller*, 709–10; *Origins* 24:42 (1995), 702–3; *Pope Speaks* 40:4 (1995), 2226–27.
4. *Vita consecrata*, 20, in *AAS* 88 (1996), 393–94; *EncMiller*, 665; *Origins* 25:41 (1996), 688; *Pope Speaks* 41:5 (1996), 269. The pope is here quoting Simeon the New Theologian (d. 1022), *Hymns*, 2.19–27, a passage that he also cited at a general audience on September 13, 2000.
5. *Tertio millennio adveniente*, 9–10, in *AAS* 85 (1995), 10–12; *Origins* 24:24 (1995), 405; *Pope Speaks* 40:2 (1995), 89–90.
6. *Dies Domini*, 37, in *AAS*, 90 (1998), 736; *Origins* 28:8 (1998), 141; *Pope Speaks* 43:6 (1998), 354.
7. Ibid., 84, in *AAS* 90 (1998), 764; *ND*, 1595; *Origins* 28:8 (1998), 149; *Pope Speaks* 43:6 (1998), 372.

CHAPTER SIX

The Sacraments and Worship

6.1 When John Paul II celebrated Mass either at home in Rome or during his many apostolic journeys (104 outside Italy and 146 within Italy), everyone could see how deeply the Eucharist mattered to him. It was also clear that he welcomed ways in which the celebration drew on elements from African, Indian, and other cultures—that is to say, was "inculturated." Right from his 1979 encyclical *Redemptor hominis* (The Redeemer of the Human Person) and the 1980 letter *Dominicae cenae* (The Lord's Supper), he wrote and spoke about the Eucharist, which his 1987 encyclical *Sollicitudo rei socialis* (Concern for Social Matters) saw as empowering work for development and peace.

The Eucharist Builds the Church

It is an essential truth, not only of doctrine but also of life, that the Eucharist builds the Church (*Lumen gentium*, 11), building it as the authentic community of the People of God, as the assembly of the faithful, bearing the same mark of unity that was shared by the Apostles and the first disciples of the Lord. The Eucharist builds ever anew this community and unity, ever building and regenerating it on the basis of the Sacrifice of Christ, since it commemorates his death on the Cross (*Sacrosanctum concilium* [The Sacred Council], 47), the price by which he redeemed us. Accordingly, in the Eucharist we touch in a way the very mystery of the Body and Blood of the Lord, as is attested by the very words used at its institution, the words that, because of that institution, have become the words with which those called to this ministry in the Church unceasingly celebrate the Eucharist.

The Church lives by the Eucharist, by the fullness of this Sacrament, the stupendous content and meaning of which have often been expressed in the Church's Magisterium from the most distant times down to our own days (cf. Pope Paul VI, *Mysterium fidei*). However, we can say with certainty that, although this teaching is sustained by the acuteness of theologians, by men and women of deep faith and prayer, and by ascetics and mystics, in complete fidelity to the Eucharistic mystery, it still reaches no more than the threshold, since it is incapable of grasping and translating into words what the Eucharist is in all its fullness, what is expressed by it and what is actuated by it. Indeed, the Eucharist is the ineffable Sacrament! The essential commitment and, above all, the visible grace and source of supernatural strength for the Church as the People of God is to persevere and advance constantly in Eucharistic life and Eucharistic piety and to develop spiritually in the climate of the Eucharist.[1]

Sacrifice, Communion, and Presence

[The Eucharist] is at one and the same time a Sacrifice-Sacrament, a Communion-Sacrament, and a Presence-Sacrament. And, although it is true that the Eucharist always was and must continue to be the most profound revelation of the human brotherhood of Christ's disciples and confessors, it cannot be treated merely as an "occasion" for manifesting this brotherhood. When celebrating the Sacrament of the Body and Blood of the Lord, the full magnitude of the divine mystery must be respected, as must the full meaning of this sacramental sign in which Christ is really present and is received, the soul is filled with grace and the pledge of future glory is given (*Sacrosanctum concilium*, 47).

This is the source of the duty to carry out rigorously the liturgical rules and everything that is a manifestation of community worship offered to God himself, all the more so because in this sacramental sign he entrusts himself to us with limitless trust, as if not taking into consideration our human weakness, our unworthiness, the force of habit, routine, or even the possibility of insult. Every member of the Church, especially bishops and priests, must be vigilant in seeing that this Sacrament of love shall be at the center of the life of the People of God, so that through all the manifestations of worship due to it Christ shall be given back love for love and truly become "the life of our souls" (cf. John 6:41, 57; 14:6; Gal 2:20). Nor can we, on the other hand, ever forget the following words of Saint Paul: "Let people examine themselves, and so eat of the bread and drink of the cup" (1 Cor 11:28).

This call by the Apostle indicates at least indirectly the close link between the Eucharist and Penance. Indeed, if the first word of Christ's teaching, the first phrase of the Gospel Good News, was "Repent, and believe in the gospel" (*metanoeite*) (Mark 1:15), the Sacrament of the Passion, Cross and Resurrection seems to strengthen and consolidate in an altogether special way this call in our souls.[2]

The Eucharist and Our Neighbor

The authentic sense of the Eucharist becomes of itself the school of active love for neighbor. We know that this is the true and full order of love that the Lord has taught us: "By this love you have for one another, everyone will know that you are my disciples" (John 13:35). The Eucharist educates us to this love in a deeper way; it shows us, in fact, what value each person, our brother or sister, has in God's eyes, if Christ offers himself equally to each one, under the species of bread and wine. If our Eucharistic worship is authentic, it must make us grow in awareness of the dignity of each person. The awareness of that dignity becomes the deepest motive of our relationship with our neighbor.

We must also become particularly sensitive to all human suffering and misery, to all injustice and wrong, and seek the way to redress them effectively. Let us learn to discover with respect the truth about the inner self that becomes the dwelling place of God present in the Eucharist. Christ comes into the hearts of our brothers and sisters and visits their consciences. How the image of each and every one changes, when we become aware of this reality, when we make it the subject of our reflections! The sense of the Eucharistic Mystery leads us to a love for our neighbor, to a love for every human being.[3]

Inculturating the Gospel and the Liturgy in Africa

One of the aspects of this evangelization is the inculturation of the Gospel, the Africanization of the Church. Several have confided to me that it concerns you very much and rightly so. That is part of the indispensable efforts to incarnate the message of Christ. The Gospel, certainly, is not identified with cultures and transcends them all. But the kingdom which the Gospel announces is lived by human beings profoundly linked to a culture; the building of the kingdom cannot be dispensed from borrowing elements of human cultures (cf. *Evangelium nuntiandi*, 20). And even, evangelization must help these cultures to bring forth from their own living tradition original expressions of Christian life, celebration and thought (cf. *Catechesi tradendae*, 53). You desire to be at the same time fully Christian and fully African. The Holy Spirit asks us to believe in fact that the leaven of the Gospel, in its authenticity, has the strength to raise up Christians in the various cultures, with all the riches of their patrimony, purified and transfigured.

On this subject, the Second Vatican Council well expressed certain principles which always illumine the road to follow in this area: "The Church...fosters and takes to herself, insofar as they are good, the ability, resources and customs of each people. Taking them to herself, she purifies, strengthens and ennobles them....In virtue of this catholicity, each individual part of the Church contributes through its special gifts to the good of the other parts and of the whole Church. Thus through the common sharing of gifts and through the common effort to attain fullness in unity, the whole and each of the parts receive increase....The chair of Peter...presides over the whole assembly of charity and protects legitimate differences, while at the same time it sees that such differences do not hinder unity but rather contribute towards it" (*Lumen gentium*, 13).

Africanization takes in large and profound areas, which have not yet been sufficiently explored, whether it is a matter of the language to be used to present the Christian message in a manner which touches the mind and heart of the Zairian, of catechesis, of theological reflection, of the most suitable expression in the liturgy or sacred art, of community forms of Christian life. It is up to you, Bishops, to promote and harmonize progress in this area, after mature reflection, in harmony among yourselves, in union also with the universal Church and with the Holy See.[4]

Social Implications of the Eucharist

Eucharistic communion is therefore the sign of the meeting of all the faithful. A truly inspiring sign, because at the holy table all differences of race or social class disappear, leaving only the participation of all in the same holy food. This participation, identical in all, signifies and realizes the suppression of all that divides people, and brings about the meeting of all at a higher level, where all opposition is eliminated. Thus the Eucharist becomes the great instrument of bringing people closer to one another. Whenever the faithful take part in it with a sincere heart, they receive a new impetus to establish a better relationship among themselves, leading to recognition of one another's rights, and corresponding duties as well. In this way the implementation of the requirements of justice is facilitated, precisely because of the particular climate of interpersonal relations that fraternal charity creates within the same community.[5]

The Eucharist Empowers Efforts for Development and Peace

The Lord unites us with himself through the Eucharist— Sacrament and Sacrifice—and he unites us with himself and with one another by a bond stronger than any natural union; and thus united, he sends us into the whole world to bear witness, through faith and works, to God's love, preparing the coming of his Kingdom and anticipating it, though in the obscurity of the present time.

All of us who take part in the Eucharist are called to discover, through this sacrament, the profound meaning of our actions in the world in favor of development and peace; and to receive from it the strength to commit ourselves ever more generously, following the example of Christ, who in this sacrament lays down his life for his friends (cf. John 15:13). Our personal commitment, like Christ's and in union with his, will not be in vain but certainly fruitful.[6]

6.2 In a 1988 apostolic letter *Vicesimus quintus annus* (The Twenty-fifth Year) written for the twenty-fifth anniversary of Vatican II's Constitution on the Sacred Liturgy, *Sacrosanctum concilium* (The Sacred Council), John Paul II offered some guidelines for vigorous liturgical renewal and for adapting the liturgy to various cultures (inculturation). He also wrote of "what Christ accomplishes by the power of his Spirit" to the "praise of the Father," espousing thus a trinitarian understanding of the liturgy that he was to develop more fully in his 2003 encyclical, *Ecclesia de Eucharistia* (The Church from the Eucharist).

Guidelines for Liturgical Renewal

From these principles [those of *Sacrosanctum concilium*] are derived certain norms and guidelines which must govern the renewal of liturgical life. While the reform of the Liturgy desired by the Second Vatican Council can be considered already in progress, the pastoral promotion of the Liturgy constitutes a permanent commitment to draw ever more abundantly from the riches of the Liturgy that vital force which spreads from Christ to the members of his Body which is the Church.

Since the Liturgy is the exercise of the priesthood of Christ, it is necessary to keep ever alive the affirmation of the disciple faced with the mysterious presence of the Lord: "It is the Lord!" (John 21:7). Nothing of what we do in the Liturgy can appear more important than what in an unseen but real manner Christ accomplishes by the power of his Spirit. A faith alive in charity, adoration, praise of the Father and silent contemplation will always be the prime objective of liturgical and pastoral care.

Since the Liturgy is totally permeated by the word of God, any other word must be in harmony with it, above all in the homily, but also in the various interventions of the minister and in the hymns which are sung. No other reading may supplant the Biblical word, and the words of humankind must be at the service of the word of God without obscuring it.

Since liturgical celebrations are not private acts but "celebrations of the Church, the *sacrament of unity*" (*Sacrosanctum concilium*, 26), their regulation is dependent solely upon the hierarchical authority of the Church (*Sacrosanctum concilium*, 22, 26). The Liturgy belongs to the whole body of the Church (*Sacrosanctum concilium*, 26). It is for this reason that it is not permitted to anyone, even the priest, or any group, to subtract or change anything whatsoever on their own initiative (*Sacrosanctum concilium*, 22). Fidelity to the rites and to the authentic texts of the Liturgy is a requirement of the *Lex orandi* [rule of the Church at prayer], which must always be in conformity with the *Lex credendi* [rule of those who believe]. A lack of fidelity on this point may even affect the very validity of the sacraments.

Since the Liturgy has great pastoral value, the liturgical books have provided for a certain degree of adaptation to the assembly and to individuals, with the possibility of openness to the traditions and cultures of different peoples (*Sacrosanctum concilium*, 37–40). The revision of the rites has sought a noble simplicity (*Sacrosanctum concilium*, 34) and signs that are easily understood, but the desired simplicity must not degenerate into an impoverishment of the signs. On the contrary, the signs, above all the sacramental signs, must be easily grasped but carry the greatest possible expressiveness. Bread and wine, water and oil, and also incense, ashes, fire and flowers, and indeed almost all the elements of creation have their place in the Liturgy as gifts to the Creator and as a contribution to the dignity and beauty of the celebration.[7]

Adaptation of the Liturgy

Another important task for the future is that of the adaptation of the Liturgy to different cultures. The Constitution set forth the principle, indicating the procedure to be followed by the bishops' conferences (*Sacrosanctum concilium*, 39). The adaptation of languages has been rapidly accomplished, even if on occasion with some difficulties. It has been followed by the adaptation of rites, which is a more delicate matter but equally necessary. There remains the considerable task of continuing to implant the Liturgy in certain cultures, welcoming from them those expressions which are compatible with aspects of the *true and authentic spirit of the Liturgy*, in respect for the *substantial unity of the Roman Rite* as expressed in the liturgical books (*Sacrosanctum concilium*, 37–40). The adaptation must take account of the fact that in the Liturgy, and notably that of the sacraments, there is a *part which is unchangeable*, because it is of divine institution, and of which the Church is the guardian. There are also *parts open to change*, which the Church has the power and on occasion also the duty to adapt to the cultures of recently evangelized peoples (*Sacrosanctum concilium*, 21). This is not a new problem for the Church. Liturgical diversity can be a source of enrichment, but it can also provoke tensions, mutual misunderstandings and even divisions. In this field it is clear that diversity must not damage unity. It can only gain expression in fidelity to the common faith, to the sacramental signs that the Church has received from Christ and to hierarchical communion. Cultural adaptation also requires conversion of heart and even, where necessary, a breaking with ancestral customs incompatible with the Catholic faith. This demands a serious formation in theology, history and culture, as well as sound judgment in discerning what is necessary or useful and what is not useful or even dangerous to faith. "A satisfactory development in this area cannot be anything less than the fruit of a progressive maturing in faith, one which encompasses spiritual discernment, theological lucidity, and a sense of the universal Church, acting in broad harmony" (*Address to a group of bishops from the Episcopal Conference of Zaire* [April 12, 1983]).[8]

6.3 In his 1998 apostolic letter *Dies Domini* (The Day of the Lord), John Paul wished to help the faithful prepare for the great jubilee of the year 2000 by rediscovering the centrality of Sunday and its eucharistic assembly. In the aftermath of the jubilee, which had been preceded by three years of reflection on the Trinity (each year being dedicated to one divine person), came the 2003 encyclical, *Ecclesia de Eucharistia* (The Church from the Eucharist). John Paul II expressed the cosmic and trinitarian nature of the Eucharist: "its goal in the communion of humankind with Christ, and in him with the Father and the Holy Spirit" (no. 22).

The Mass and Daily Life

Receiving the Bread of Life, the disciples of Christ ready themselves to undertake, with the strength of the Risen Lord and his Spirit, the tasks which await them in their ordinary life. For the faithful who have understood the meaning of what they have done, the Eucharistic celebration does not stop at the church door. Like the first witnesses of the Resurrection, Christians who gather each Sunday to experience and proclaim the presence of the Risen Lord are called *to evangelize and bear witness* in their daily lives. Given this, the Prayer after Communion and the Concluding Rite (the Final Blessing and the Dismissal) need to be better valued and appreciated, so that all who have shared in the Eucharist may come to a deeper sense of the responsibility which is entrusted to them. Once the assembly disperses, Christ's disciples return to their everyday surroundings with the commitment to make their whole life a gift, a spiritual sacrifice pleasing to God (cf. Rom 12:1). They feel indebted to their brothers and sisters because of what they have received in the celebration, not unlike the disciples of Emmaus who, once they had recognized the Risen Christ "in the breaking of the bread" (cf. Luke 24:30–32), felt the need to return immediately to share with their brothers and sisters the joy of meeting the Lord (cf. Luke 24:33–35).[9]

Sunday Worship

It is crucially important that all the faithful should be convinced that they cannot live their faith or share fully in the life of the Christian community unless they take part regularly in the Sunday Eucharistic Assembly.[10]

The Altar of the World

When I think of the Eucharist and look at my life as a priest, as a bishop and as the Successor of Peter, I naturally recall the many times and places in which I was able to celebrate it. I remember the parish church of Niegowić, where I had my first pastoral assignment, the collegiate church of Saint Florian in Krakow, Wawel Cathedral, Saint Peter's Basilica and so many basilicas and churches in Rome and throughout the world. I have been able to celebrate Holy Mass in chapels built along mountain paths, on lakeshores and seacoasts; I have celebrated it on altars built in stadiums and in city squares....This varied scenario of celebrations of the Eucharist has given me a powerful experience of its universal and, so to speak, cosmic character. Yes, cosmic! Because even when it is celebrated on the humble altar of a country church, the Eucharist is always in some way celebrated *on the altar of the world.* It unites heaven and earth. It embraces and permeates all creation. The Son of God became man in order to restore all creation, in one supreme act of praise, to the One who made it from nothing. He, the Eternal High Priest who by the blood of his Cross entered the eternal sanctuary, thus gives back to the Creator and Father all creation redeemed. He does so through the priestly ministry of the Church, to the glory of the Most Holy Trinity. Truly this is the *mysterium fidei* which is accomplished in the Eucharist: the world which came forth from the hands of God the Creator now returns to him redeemed by Christ.[11]

The Trinity and the Liturgy

The joint and inseparable activity of the Son and of the Holy Spirit, which is at the origin of the Church, of her consolidation and her continued life, is at work in the Eucharist. This was clearly evident to the author of the *Liturgy of Saint James*: in the epiclesis of the Anaphora, God the Father is asked to send the Holy Spirit upon the faithful and upon the offerings, so that the body and blood of Christ "may be a help to all those who partake of it…for the sanctification of their souls and bodies" (*Patrologia Orientalis*, 26.206). The Church is fortified by the divine Paraclete through the sanctification of the faithful in the Eucharist.[12]

6.4 Right from his 1979 encyclical, *Redemptor hominis* (The Redeemer of Human Person), John Paul II had much to say and write about the sacrament of penance or reconciliation. His 1984 apostolic exhortation *Reconciliatio et paenitentia* (Reconciliation and Penance) attended to the mission of reconciliation and the sacrament of penance. In view of the great jubilee of 2000, his apostolic letter *Tertio millennio adveniente* (The Arrival of the Third Millennium) developed the theme of conversion and an examination of conscience. The bull with which John Paul II formally proclaimed the jubilee, *Incarnationis mysterium* (The Mystery of the Incarnation) specified the conversion, forgiveness, and charity that he hoped for; it also anticipated the dramatic confession of various categories of sins (for example, sins which have harmed the unity of the body of Christ, sins against the people of Israel, and sins against the dignity of women) at the Eucharist over which the pope presided on the first Sunday of Lent in 2000. During his pontificate, John Paul II proved himself an outstanding role model in trying to reconcile people. Over ninety times he very publicly acknowledged grave sins and errors committed by Catholics against others, asking pardon from Jews and Muslims, as well as from Protestant and Orthodox Christians.

The Individual Celebration
of the Sacrament of Penance

In the last years much has been done to highlight in the Church's practice in conformity with the most ancient tradition of the Church, the community aspect of penance and especially of the sacrament of Penance. We cannot however forget that conversion is a particularly profound inward act in which the individual cannot be replaced by others and cannot make the community to be a substitute for oneself. Although the participation by the fraternal community of the faithful in the penitential celebration is a great help for the act of personal conversion, nevertheless, in the final analysis, it is necessary that in this act there should be a pronouncement by the individual with the whole depth of human conscience.[13]

A Reconciled Church

The Church, if she is to be reconciling, must begin by being a reconciled church. Beneath this simple and indicative expression lies the conviction that the Church, in order ever more effectively to proclaim and propose reconciliation to the world, must become ever more genuinely a community of disciples of Christ (even though it were only "the little flock" of the first days), united in the commitment to be continually converted to the Lord and to live as new people in the spirit and practice of reconciliation.

To the people of our time, so sensitive to the proof of concrete living witness, the Church is called upon to give an example of reconciliation particularly within herself. And for this purpose we must all work to bring peace to people's minds, to reduce tensions, to overcome divisions and to heal wounds that may have been inflicted by one on the other when the contrast of choices in the field of what is optional becomes acute. On the contrary, we must try to be united in what is essential for Christian faith and life, in accordance with the ancient maxim: In what is doubtful, freedom; in what is necessary, unity; in all things, charity.[14]

Method of Dialogue

The Church in fact uses the method of dialogue in order the better to lead people—both those who through baptism and the profession of faith acknowledge their membership of the Christian community and also those who are outside—to conversion and repentance, along the path of a profound renewal of their own consciences and lives in the light of the mystery of the redemption and salvation accomplished by Christ and entrusted to the ministry of his church. Authentic dialogue, therefore, is aimed above all at the rebirth of individuals through interior conversion and repentance, but always with profound respect for consciences and with patience and at the step-by-step pace indispensable for modern conditions.[15]

Catechesis on Reconciliation and Penance

From the pastors of the church one expects, first of all, catechesis on reconciliation. This must be founded on the teaching of the Bible, especially the New Testament, on the need to rebuild the covenant with God in Christ the redeemer and reconciler. And in the light of this new communion and friendship, and as an extension of it, it must be founded on the teaching concerning the need to be reconciled with one's brothers and sisters, even if this means interrupting the offering of the sacrifice (Matt 5:23–24). Jesus strongly insists on this theme of familial reconciliation: for example, when he invites us to turn the other cheek to the one who strikes us, and to give our cloak too to the one who has taken our coat (cf. Matt 5:38–40), or when he instills the law of forgiveness: forgiveness which each one receives in the measure that he or she sees fit to offer forgiveness even to enemies (cf. Matt 5:43ff.), forgiveness to be granted seventy times seven times (cf. Matt 18:21ff.), which means in practice without any limit.

The pastors of the Church are also expected to provide catechesis on penance. Here too the richness of the biblical message must be its source. With regard to penance this message emphasizes particularly its value for conversion, which is the term that attempts to translate the word in the Greek text, *metanoia* (cf. Mark 1:14; Matt 3:2; 4:17; Luke 3:8), which literally means to allow the spirit to be overturned in order to make it turn toward God.[16]

Renewal of the Sacrament of Reconciliation

It is good to renew and reaffirm this faith at a moment when it might be weakening, losing something of its completeness or entering into an area of shadow and silence, threatened as it is by the negative elements of the above-mentioned crisis. For the sacrament of confession is indeed being undermined, on the one hand by the obscuring of the moral and religious conscience, the lessening of a sense of sin, the distortion of the concept of repentance and the lack of effort to live an authentically Christian life. And on the other hand, it is being undermined by the sometimes widespread idea that one can obtain forgiveness directly from God, even in a habitual way, without approaching the sacrament of reconciliation. A further negative influence is the routine of a sacramental practice sometimes lacking in fervor and real spontaneity, deriving perhaps from a mistaken and distorted idea of the effects of the sacrament.[17]

The Minister of Penance

For the effective performance of this ministry, the confessor must necessarily have human qualities of prudence, discretion, discernment and a firmness tempered by gentleness and kindness. He must likewise have a serious and careful preparation, not fragmentary but complete and harmonious, in the different branches of theology, pedagogy and psychology, in the methodology of dialogue and above all in a living and communicable knowledge of the word of God. But it is even more necessary that he should live an intense and genuine spiritual life. In order to lead others along the path of Christian perfection, the minister of penance himself must first travel this path. More by actions than by long speeches he must give proof of real experience of lived prayer, the practice of the theological and moral virtues of the Gospel, faithful obedience to the will of God, love of the Church and docility to her Magisterium.[18]

Importance and Function of Penance

The first conviction is that for a Christian the sacrament of penance is the primary way of obtaining forgiveness and the remission of serious sin committed after baptism. Certainly the Savior and his salvific action are not so bound to a sacramental sign as to be unable in any period or area of the history of salvation to work outside and above the sacraments. But in the school of faith we learn that the same Savior desired and provided that the simple and precious sacraments of faith would ordinarily be the effective means through which his redemptive power passes and operates. It would therefore be foolish, as well as presumptuous, to wish arbitrarily to disregard the means of grace and salvation which the Lord has provided and, in the specific case, to claim to receive forgiveness while doing without the sacrament which was instituted by Christ precisely for forgiveness. The renewal of the rites carried out after the Council does not sanction any illusion or alteration in this direction. According to the Church's intention, it was and is meant to stir up in each one of us a new impulse toward the renewal of our interior attitude; toward a deeper understanding of the nature of the sacrament of penance; toward a reception of the sacrament which is more filled with faith, not anxious but trusting; toward a more frequent celebration of the sacrament which is seen to be completely filled with the Lord's merciful love.

The second conviction concerns the function of the sacrament of penance for those who have recourse to it. According to the most ancient traditional idea, the sacrament is a kind of judicial action; but this takes place before a tribunal of mercy rather than of strict and rigorous justice, which is comparable to human tribunals only by analogy, namely insofar as sinners reveal their sins and their condition as creatures subject to sin; they commit themselves to renouncing and combating sin; they accept the punishment (sacramental penance) which the confessor imposes on them and receive absolution from him.[19]

Forms of Celebration

The first form (reconciliation of individual penitents) is the only normal and ordinary way of celebrating the sacrament, and it cannot and must not be allowed to fall into disuse or be neglected. The second form (reconciliation of a number of penitents with individual confession and absolution), even though in the preparatory acts it helps to give greater emphasis to the community aspects of the sacrament, is the same as the first form in the culminating sacramental act, namely individual confession and individual absolution of sins. It can thus be regarded as equal to the first form as regards the normality of the rite. The third form however (reconciliation of a number of penitents with general confession and absolution) is exceptional in character. It is therefore not left to free choice but is regulated by a special discipline.[20]

Counterwitness and Scandal

Hence it is appropriate that, as the Second Millennium of Christianity draws to a close, the Church should become more fully conscious of the sinfulness of her children, recalling all those times in history when they departed from the spirit of Christ and his Gospel and, instead of offering to the world the witness of a life inspired by the values of faith, indulged in ways of thinking and acting which were truly *forms of counterwitness and scandal.*

Although she is holy because of her incorporation into Christ, the Church does not tire of doing penance: before God and humankind *she always acknowledges as her own her sinful sons and daughters.* As *Lumen gentium* [8] affirms: "The Church, embracing sinners to her bosom, is at the same time holy and always in need of being purified, and incessantly pursues the path of penance and renewal."

The Holy Door of the Jubilee of the Year 2000 should be symbolically wider than those of previous Jubilees, because humanity, upon reaching this goal, will leave behind not just a century but a millennium. It is fitting that the Church should make this passage with a clear awareness of what has happened to her during the last ten centuries. She cannot cross the threshold of the new millennium without encouraging her children to purify themselves, through repentance, of past errors, and instances of infidelity, inconsistency, and slowness to act. Acknowledging the weaknesses of the past is an act of honesty and courage which helps us to strengthen our faith, which alerts us to face today's temptations and challenges and prepares us to meet them.[21]

Sins against Unity

Among the sins which require a greater commitment to repentance and conversion should certainly be counted those which *have been detrimental to the unity willed by God for his people.* In the course of the thousand years now drawing to a close, even more than in the first millennium, ecclesial communion has been painfully wounded, a fact "for which, at times, men and women of both sides were to blame" (*Unitatis redintegratio*, 3). Such wounds openly contradict the will of Christ and are a cause of scandal to the world (*Unitatis redintegratio*, 1). These sins of the past unfortunately still burden us and remain ever present temptations. It is necessary to make amends for them, and earnestly to beseech Christ's forgiveness.[22]

Sins of Intolerance and Violence

Another painful chapter of history to which the sons and daughters of the Church must return with a spirit of repentance is that of the acquiescence given, especially in certain centuries, to *intolerance and even the use of violence* in the service of truth. It is true that an accurate historical judgment cannot prescind from careful study of the cultural conditioning of the times, as a result of which many people may have held in good faith that an authentic witness to the truth could include suppressing the opinions of others or at least paying no attention to them. Many factors frequently converged to create assumptions which justified intolerance and fostered an emotional climate from which only great spirits, truly free and filled with God, were in some way able to break free. Yet the consideration of mitigating factors does not exonerate the Church from the obligation to express profound regret for the weaknesses of so many of her sons and daughters who sullied her face, preventing her from fully mirroring the image of her crucified Lord, the supreme witness of patient love and of humble meekness. From these painful moments of the past a lesson can be drawn for the future, leading all Christians to adhere fully to the sublime principle stated by the Council: "The truth cannot impose itself except by virtue of its own truth, as it wins over the mind with both gentleness and power" (*Dignitatis humanae*, 1).[23]

The Evils of Our Day

Many cardinals and bishops expressed the desire for a serious examination of conscience above all on the part of *the Church of today*. On the threshold of the new millennium, Christians need to place themselves humbly before the Lord and examine themselves on *the responsibility which they too have for the evils of our day*. The present age, in fact, together with much light, also presents not a few shadows.

How can we remain silent, for example, about the *religious indifference* which causes many people today to live as if God did not exist, or to be content with a vague religiosity, incapable of coming to grips with the question of truth and the requirement of consistency? To this must also be added the widespread loss of the transcendent sense of human life, and confusion in the ethical sphere, even about the fundamental values of respect for life and the family. The sons and daughters of the Church too need to examine themselves in this regard. To what extent have they been shaped by the climate of secularism and ethical relativism? And what responsibility do they bear, in view of the increasing lack of religion, for not having shown the true face of God, by having "failed in their religious, moral, or social life" (*Gaudium et spes*, 19)?

It cannot be denied that, for many Christians, the spiritual life is passing through a *time of uncertainty* which affects not only their moral life but also their life of prayer and the *theological correctness of their faith*. Faith, already put to the test by the challenges of our times, is sometimes disoriented by erroneous theological views, the spread of which is abetted by the crisis of obedience vis-à-vis the Church's Magisterium.

And with respect to the Church of our time, how can we not lament *the lack of discernment*, which at times became even acquiescence, shown by many Christians concerning the violation of fundamental human rights by totalitarian regimes? And should we not also regret, among the shadows of our own day, the responsibility shared by so many Christians *for grave forms of injustice and exclusion*? It must be asked how many Christians really know and put into practice the principles of the Church's social doctrine.

An examination of conscience must also consider the *reception given to the Council*, this great gift of the Spirit to the Church at the end of the second millennium. To what extent has the word of God become more fully the soul of theology and the inspiration of the whole of Christian living, as *Dei Verbum* sought? Is the liturgy lived as the "origin and summit" of ecclesial life, in accordance with the teaching of *Sacrosanctum concilium*? In the universal Church and in the particular Churches, is the ecclesiology of communion described in *Lumen gentium* being strengthened? Does it leave room for charisms, ministries, and different forms of participation by the People of God, without adopting notions borrowed from democracy and sociology which do not reflect the Catholic vision of the Church and the authentic spirit of Vatican II? Another serious question is raised by the nature of relations between the Church and the world. The Council's guidelines, set forth in *Gaudium et spes* and other documents, of open, respectful and cordial dialogue, yet accompanied by careful discernment and courageous witness to the truth, remain valid and call us to a greater commitment.[24]

Penance and Conversion

The Sacrament of Penance offers the sinner "a new possibility to convert and to recover the grace of justification" (*Catechism of the Catholic Church*, 1446) won by the sacrifice of Christ. The sinner thus enters the life of God anew and shares fully in the life of the Church. Confessing their sins, believers truly receive pardon and can once more take part in the Eucharist as the sign that they have again found communion with the Father and with his Church. From the first centuries, however, the Church has always been profoundly convinced that pardon, freely granted by God, implies in consequence a real change of life, the gradual elimination of evil within us, a renewal in our way of living. The sacramental action had to be combined with an existential act, with a real cleansing from fault, precisely what is called penance. Pardon does not imply that this existential process becomes superfluous, but rather that it acquires a meaning, that it is accepted and welcomed. Reconciliation with God does not mean that there are no enduring consequences of sin from which we must be purified.[25]

Purification of Memory

Nor will the People of God fail to recognize other possible signs of the mercy of God at work in the Jubilee. In my Apostolic Letter *Tertio millennio adveniente*, I suggested some which may help people to live the exceptional grace of the Jubilee with greater fervor (cf. nos. 33, 37, 51). I recall them briefly here. First of all, the sign of *the purification of memory*; this calls everyone to make an act of courage and humility in recognizing the wrongs done by those who have borne or who bear the name of Christian.

By its nature, the Holy Year is a time when we are called to conversion. This is the first word of the preaching of Jesus, which significantly enough is linked with readiness to believe: "Repent and believe the Good News" (Mark 1:15). The imperative put by Christ flows from realization of the fact that "the time is fulfilled" (Mark 1:15). The fulfillment of God's time becomes a summons to conversion, which is in the first place an effect of grace. It is the Spirit who impels each of us to "return into ourselves" and to see the need to go back to the Father's house (cf. Luke 15:17–20). Examination of conscience is therefore one of the most decisive moments of life. It places each individual before the truth of his own life. Thus we discover the distance which separates our deeds from the ideal which we have set for ourselves.

The history of the Church is a history of holiness. The New Testament strongly states this mark of the baptized: they are "saints" to the extent that, being separate from the world insofar as the latter is subject to the Evil One, they consecrate themselves to worshipping the one true God. In fact, this holiness is evident not only in the lives of the many Saints and Blessed recognized by the Church, but also in the lives of the immense host of unknown men and women whose number it is impossible to calculate (cf. Rev 7:9). Their lives attest to the truth of the Gospel and offer the world a visible sign that perfection is possible. Yet it must be acknowledged that history also records events which constitute a counter-testimony to Christianity. Because of the bond which unites us to one another in the Mystical Body, all of us, though not personally responsible and without encroaching on the judgment of God who alone knows every heart, bear the burden of the errors and faults of those who have gone before us. Yet we too, sons and daughters of the Church, have sinned and have hindered the Bride of Christ from shining forth in all her beauty. Our sin has impeded the Spirit's working in the hearts of many people. Our meager faith has meant that many have lapsed into apathy and been driven away from a true encounter with Christ.[26]

Implore Forgiveness

As the Successor of Peter, I ask that in this year of mercy the Church, strong in the holiness which she receives from her Lord, should kneel before God and implore forgiveness for the past and present sins of her sons and daughters. All have sinned and none can claim righteousness before God (cf. 1 Kgs 8:46). Let it be said once more without fear: "We have sinned" (Jer 3:25), but let us keep alive the certainty that "where sin increased, grace abounded even more" (Rom 5:20).[27]

The Sign of Charity

One sign of the mercy of God which is especially necessary today is the sign of *charity*, which opens our eyes to the needs of those who are poor and excluded. Such is the situation affecting vast sectors of society and casting its shadow of death upon whole peoples. The human race is facing forms of slavery which are new and more subtle than those of the past; and for too many people freedom remains a word without meaning. Some nations, especially the poorer ones, are oppressed by a debt so huge that repayment is practically impossible. It is clear, therefore, that there can be no real progress without effective cooperation between the peoples of every language, race, nationality and religion. The abuses of power which result in some dominating others must stop: such abuses are sinful and unjust. Whoever is concerned to accumulate treasure only on earth (cf. Matt 6:19) "is not rich in the sight of God" (Luke 12:21).

There is also a need to create a new culture of international solidarity and cooperation, where all (particularly the wealthy nations and the private sector) accept responsibility for an economic model which serves everyone. There should be no more postponement of the time when the poor Lazarus can sit beside the rich man to share the same banquet and be forced no more to feed on the scraps that fall from the table (cf. Luke 16:19–31). Extreme poverty is a source of violence, bitterness and scandal; and to eradicate it is to do the work of justice and therefore the work of peace.

The Jubilee is a further summons to conversion of heart through a change of life. It is a reminder to all that they should give absolute importance neither to the goods of the earth, since these are not God, nor to human domination or claim to domination, since the earth belongs to God and to him alone: "the earth is mine and you are strangers and sojourners with me" (Lev 25:23). May this year of grace touch the hearts of those who hold in their hands the fate of the world's peoples![28]

6.5 During his long pontificate, John Paul spoke and wrote about the other five sacraments: baptism, confirmation, anointing of the sick, the hierarchical and ministerial priesthood, and sacramental marriage. To prepare for the great jubilee of the year 2000, he proclaimed a Year of the Family for the Catholic Church and developed an appropriate theology and spirituality in his "Letter to Families" of February 2, 1994. A year later he addressed his "Letter to Women" of June 29, 1995, to "women throughout the world," and published it before the Fourth World Conference that the United Nations organized in Beijing the following September.

The Marital Covenant and Communion

The family has always been considered as the first and basic expression of human beings' *social nature*. Even today this way of looking at things remains unchanged. Nowadays, however, emphasis tends to be laid on how much the family, as the smallest and most basic human community, owes to the personal contribution of a man and a woman. The family is in fact a community of persons whose proper way of existing and living together is communion: *communio personarum*. Here too, while always acknowledging the absolute transcendence of the Creator with regard to his creatures, we can see the family's ultimate relationship to the divine "We." *Only persons are capable of living "in communion."* The family originates in a marital communion described by the Second Vatican Council as a "covenant," *in which man and woman "give themselves to each other and accept each other."*

The Book of Genesis helps us to see this truth when it states, in reference to the establishment of the family through marriage, that "a man leaves his father and his mother and cleaves to his wife, and they become one flesh" (Gen 2:24). In the Gospel, Christ, disputing with the Pharisees, quotes these same words and then adds: "So they are no longer two but one flesh. What therefore God has joined together, let not man put asunder" (Matt 19:6). In this way, he reveals anew the binding content of a fact which exists "from the beginning" (Matt 19:8) and which always preserves this content. If the Master confirms it "now," he does so in order to make clear and unmistakable to all, at the dawn of the New Covenant, the *indissoluble character* of marriage as the *basis of the common good of the family*.

When, in union with the Apostle, we bow our knees before the Father from whom all fatherhood and motherhood is named (cf. Eph 3:14–15), we come to realize that parenthood is the event whereby the family, already constituted by the conjugal covenant of marriage, is brought about "in the full and specific sense." *Motherhood necessarily implies fatherhood*, and in turn, *fatherhood necessarily implies motherhood*. This is the result of the duality bestowed by the Creator upon human beings "from the beginning."

I have spoken of two closely related yet not identical concepts: the concept of "communion" and that of "community." *"Communion"* has to do with the personal relationship between the "I" and the "thou." *"Community"* on the other hand transcends this framework and moves towards a "society," a "we." The family, as a community of persons, is thus the first human "society." It arises whenever there comes into being the conjugal covenant of marriage, which opens the spouses to a lasting communion of love and of life, and it is brought to completion in a full and specific way with the procreation of children: the "communion" of the spouses gives rise to the "community" of the family. The "community" of the family is completely pervaded by the very essence of "communion." On the human level, can there be any other *"communion"* comparable to that *between a mother and a child* whom she has carried in her womb and then brought to birth?

In the family thus constituted there appears a new unity, in which the relationship "of communion" between the parents attains complete fulfillment. Experience teaches that this fulfillment represents both a task and a challenge. The task involves the spouses in living out their original covenant. *The children* born to them (and here is the challenge) *should consolidate that covenant*, enriching and deepening the conjugal communion of the father and mother. When this does not occur, we need to ask if the selfishness which lurks even in the love of man and woman as a result of the human inclination to evil is not stronger than this love. Married couples need to be well aware of this. From the outset they need to have their hearts and thoughts turned towards the God "from whom every family is named," *so that their fatherhood and motherhood will draw from that source the power to be continually renewed in love.*

Fatherhood and motherhood are themselves a particular proof of love; they make it possible to discover love's extension and original depth. But this does not take place automatically. Rather, it is a task entrusted to both husband and wife. In the life of husband and wife together, fatherhood and motherhood represent such a sublime "novelty" and richness as can only be approached "on one's knees."[29]

The Love of Man and Woman

Only "persons" are capable of saying those words [of reciprocal acceptance]; only they are able to live "in communion" on the basis of a mutual choice which is, or ought to be, fully conscious and free. The Book of Genesis, in speaking of a man who leaves father and mother in order to cleave to his wife (cf. Gen 2:24), highlights the *conscious and free choice* which gives rise to marriage, making the son of a family a husband, and the daughter of a family a wife. How can we adequately understand this mutual choice, unless we take into consideration the full truth about the person, who is a rational and free being? The Second Vatican Council, in speaking of the likeness of God, uses extremely significant terms. It refers not only to the divine image and likeness which every human being as such already possesses, but also and primarily to "a certain similarity between the union of the divine persons and the union of God's children in truth and love."

This rich and meaningful formulation first of all confirms what is central to the identity of every man and every woman. This identity consists in the *capacity to live in truth and love*; even more, it consists in the need of truth and love as an essential dimension of the life of the person. Human beings' need for truth and love opens them both to God and to creatures: it opens them to other people, to life "in communion," and in particular to marriage and to the family. In the words of the Council, the "communion" of persons is drawn in a certain sense from the mystery of the trinitarian "We," and therefore "conjugal communion" also refers to this mystery (*Gaudium et spes*, 48). The family, which originates in the love of man and woman, ultimately derives from the mystery of God. This conforms to the innermost being of man and woman, to their innate and authentic dignity as persons.

In marriage man and woman are so firmly united as to become (to use the words of the Book of Genesis) "one flesh" (Gen 2:24). Male and female in their physical constitution, the two human subjects, even though physically different, *share equally in the capacity to live "in truth and love."* This capacity, characteristic of the human being as a person, has at the same time both a spiritual and a bodily dimension. It is also through the body that man and woman are predisposed to form a "communion of persons" in marriage. When they are united by the conjugal covenant in such a way as to become "*one flesh*" (Gen 2:24), their *union* ought to take place "*in truth and love*," and thus express the maturity proper to persons created in the image and likeness of God.

The family which results from this union draws its inner solidity from the covenant between the spouses, which Christ raised to a sacrament. The family draws its proper character as a community, its traits of "communion," from that fundamental communion of the spouses which is prolonged in their children. "*Will you accept children lovingly from God, and bring them up according to the law of Christ and his Church?*" the celebrant asks during the Rite of Marriage. The answer given by the spouses reflects the most profound truth of the love which unites them. Their unity, however, rather than closing them up in themselves, opens them towards a new life, towards a new person. As parents, they will be capable of giving life to a being like themselves, not only bone of their bones and flesh of their flesh (cf. Gen 2:23), but an image and likeness of God: a person.

When the Church asks "Are you willing?" she is reminding the bride and groom that they stand *before the creative power of God*. They are called to become parents, to cooperate with the Creator in giving life. Cooperating with God to call new human beings into existence means contributing to the transmission of that divine image and likeness of which everyone "born of a woman" is a bearer.[30]

The Common Good of Marriage and the Family

Marital consent defines and consolidates *the good common to marriage and to the family*. "I, N., take you, N., to be my wife/husband. I promise to be true to you in good times and in bad, in sickness and in health. I will love you and honor you all the days of my life." Marriage is a unique communion of persons, and it is on the basis of this communion that the family is called to become a community of persons. This is a commitment which the bride and groom undertake "before God and his Church," as the celebrant reminds them before they exchange their consent. Those who take part in the rite are witnesses of this commitment, for in a certain sense they represent the Church and society, the setting in which the new family will live and grow.

The words of consent define the common good of the *couple and of the family*. First, the common good of the spouses: love, fidelity, honor, the permanence of their union until death, "all the days of my life." The good of both, which is at the same time the good of each, must then become the good of the children. The common good, by its very nature, both unites individual persons and ensures the true good of each. If the Church (and the State for that matter) receives the consent which the spouses express in the words cited above, she does so because that consent is "written in their hearts" (Rom 2:15). It is the spouses who give their consent to each other by a solemn promise, that is, by confirming the truth of that consent in the sight of God. As baptized Christians, they are the ministers of the Sacrament of Matrimony in the Church. Saint Paul teaches that this mutual commitment of theirs is a "great mystery" (Eph 5:32).

The words of consent, then, express what is essential to the common good of the spouses, and *they indicate what ought to be the common good of the future family*. In order to bring this out, the Church asks the spouses if they are prepared to accept the children God grants them and to raise the children as Christians. This question calls to mind the common good of the future family unit, evoking the genealogy of persons which is part of the constitution of marriage and of the family itself. The question about children and their education is profoundly linked to marital consent, with its solemn promise of love, conjugal respect, and fidelity until death. The acceptance and education of children, two of the primary ends of the family, are conditioned by how that commitment will be fulfilled. Fatherhood and motherhood represent a *responsibility which is not simply physical but spiritual in nature*; indeed, through these realities there passes the genealogy of the person, which has its eternal beginning in God and which must lead back to him.[31]

Men and Women

After creating human beings male and female, God says to both: *"Fill the earth and subdue it"* (Gen 1:28). Not only does he give them the power to procreate as a means of perpetuating the human species throughout time, *he also gives them the earth, charging them with the responsible use of its resources.* As rational and free beings, humans are called to transform the face of the earth. In this task, which is essentially that of culture, *man and woman alike* share equal responsibility from the start. In their fruitful relationship as husband and wife, in their common task of exercising dominion over the earth, woman and man are marked neither by a static and undifferentiated equality nor by an irreconcilable and inexorably conflictual difference. Their most natural relationship, which corresponds to the plan of God, is the "unity of the two," a relational "uni-duality," which enables each to experience their interpersonal and reciprocal relationship as a gift which enriches and which confers responsibility.

To this "unity of the two" God has entrusted not only the work of procreation and family life, but the creation of history itself. While the *1994 International Year of the Family* focused attention on *women as mothers,* the Beijing Conference, which has as its theme "Action for Equality, Development and Peace," provides an auspicious occasion for heightening awareness of *the many contributions made by women to the life of whole societies and nations.* This contribution is primarily spiritual and cultural in nature, but socio-political and economic as well. The various sectors of society, nations and states, and the progress of all humanity, are certainly deeply indebted to the contribution of women![32]

NOTES

1. *Redemptor hominis*, 20, in *AAS* 71 (1979), 311–12; *EncMiller*, 82; *Origins* 8:40 (1979), 640; *Pope Speaks* 24:2 (1979), 137–38.

2. Ibid., 20, in *AAS* 71 (1979), 312–13; *EncMiller*, 82; *Origins* 8:40 (1979), 640; *Pope Speaks* 24:2 (1979), 138–38.

3. *Dominicae cenae*, 6, in *AAS* 72 (1980), 123–24; *ND*, 1590; *Origins* 9:41 (1980), 657; *Pope Speaks* 25:2 (1980), 146–47.

4. *Address to the Bishops of Zaire (1980)*, 4–5, in *AAS* 72 (1980), 432–33; *Origins* 10:1 (1980), 5.

5. *Sollicitudo rei socialis*, 48, in *AAS* 80 (1988), 584; *EncMiller*, 419; *ND*, 1592; *Origins* 17:38 (1988), 658; *Pope Speaks* 33:2 (1988), 154–55.

6. Ibid., 48, in *AAS* 80 (1988), 584; *EncMiller*, 419; *ND*, 1592; *Origins* 17:38 (1988), 658; *Pope Speaks* 33:2 (1988), 154–55.

7. *Vicesimus quintus annus*, 10, in *AAS* 81 (1989), 906–8; *ND*, 1240; *Origins* 19:2 (1989), 21; *Pope Speaks* 34:3 (1989), 226–27.

8. Ibid., 16, in *AAS* 81 (1989), 912–13; *ND*, 1241; *Origins* 19:2 (1989), 16; *Pope Speaks* 34:3 (1989), 228–29.

9. *Dies Domini*, 45, in *AAS* 90 (1998), 741–42; *ND*, 1593; *Origins* 28:9 (1998), 143; *Pope Speaks* 43:6 (1998), 358.

10. Ibid., 81, in *AAS* 90 (1998), 763; *ND*, 1250e; *Origins* 28:9 (1998), 149; *Pope Speaks* 43:6 (1998), 371.

11. *Ecclesia de Eucharistia*, 8, in *AAS* 95 (2003), 437–38; *Pope Speaks* 48:5 (2003), 285.

12. Ibid., 23, in *AAS* 95 (2003), 449; *Pope Speaks*.48:5 (2003), 292.

13. *Redemptor hominis*, 20, in *AAS* 71 (1979), 314; *EncMiller*, 83; *ND*, 1672; *Origins* 8:40 (1979), 640–41; *Pope Speaks* 24:2 (1979), 139–40.

14. *Reconciliatio et paenitentia*, 9, in *AAS* 77 (1985), 202–3; *ApExMiller*, 275; *ND*, 1673; *Origins* 14:27 (1984), 438; *Pope Speaks* 30:1 (1985), 33.

15. Ibid., 25, in *AAS* 77 (1985), 236–37; *ApExMiller*, 301; *ND*, 1674; *Origins* 14:27 (1984), 446; *Pope Speaks* 30:1 (1985), 56.

16. Ibid., 26, in *AAS* 77 (1985), 242–43; *ApExMiller*, 305–6; *ND*, 1675; *Origins* 14:27 (1984), 447; *Pope Speaks* 30:1 (1985), 60.

17. Ibid., 28, in *AAS* 77 (1985), 251–52; *ApExMiller*, 312; *ND*, 1676a; *Origins* 14:27 (1984), 449; *Pope Speaks* 30:1 (1985), 66.

18. Ibid., 29, in *AAS* 77 (1985), 254–55; *ApExMiller*, 314; *ND*, 1676b; *Origins* 14:27 (1984), 450; *Pope Speaks* 30:1 (1985), 68.

19. Ibid., 31, in *AAS* 77 (1985), 258–59; *ApExMiller*, 316–17; *ND*, 1676c and d; *Origins* 14:27 (1984), 451; *Pope Speaks* 30:1 (1985), 70–71.

20. Ibid., 32, in *AAS* 77 (1985), 267; *ApExMiller*, 323–24; *ND*, 1676e; *Origins* 14:27 (1984), 453; *Pope Speaks* 30:1 (1985), 77.

21. *Tertio millennio adveniente*, 33, in *AAS* 87 (1995), 25–26; *ND*, 1677b; *Origins* 24:24 (1994), 410; *Pope Speaks* 40:2 (1995), 101.

22. Ibid., 34, in *AAS* 87 (1995), 26; *ND*, 1677c; *Origins* 24:24 (1994), 410; *Pope Speaks* 40:2 (1995), 101.

23. Ibid., 35, in *AAS* 87 (1995), 27; *ND*, 1677d; *Origins* 24:24 (1994), 411; *Pope Speaks* 40:2 (1995), 102.

24. Ibid., 36, in *AAS* 87 (1995), 27–29; *ND*, 1677e; *Origins* 24:24 (1994), 411; *Pope Speaks* 40:2 (1995), 102–3.

25. *Incarnationis mysterium*, 9, in *AAS* 91 (1999), 137; *ND*, 1680a; *Origins* 28:26 (1998), 449; *Pope Speaks* 44:2 (1999), 186.

26. Ibid., 11, in *AAS* 91 (1999), 139–40; *ND*, 1680b; *Origins* 28:26 (1998), 450; *Pope Speaks* 44:3 (1999), 187–88.

27. Ibid., 11, in *AAS* 91 (1999), 140; *ND*, 1680b; *Origins* 28:26 (1998), 450; *Pope Speaks* 44:3 (1999), 188.

28. Ibid., 12, in *AAS* 91 (1999), 141–42; *Origins* 28:26 (1998), 451; *Pope Speaks* 44:3 (1999), 189.

29. "Letter to Families," 7, in *AAS* 86 (1994), 874–76; *ND*, 1852a; *Origins* 23:37 (1994), 641; *Pope Speaks* 39:4 (1994), 212–13.

30. Ibid., 8, in *AAS* 86 (1994), 876–78; *ND*, 1852b; *Origins* 23:37 (1994), 642; *Pope Speaks* 39:4 (1994), 213–14.

31. Ibid., 10, in *AAS* 86 (1994), 880–81; *ND*, 1852c; *Origins* 23:37 (1994), 643; *Pope Speaks* 39:4 (1994), 215–16.

32. "Letter to Women," 8, in *AAS* 87 (1995), 808–9; *ND*, 1854; *Origins* 25:9 (1995), 141; *Pope Speaks* 40:6 (1995), 406–7.

CHAPTER SEVEN

The Church and Her Mission

The major texts John Paul II published on the church and her mission must include the 1988 apostolic exhortation *Christifideles laici* (The Lay Faithful), the 1990 encyclical *Redemptoris missio* (The Mission of the Redeemer), and the 2003 apostolic exhortation *Pastores gregis* (Shepherds of the Flock). While presenting the church as communion and mission, *Christifideles laici* followed Vatican II by emphasizing the way in which all the baptized participate in the priestly, prophetic, and kingly mission of Christ and enjoy diverse charisms that contribute to the well-being of the whole church. *Redemptoris missio* broke new ground by acknowledging that the church is "ordered toward" the kingdom of God. While not separated from the church, the kingdom is the greater reality. *Pastores gregis*, recognizing that the hierarchical and ministerial priesthood shares in a particular way in the triple "office" of Christ as priest, prophet, and king, proposed a demanding pattern of spiritual and pastoral life for bishops.

We can also glean some important passages about the church and her mission from other texts, such as the 1979 apostolic exhortation *Catechesi tradendae* (Handing on Catechesis), a 1980 address to workers in São Paulo (Brazil), the 1984 apostolic exhortation *Reconciliatio et paenitentia* (Reconciliation and Penance), the 1985 encyclical *Slavorum apostoli* (The Apostles of the Slavs), a 1992 address to the Fourth General Conference of Latin American Bishops at Santo Domingo, and the 1998 encyclical *Fides et ratio* (Faith and Reason).

The Church and Her Mission

[As I said recently to the members of the Biblical Commission:] The term "acculturation" or "inculturation" may be a neologism, but it expresses very well one factor of the great mystery of the incarnation. We can say of catechesis, as well as of evangelization in general, that it is called to bring the power of the Gospel into the very heart of culture and cultures. For this purpose, catechesis will seek to know these cultures and their essential components; it will learn their most significant expressions; it will respect their particular values and riches. In this manner it will be able to offer these cultures the knowledge of the hidden mystery (cf. Rom 16:25; Eph 3:5) and help them to bring forth from their own living tradition original expressions of Christian life, celebration and thought. Two things must however be kept in mind.

On the one hand the Gospel message cannot be purely and simply isolated from the culture in which it was first inserted (the biblical world or, more concretely, the cultural milieu in which Jesus of Nazareth lived), nor, without serious loss, from the cultures in which it has already been expressed down the centuries; it does not spring spontaneously from any cultural soil; it has always been transmitted by means of an apostolic dialogue which inevitably becomes part of a certain dialogue of cultures.

On the other hand, the power of the Gospel everywhere transforms and regenerates. When that power enters into a culture, it is no surprise that it rectifies many of its elements. There would be no catechesis if it were the Gospel that had to change when it came into contact with the cultures. To forget this would simply amount to what St. Paul very forcefully calls "emptying the cross of Christ of its power" (1 Cor 1:17). It is a different matter to take, with wise discernment, certain elements, religious or otherwise, that form part of the cultural heritage of a human group and use them to help its members to understand better the whole of the Christian mystery.[1]

Promoting Justice Belongs to the Church's Mission

This message of salvation which the Church, by virtue of her mission, brings to every person, to the family, to the different social environments, to the nations and to the whole of humankind, is a message of love and kinship, a message of justice and solidarity, in the first place for the neediest. In a word, it is a message of peace and of a just social order....

The world willed by God is a world of justice. The order [of justice] must be continually realized in this world, and it must always be realized anew, as situations and social systems grow and develop, in proportion to new conditions and economic possibilities, new possibilities of technology and production, and at the same time new possibilities and necessities of distributing goods. The Church, when she proclaims the Gospel, also tries to ensure, without, however, forgetting her specific task of evangelization, that all aspects of social life in which injustice is manifested undergo a change towards justice.[2]

The Church, the Sacrament of Reconciliation

The Church has the mission of proclaiming reconciliation and as it were of being its sacrament in the world. The Church is the sacrament, that is to say, the sign and means of reconciliation in different ways which differ in value but which all come together to obtain what the divine initiative of mercy desires to grant to humanity. She is a sacrament in the first place by her very existence as a reconciled community which witnesses to and represents in the world the work of Christ.

She is also a sacrament through her service as the custodian and interpreter of sacred Scripture, which is the good news of reconciliation inasmuch as it tells each succeeding generation about God's loving plan and shows to each generation the paths to universal reconciliation in Christ.

109

Finally she is a sacrament by reason of the seven sacraments which, each in its own way, "make the church" (St. Augustine, *De Civitate Dei*, 22.17). For since they commemorate and renew Christ's paschal mystery, all the sacraments are a source of life for the Church, and in the Church's hands they are means of conversion to God and of reconciliation among people.[3]

The Catholicity of the Church

The Church is catholic also because she is able to present in every human context the revealed truth, preserved by her intact in its divine content, in such a way as to bring it into contact with the lofty thoughts and just expectations of every individual and every people. Moreover, the entire patrimony of good which every generation transmits to posterity, together with the priceless gift of life, forms as it were an immense and many-colored collection of tiles that together make up the living mosaic of the Pantocrator [universal ruler], who will manifest himself in his total splendor only at the moment of the parousia.

The Gospel does not lead to the impoverishment or extinction of those things which every individual, people and nation and every culture throughout history recognize and bring into being as goodness, truth and beauty. On the contrary, it strives to assimilate and to develop all these values, to live them with magnanimity and joy, and to perfect them by the mysterious and ennobling light of revelation.

The concrete dimension of catholicity, inscribed by Christ the Lord in the very makeup of the Church, is not something static, outside history and flatly uniform. In a certain sense it wells up and develops every day as something new from the unanimous faith of all those who believe in God, one and three, revealed by Jesus Christ and preached by the Church through the power of the Holy Spirit. This dimension issues quite spontaneously from mutual respect proper to fraternal love: for every person and every nation, great or small, and from the honest acknowledgment of the qualities and rights of brothers and sisters in the faith.[4]

The Vocation of the Lay Faithful

In giving a response to the question, "Who are the lay faithful?" the Council went beyond previous interpretations which were predominantly negative. Instead it opened itself to a decidedly positive vision and displayed a basic intention of asserting *the full belonging of the lay faithful to the Church and to its mystery.*

At the same time it insisted on the unique character of their vocation, which is in a special way to "seek the Kingdom of God by engaging in temporal affairs and ordering them according to the plan of God" (*Lumen gentium*, 31). "The term *lay faithful*," we read in the Constitution on the Church, *Lumen gentium*, "is here understood to mean all the faithful except those in Holy Orders and those who belong to a religious state sanctioned by the Church. Through baptism the lay faithful are made one body with Christ and are established among the People of God. They are in their own way made sharers in the priestly, prophetic and kingly office of Christ. They carry out their own part in the mission of the whole Christian people with respect to the Church and the world" (*Lumen gentium*, 31).

Pius XII once stated: 'The faithful, more precisely the lay faithful, find themselves on the front lines of the Church's life; for them the Church is the animating principle for human society. Therefore, they in particular, ought to have an ever-clearer consciousness *not only of belonging to the Church, but of being the Church*, that is to say, the community of the faithful on earth under the leadership of the Pope, the head of all, and of the bishops in communion with him. These *are the Church*" (*Address to the New Cardinals, February 20, 1946).*[5]

An Organic Communion

Ecclesial communion is more precisely likened to an "organic" communion, analogous to that of a living and functioning body. In fact, at one and the same time it is characterized by a *diversity* and a *complementarity* of vocations and states in life, of ministries, of charisms and responsibilities. Because of this diversity and complementarity, every

111

member of the lay faithful is seen *in relation to the whole body* and offers a *totally unique contribution* on behalf of the whole body.[6]

The Ministries and Mission of the Lay Faithful

The Church's mission of salvation in the world is realized not only by the ministers in virtue of the Sacrament of Orders but also by all the lay faithful; indeed, because of their baptismal state and their specific vocation, in the measure proper to each person, the lay faithful participate in the priestly, prophetic and kingly mission of Christ. The pastors, therefore, ought to acknowledge and foster the ministries, the offices and roles of the lay faithful that find their *foundation in the Sacraments of Baptism and Confirmation*, indeed, for a good many of them, *in the Sacrament of Matrimony*.

When necessity and expediency in the Church require it, the pastors, according to established norms from universal law, can entrust to the lay faithful certain offices and roles that are connected to their pastoral ministry but do not require the character of Orders. The Code of Canon Law states: "When the necessity of the Church warrants it and when ministers are lacking, lay persons, even if they are not lectors or acolytes, can also supply for certain of their offices, namely, to exercise the ministry of the word, to preside over liturgical prayers, to confer baptism, and to distribute Holy Communion in accord with the prescriptions of the law" (cf. *Canon* 230, 3). However, *the exercise of such tasks does not make pastors of the lay faithful*: in fact, a person is not a minister simply in performing a task, but through sacramental ordination. Only the Sacrament of Orders gives the ordained minister a particular participation in the office of Christ, the Shepherd and Head, and in his Eternal Priesthood (cf. *Presbyterorum ordinis*, 2, 5). The task exercised in virtue of a substitute takes its legitimacy formally and immediately from the official deputation given by the pastors, as well as from its concrete exercise under the guidance of ecclesiastical authority (cf. *Apostolicam actuositatem*, 24).[7]

Criteria for Ecclesiality

It is always from the perspective of the Church's communion and mission, and not in opposition to the freedom to associate, that one understands the necessity of having *clear and definite criteria for discerning and recognizing* such lay groups, also called "Criteria of Ecclesiality." The following basic criteria might be helpful in evaluating an association of the lay faithful in the Church:

—*The primacy given to the call of every Christian to holiness*, as it is manifested "in the fruits of grace which the spirit produces in the faithful" (*Lumen gentium*, 39) and in a growth towards the fullness of Christian life and the perfection of charity (*Lumen gentium*, 40)....

—*The responsibility of professing the Catholic faith*, embracing and proclaiming the truth about Christ, the Church and humanity, in obedience to the Church's Magisterium, as the Church interprets it....

—*The witness to a strong and authentic communion* in filial relationship to the Pope, in total adherence to the belief that he is the perpetual and visible center of unity of the universal Church (cf. *Lumen gentium*, 23), and with the local bishop, "the visible principle and foundation of unity" (*ibid.*) in the particular Church, and in "mutual esteem for all forms of the Church's apostolate" (*Apostolicam actuositatem*, 23)....

—*Conformity to and participation in the Church's apostolic goals*, that is, "the evangelization and sanctification of humanity and the Christian formation of people's conscience, so as to enable them to infuse the spirit of the gospel into the various communities and spheres of life" (*Apostolicam actuositatem*, 20)....

—*A commitment to a presence in human society*, which in light of the Church's social doctrine, places it at the service of the total dignity of the person.[8]

The Church, the Instrument of Salvation for All

It is necessary to keep these two truths together, namely, the real possibility of salvation in Christ for all humankind and the necessity of the Church for salvation. Both these truths help us to understand the *one mystery of salvation*, so that we can come to know God's mercy and our own responsibility. Salvation, which always remains a gift of the Holy Spirit, requires one's cooperation, both to save oneself and to save others. This is God's will, and this is why he established the Church and made her a part of his plan of salvation. Referring to "this messianic people," the Council says; "It has been set up by Christ as a communion of life, love and truth; by him too it is taken up as the instrument of salvation for all, and sent on a mission to the whole world as the light of the world and the salt of the earth" (*Lumen gentium*, 9).[9]

The Universal Kingdom of God

The kingdom aims at transforming human relationships; it grows gradually as people slowly learn to love, forgive and serve one another. Jesus sums up the whole Law, focusing it on the commandment of love (cf. Matt 22:34–40; Luke 10:25–28). Before leaving his disciples, he gives them a "new commandment": "Love one another; even as I have loved you" (John 13:34; cf. 15:12). Jesus' love for the world finds its highest expression in the gift of his life for humankind (cf. John 15:13), which manifests the love which the Father has for the world (cf. John 3:16). The kingdom's nature, therefore, is one of communion among all human beings, with one another and with God.

The kingdom is the concern of everyone: individuals, society, and the world. Working for the kingdom means acknowledging and promoting God's activity, which is present in human history and transforms it. Building the kingdom means working for liberation from evil in all its forms. In a word, the kingdom of God is the manifestation and the realization of God's plan of salvation in all its fullness.[10]

The Motivation for the Church's Mission

To the question, "*why mission?*" we reply with the Church's faith and experience that true liberation consists in opening oneself to the love of Christ. In him, and only in him, are we set free from all alienation and doubt, from slavery to the power of sin and death. Christ is truly "our peace" (Eph 2:14); "the love of Christ impels us" (2 Cor 5:14), giving meaning and joy to our life. *Mission is an issue of faith*, an accurate indicator of our faith in Christ and his love for us.[11]

The Kingdom Is Inseparable from Christ and the Church

There are also conceptions which deliberately emphasize the kingdom and which describe themselves as "kingdom-centered." They stress the image of a Church which is not concerned about herself, but which is totally concerned with bearing witness to and serving the kingdom. It is a "Church for others" just as Christ is the "man for others." The Church's task is described as though it had to proceed in two directions: on the one hand promoting such "values of the kingdom" as peace, justice, freedom, brotherhood, etc., while on the other hand fostering dialogue between peoples, cultures and religions, so that through a mutual enrichment they might help the world to be renewed and to journey ever closer to the kingdom.

Together with positive aspects, these conceptions often reveal negative aspects as well. First, they are silent about Christ: the kingdom of which they speak is "theocentrically" based, since, according to them, Christ cannot be understood by those who lack Christian faith, whereas different peoples, cultures and religions are capable of finding common ground in the one divine reality, by whatever name it is called....Furthermore, the kingdom, as they understand it, ends up either leaving very little room for the Church or undervaluing the Church in reaction to a presumed "ecclesiocentrism" of the past, and because they consider the Church herself only a sign, for that matter a sign not without ambiguity. This is not the kingdom of God as we know it from Revelation. The kingdom cannot be detached either from Christ or from the Church....

The kingdom of God is not a concept, a doctrine, or a program subject to free interpretation, but it is before all else *a person* with the face and name of Jesus of Nazareth, the image of the invisible God (cf. *Gaudium et spes*, 22). If the kingdom is separated from Jesus, it is no longer the kingdom of God which he revealed. The result is a distortion of the meaning of the kingdom, which runs the risk of being transformed into a purely human or ideological goal, and a distortion of the identity of Christ, who no longer appears as the Lord to whom everything must one day be subjected (cf. 1 Cor 15:27).

Likewise, one may not separate the kingdom from the Church. It is true that the Church is not an end unto herself, since she is ordered toward the kingdom of God of which she is the seed, sign and instrument. Yet, while remaining distinct from Christ and the kingdom, the Church is indissolubly united to both. Christ endowed the Church, his body, with the fullness of the benefits and means of salvation. The Holy Spirit dwells in her, enlivens her with his gifts and charisms, sanctifies, guides and constantly renews her (cf. *Lumen gentium*, 4). The result is a unique and special relationship which, while not excluding the action of Christ and the Spirit outside the Church's visible boundaries, confers upon her a specific and necessary role; hence the Church's special connection with the kingdom of God and of Christ, which she has "the mission of announcing and inaugurating among all peoples" (cf. *Lumen gentium*, 4).[12]

The Kingdom beyond the Church

The Church serves the kingdom by spreading throughout the world the "gospel values," which are an expression of the kingdom and which help people to accept God's plan. It is true that the inchoate reality of the kingdom can also be found beyond the confines of the Church among peoples everywhere, to the extent that they live "gospel values" and are open to the working of the Spirit who breathes when and where he wills (cf. John 3:8). But it must immediately be added that this temporal dimension of the kingdom remains incomplete unless it is related to the kingdom of Christ, present in the Church and straining towards eschatological fullness (cf. *Evangelium nuntiandi*, 34).[13]

Proclamation as the Center of Missionary Activity

Proclamation is the permanent priority of mission. The Church cannot elude Christ's explicit mandate, nor deprive men and women of the "Good News" about their being loved and saved by God....All forms of missionary activity are directed to this proclamation, which reveals and gives access to the mystery hidden for ages and made known in Christ (cf. Eph 3:3–9; Col 1:25–29), the mystery which lies at the heart of the Church's mission and life, as the hinge on which all evangelization turns.

In the complex reality of mission, initial proclamation has a central and irreplaceable role, since it introduces human beings "into the mystery of the love of God, who invites them to enter into a personal relationship with himself in Christ" (cf. *Ad gentes*, 13) and opens the way to conversion....Just as the whole economy of salvation has its center in Christ, so too all missionary activity is directed to the proclamation of his mystery.[14]

Basic Ecclesial Communities

A rapidly growing phenomenon in the young churches, one sometimes fostered by the bishops and their conferences as a pastoral priority, is that of "ecclesial basic communities" (also known by other names) which are proving to be good centers for Christian formation and missionary outreach. These are groups of Christians who, at the level of the family or in a similarly restricted setting, come together for prayer, scripture reading, catechesis, and discussion on human and ecclesial problems with a view to a common commitment. These communities are a sign of vitality within the Church, an instrument of formation and evangelization, and a solid starting point for a new society based on a "civilization of love."[15]

Inculturating the Gospel

Through inculturation the Church makes the Gospel incarnate in different cultures and at the same time introduces peoples, together with their cultures, into her own community. She transmits to them her own values, at the same time taking the good elements that already exist in them and renewing them from within (cf. *Catechesi tradendae*, 53). Through inculturation the Church, for her part, becomes a more intelligible sign of what she is, and a more effective instrument of mission.

Thanks to this action within the local churches, the universal Church herself is enriched with forms of expression and values in the various sectors of Christian life, such as evangelization, worship, theology and charitable works. She comes to know and to express better the mystery of Christ, all the while being motivated to continual renewal.[16]

Various Expressions of Faith

Developing ecclesial communities, inspired by the Gospel, will gradually be able to express their Christian experience in original ways and forms that are consonant with their own cultural traditions, provided that those traditions are in harmony with the objective requirements of the faith itself. To this end, especially in the more delicate areas of inculturation, particular churches of the same region should work in communion with each other (cf. *Ad gentes*, 22) and with the whole Church, convinced that only through attention both to the universal Church and to the particular churches will they be capable of translating the treasure of faith into a legitimate variety of expressions (cf. *Evangelium nuntiandi*, 64). Groups which have been evangelized will thus provide the elements for a "translation" of the gospel message (cf. *ibid.*, 63), keeping in mind the positive elements acquired down the centuries from Christianity's contact with different cultures and not forgetting the dangers of alterations which have sometimes occurred.[17]

New Evangelization

The *new evangelization* is the main concern of the whole theme of this conference [in Santo Domingo in 1992]. Since my meeting in Haiti with the bishops of CELAM in 1983, I have placed particular emphasis on this expression, using it to indicate a new fervor and new desires for evangelization in America and the whole world; it is meant to give pastoral action "a new stimulus, which would introduce the Church, now thoroughly imbued with the strength and power of Pentecost, into a new and more fruitful era of evangelization" (*Evangelium nuntiandi*, 2).

The new evangelization does not consist of a "new Gospel," which would arise from us, from our culture, or our analyses of the needs of humankind. In that case, it would not be the "Gospel," but a mere human invention, and salvation would not be found in it. Neither does it involve removing from the Gospel whatever seems difficult for the modern mentality to accept. Culture is not the measure of the Gospel, but it is Jesus Christ who is the measure of every culture and every human action. No, the new evangelization is not born of the desire for "currying favor with human beings" or "seeking to please people" (Gal 1:10), but of the responsibility for the gift which God has given us in Christ, in which we learn the truth about God and humankind, and the possibility for true life.

The new evangelization has as its point of departure the certitude that in Christ there are "inscrutable riches" (Eph 3:8) which no culture nor era can exhaust, and which we must always bring to people in order to enrich them (cf. Special Assembly for Europe of the Synod of Bishops, *Final Declaration*, 3). These riches are, first of all, Christ himself, his person, because he himself is our salvation. Drawing near to him in faith and being incorporated into his body, the Church, the men and women of every age and culture can find the answer to those questions, ever ancient yet ever new, with which people face the mystery of existence and which have been indelibly engraved on our hearts since creation and the wound of sin.[18]

Faithfulness to the Gospel

This *newness* does not affect the content of the Gospel message, which is unchangeable because Christ is "the same yesterday, today, and forever." Therefore, the Gospel must be preached *in total fidelity and purity*, as it has been preserved and handed on by the Church's tradition. Evangelization means proclaiming a person, Christ. Indeed, "there is no true evangelization if the name, the teaching, the life, the promises, the kingdom and the mystery of Jesus of Nazareth, the son of God, are not proclaimed" (*Evangelium nuntiandi*, 22). Therefore, *reductive Christologies*, whose errors I have pointed out on various occasions (cf. inaugural address to the Puebla Conference, January 29, 1979, 1.4), are unacceptable as tools of the new evangelization. In evangelizing, the unity of the Church's faith must shine forth not only in the authentic Magisterium of the bishops, but also in the service of the truth offered by pastors of souls, theologians, catechists and all whose who are involved in the preaching and the proclamation of the faith.[19]

Cultural Pluralism

While it demands of all who hear it the adherence of faith, the proclamation of the Gospel in different cultures allows people to preserve their own cultural identity. This in no way creates division, because the community of the baptized is marked by a universality which can embrace every culture and help to foster whatever is implicit in them to the point where it will be fully explicit in the light of truth.

This means that no one culture can ever become the criterion of judgment, much less the ultimate criterion of truth with regard to God's revelation. The Gospel is not opposed to any culture, as if in engaging a culture the Gospel would seek to strip it of its native riches and force it to adopt forms which are alien to it. On the contrary, the message which believers bring to the world and to cultures is a genuine liberation from all the disorders caused by sin and is, at the same time, a call to the fullness of truth. Cultures are not only not diminished by this encounter; rather, they are prompted to open themselves to the newness of the Gospel's truth and to be stirred by this truth to develop in new ways.[20]

Inculturation, Especially in India

In preaching the Gospel, Christianity first encountered Greek philosophy; but this does not mean at all that other approaches are precluded. Today, as the Gospel gradually comes into contact with cultural worlds which once lay beyond Christian influence, there are new tasks of inculturation, which mean that our generation faces problems not unlike those faced by the Church in the first centuries.

My thoughts turn immediately to the lands of the East, so rich in religious and philosophical traditions of great antiquity. Among these lands, India has a special place. A great spiritual impulse leads Indian thought to seek an experience which would liberate the spirit from the shackles of time and space and would therefore acquire absolute value. The dynamic of this quest for liberation provides the context for great metaphysical systems.

In India particularly, it is the duty of Christians now to draw from this rich heritage the elements compatible with their faith, in order to enrich Christian thought. In this work of discernment, which finds its inspiration in the Council's Declaration *Nostra aetate*, certain criteria will have to be kept in mind. The first of these is the universality of the human spirit, whose basic needs are the same in the most disparate cultures. The second, which derives from the first, is this: in engaging great cultures for the first time, the Church cannot abandon what she has gained from her inculturation in the world of Greco-Latin thought. To reject this heritage would be to deny the providential plan of God who guides his Church down the paths of time and history. This criterion is valid for the Church in every age, even for the Church of the future, who will judge herself enriched by all that comes from today's engagement with Eastern cultures and will find in this inheritance fresh cues for fruitful dialogue with the cultures which will emerge as humanity moves into the future. Thirdly, care will need to be taken lest, contrary to the very nature of the human spirit, the legitimate defense of the uniqueness and originality of Indian thought be confused with the idea that a particular cultural tradition should remain closed in its difference and affirm itself by opposing other traditions.

What has been said here of India is no less true for the heritage of the great cultures of China, Japan and the other countries of Asia, as also for the riches of the traditional cultures of Africa, which are for the most part orally transmitted.[21]

The Spiritual Life of Bishops

A bishop can be considered a genuine minister of communion and hope for God's holy people only when he walks in the presence of the Lord. It is not possible to be a servant of others unless one is first a "servant of God." And one can only be a servant of God if one is a "man of God." For this reason I stated in my homily at the beginning of the Synod: "The pastor must be a man of God; his existence and his ministry are entirely under his divine glory and from the supereminent mystery of God they derive their light and vigor" (cf. *Novo millennio ineunte*, 5).

For bishops the call to holiness is inherent in the sacramental event that stands at the origin of their ministry, that is, their episcopal ordination. The ancient *Euchology of Serapion* formulates the ritual invocation of the consecration thus: "God of truth, make thy servant a living bishop, a holy bishop in the succession of the holy Apostles" (*Sacramentarium Serapionis*, 28). Since episcopal ordination does not infuse the perfection of the virtues, "the bishop is called to pursue his path of perfection with greater intensity so as to attain to the stature of Christ, the perfect Man" (*Homily for the Opening of the Tenth Ordinary General Assembly of the Synod of Bishops* [September 30, 2001], 5).

The Christological and Trinitarian character of his mystery and ministry demands of the bishop a journey of holiness which consists in a progressive advance towards an ever more profound spiritual and apostolic maturity marked by the primacy of pastoral charity. This journey is obviously experienced together with his people, along a path which is at once personal and communitarian, like the life of the Church itself. Along this path, however, the bishop becomes, in intimate communion with Christ and attentive docility to the Holy

Spirit, a witness, a model, and a source of encouragement and help. This same idea is expressed by canon law: "Mindful that he is bound to give an example of holiness, charity, humility and simplicity of life, the diocesan bishop is to seek in every way to promote the holiness of Christ's faithful according to the special vocation of each. Since he is the principal dispenser of the mysteries of God, he is to strive constantly that the faithful entrusted to his care may grow in grace through the celebration of the sacraments, and may know and live the Paschal mystery" (*Code of Canon Law*, c. 387; cf. *Code of Canons of Eastern Churches*, c. 197).

The spiritual journey of the bishop, like that of every Christian, is rooted in the sacramental grace of Baptism and Confirmation. He shares this grace in common with all the faithful since, as the Second Vatican Council notes, "all the faithful of whatever condition or rank are called to the fullness of Christian life and to the perfection of charity" (*Lumen gentium*, 40). Here the celebrated expression of Saint Augustine, with its rich realism and supernatural wisdom, proves especially true: "If I am in fear because I am for you, I am consoled to be with you. Because for you I am a bishop, with you I am a Christian. The first name is one of responsibility, the second, one of grace. The former is the name of a danger, the latter of salvation" (*Sermo* 340, 1). Thanks to pastoral charity, however, responsibility becomes a form of service and peril is transformed into an opportunity for growth and maturation. The episcopal ministry is not only a source of holiness for others, but is already a cause of sanctification for one who allows the charity of God to pass through his own heart and life....

To all his disciples, and especially to those who while still on this earth wish to follow him more closely like the Apostles, the Lord proposes the way of the evangelical counsels. In addition to being a gift of the Holy Trinity to the Church, the counsels are a reflection of the life of the Trinity in each believer (cf. *Vita consecrata*, 20–21). This is especially the case in the bishop, who, as a successor of the Apostles, is called to follow Christ along the path leading to the perfection of charity. For this reason he is consecrated, even as Jesus was consecrated. The bishop's life is radically dependent on Christ and a completely transparent image of Christ before the Church and the world. The life of the bishop must radiate the life of Christ and consequently Christ's own obedience to the Father, even unto death, death on a cross (cf.

Phil 2:8), his chaste and virginal love, and his poverty which is absolute detachment from all earthly goods.

In this way the bishops can lead by their example not only those members of the Church who are called to follow Christ in the consecrated life but also priests, to whom the radicalism of holiness in accordance with the spirit of the evangelical counsels is also proposed. Indeed, this radicalism is incumbent on all the faithful, including lay people, for it is "a fundamental, undeniable demand flowing from the call of Christ to follow and imitate him by virtue of the intimate communion of life with him brought about by the Spirit" (cf. *Pastores dabo vobis*, 27).

The faithful ought to be able to contemplate on the face of their bishop the grace-given qualities which in the various beatitudes make up the self-portrait of Christ: the face of poverty, meekness and the thirst for righteousness; the merciful face of the Father and of the peaceful and peace giving man; the pure face of one who constantly looks to God alone. The faithful should also be able to see in their bishop the face of one who relives Jesus' own compassion for the afflicted, and, today as much as in the past, the face filled with strength and interior joy of one persecuted for the truth of the Gospel.[22]

NOTES

1. *Catechesi tradendae*, 53, in *AAS* 71 (1979), 1319–21; *ApExMiller*, 101–2; *ND*, 1161; *Origins* 9:21 (1979), 342; *Pope Speaks* 25:1 (1980), 69–70.

2. *Address to Workers in São Paulo, Brazil (1980)*, 3, in *AAS* 72 (1980), 859–60; *ND*, 1162; *Origins* 10:9 (1980), 137–38. In his 1991 encyclical *Centesimus annus* (The Hundredth Year), John Paul II was to state: "To teach and to spread her social doctrine belongs to the Church's evangelizing mission and is an essential part of the Christian message, since this doctrine points out the direct consequences of that message in the life of society and situates daily work and struggles for justice in the context of bearing witness to Christ the Savior" (no. 5).

3. *Reconciliatio et paenitentia*, 11, in *AAS* 77 (1985), 206–7; *ApExMiller*, 278; *ND*, 885; *Origins* 17:27 (1984), 439; *Pope Speaks* 30:4 (1985), 35–36.

4. *Slavorum apostoli*, 18, in *AAS*, 77 (1985), 800; *EncMiller*, 220; *ND*, 1165; *Origins* 15:8 (1985), 121; *Pope Speaks* 30:6 (1985), 266.

5. *Christifideles laici*, 9, in *AAS* 81 (1989), 405–6; *ApExMiller*, 371–72; *ND*, 894; *Origins* 18:35 (1989); *Pope Speaks* 34:2 (1989), 109–11.

6. Ibid., 20, in *AAS* 81 (1989), 425; *ApExMiller*, 387; *ND*, 895; *Origins* 18:35 (1989), 570; *Pope Speaks* 34:2 (1989), 119.

7. Ibid., 23, in *AAS* 81 (1989), 429–30; *ApExMiller*, 390–91; *ND*, 896; *Origins* 18:35 (1989), 571; *Pope Speaks* 34:2 (1989), 122.

8. Ibid., 30, in *AAS* 81 (1989), 446–47; *ApExMiller*, 403–4; *ND*, 896a; *Origins* 18:35 (1989), 575; *Pope Speaks* 34:2 (1989), 130–31.

9. *Redemptoris missio*, 9, in *AAS* 83 (1991) 258; *EncMiller*, 442; *ND*, 1167; *Origins* 29:34 (1991), 545; *Pope Speaks* 36:3 (1991), 143.

10. Ibid., 15, in *AAS* 83 (1991), 263; *EncMiller*, 445–46; *ND*, 1169; *Origins* 20:34 (1991), 546; *Pope Speaks* 36:3 (1991), 145–46.

11. Ibid., 11, in *AAS* 83, (1991), 259; *EncMiller*, 443; *ND*, 899b; *Origins* 20:34 (1991), 545; *Pope Speaks* 36:3 (1991), 144.

12. Ibid., 17–18, in *AAS* 83 (1991), 264–66; *EncMiller*, 446–47; *ND*, 1170; *Origins* 20:34 (1991), 547; *Pope Speaks* 36:3 (1991), 146–47.

13. Ibid., 20, in *AAS* 93 (1991), 267; *EncMiller*, 448; *ND*, 1171; *Origins* 20:34 (1991), 548; *Pope Speaks* 36:3 (1991), 148.

14. Ibid., 44, in *AAS* 93 (1991), 290–91; *EncMiller*, 464; *ND*, 1173; *Origins* 20:34 (1991), 554; *Pope Speaks* 159–60.

15. Ibid., 51, in *AAS* 83 (1991), 298; *EncMiller*, 469; *ND*, 899e; *Origins* 20:34 (1991); 556, *Pope Speaks* 36:3 (1991), 163.

16. Ibid., 52, in *AAS* 83 (1991), 300; *ND*, 1174; *Origins* 20:34 (1991), 556; *Pope Speaks* 36:3 (1991), 154.

17. Ibid., 53, in *AAS* 83 (1991), 301; *EncMiller*, 471–72; *ND*, 1175; *Origins* 20:34 (1991), 556–57; *Pope Speaks* 36:3 (1991), 164–65.

18. *Address at Santo Domingo, October 12, 1992*, 6, in *AAS* 85 (1993), 812–13; *ND*, 1180; *OREnglish* 42 (October 21, 1992), 7; *Origins* 22:19 (1992), 324–25; *Pope Speaks* 38:2 (1993), 87–88.
19. Ibid., 7, in *AAS* 85 (1993), 813; *ND*, 1181; *OREnglish* 42 (October 21, 1992), 7; *Origins* 22:19 (1992), 325; *Pope Speaks* 38:2 (1993), 88.
20. *Fides et ratio*, 71, in *AAS* 91 (1999), 60; *EncMiller*, 892; *ND*, 1182; *Origins* 28:19 (1998), 336; *Pope Speaks* 44:1 (1999), 40.
21. Ibid., 72, in *AAS* 91 (1999), 61; *EncMiller*, 892–93; *ND*, 1183; *Origins* 28:19 (1998), 336–37; *Pope Speaks* 44:1 (1999), 40–41.
22. *Pastores gregis*, 13, 18, in *AAS* 96 (2004), 842–43, 850; *Pope Speaks* 49:3 (2004), 141–42, 147.

CHAPTER EIGHT

Other Christians
and Other Religions

8.1 Among the texts John Paul II wrote on the ecumenical movement, or relationships between the Catholic Church and other Christian churches and ecclesial communities, the 1995 encyclical *Ut unum sint* (That They May Be One) stands out. But, as we shall see, there are other texts to quote that reveal his commitment to Christian unity and desire to make common cause on matters of world concern: for example, the 1994 apostolic letter *Tertio millennio adveniente* (The Arrival of the Third Millennium) and a "Common Declaration on Environmental Ethics" (signed by the pope and by the ecumenical patriarch, Bartholomew I, on June 10, 2003). We have already seen (at the end of chapter 3) three texts from the 1990s that aimed at reestablishing full communion with the Armenians, the Assyrian Church of the East, the Armenian Orthodox, and the Greek and Russian Orthodox by clarifying traditional points of difference about belief in the Son of God and the Holy Spirit.

We need to recall also the many actions and gestures of John Paul II that contributed to the cause of Christian unity: for instance, his visit for the feast of St. Andrew (November 30, 1979) to Patriarch Dimitrios I in Istanbul when they signed a declaration announcing the inauguration of theological dialogue between the Catholic and the Orthodox churches; his sharing in a 1982 ecumenical service with the archbishop of Canterbury (Robert Runcie)—this being the first time a pope had ever visited England

and Canterbury Cathedral; preaching at a Lutheran church in Rome on the five-hundredth anniversary of Martin Luther's birth.[1]

Rome and Constantinople are Sister Churches

This apostle [Andrew], the patron saint of the illustrious Church of Constantinople, is Peter's brother. Certainly, all the apostles are bound to one another by this new brotherhood that unites all those who hearts are renewed by the Spirit of the Son (cf. Rom 8:15) and to whom the ministry of reconciliation is entrusted (cf. 2 Cor 5:18), but that does not suppress, far from it, the special bonds created by birth and upbringing in the same family. Andrew is Peter's brother. Andrew and Peter were brothers and, within the apostolic college, a greater intimacy must have bound them, a closer collaboration must have united them in the apostolic task.

Here again today's celebration reminds us that special bonds of brotherhood and intimacy exist between the Church of Rome and the Church of Constantinople, that a closer collaboration is natural between these two Churches.[2]

Peter's Ministry of Unity

Peter, Andrew's brother, is the leader of the apostles. Thanks to the inspiration of the Father, he fully recognized, in Jesus Christ, the Son of the living God (cf. Matt 16:16); owing to his faith, he received the name of Peter in order that the Church may rest on this rock (cf. Matt 16:18). He had the task of ensuring the harmony of apostolic preaching. A brother among brothers, he received the mission of strengthening them in faith (cf. Luke 22:32); he is the first to have the responsibility of watching over the union of all, of ensuring the symphony of the holy Churches of God in faithfulness to "the faith which was once for all delivered to the saints" (Jude 3). It is in this spirit, animated by these sentiments, that Peter's successor has wished on this day to visit the Church whose patron saint is Andrew....[3]

Union with the Orthodox Church Is Basic for Ecumenism

This visit to the first see of the Orthodox Church shows clearly the will of the whole Catholic Church to go forward in the march towards the unity of all, and also its conviction that the re-establishment of full communion with the Orthodox Church is a fundamental stage of the decisive progress of the whole ecumenical movement. Our division may not, perhaps, have been without an influence on the other divisions that followed it.[4]

Theological Dialogue between Catholics and Orthodox

This theological dialogue which is about to begin now will have the task of overcoming the misunderstandings and disagreements which still exist between us, if not at the level of faith, at least at the level of theological formulation. It should take place not only in the atmosphere of the dialogue of charity, which must be developed and intensified, but also in an atmosphere of worship and availability.[5]

The Duty to Be United

It is only in worship, with a keen sense of the transcendence of the inexpressible mystery "which surpasses knowledge" (Eph 3:19), that we will be able to size up our divergences and "to lay...no greater burden than these necessary things" (Acts 15:28) to reestablish communion (cf. decree *Unitatis redintegratio*, 18). It seems to me, in fact, that the question we must ask ourselves is not so much whether we still have the right to remain separated. We must ask ourselves this question in the very name of our faithfulness to [Christ's] Church....[6]

Growing Union with Other Christians in Germany

The ecumenical movement in the last few decades has clearly shown you how much evangelical Christians are united with you in their concerns and joys, and how much you have in common with them when you live faith in our Lord Jesus Christ together, sincerely, and consistently. So let us thank God from the bottom of our hearts that the various ecclesial communities in your regions are no longer divided by misunderstanding or even barricaded against one another in fear. You rather have already had the happy experience that mutual understanding and acceptance were particularly easy when both sides knew their own faith well, professed it joyfully, and encouraged concrete communion with their own brothers in faith. I would like to encourage you to continue along this way.

Live your faith as Catholics with gratitude to God and to your ecclesial community; bear a credible witness, in all humility and without any complacency, to the deep values of your faith, and encourage, discreetly and amiably, also your evangelical fellow Christians to strengthen and deepen in Christ their own convictions and forms of religious life. If all Churches and communities really grow in the fullness of the Lord, his Spirit will certainly indicate to us the way to reach full internal and external unity of the Church.[7]

Need for Conversion and Full Unity in Faith

There is no Christian life without repentance. "There can be no ecumenism worthy of the name without interior conversion" (*Unitatis redintegratio*, 7). "Let us no more pass judgment on one another" (Rom 14:13). Let us rather recognize our guilt. "All have sinned" (Rom 3:23) applies also with regard to the grace of unity. We must see and say this in all earnestness and draw our conclusions from it. The most important thing is to recognize more and more deeply what consequences the Lord draws from human failing. Paul reduces it to the same denominator: "where sin increased, grace abounded all the more" (Rom 5:20). God does not cease to "have mercy upon us all" (Rom 11:32). He gives his Son, he gives himself, he gives forgiveness, justification, grace, eternal life. We can recognize all this together.

You know that decades of my life have been marked by the experience of Christianity being challenged by atheism and non-belief. It appears to me all the more clearly how important is our common profession of Jesus Christ, of his word and work in this world, and how we are driven by the urgency of the hour to overcome the differences that divide us and bear witness to our growing union....

All the gratitude for what remains to us in common and unites us cannot make us blind to what still divides us. We must examine it together as far as possible, not to widen the gaps, but to bridge them. We cannot stop at the acknowledgement: "We are and remain divided for ever and against each other." We are called to strive together in the dialogue of truth and love, to the full unity in faith. Only full unity gives us the possibility of gathering with the same sentiments and the same faith at the Lord's one table.[8]

Luther on Christ and the Church

We can let the lectures given by Luther on the Letter to the Romans in the years 1516–17 tell us what this effort [of mutual understanding] consists of. He teaches that "faith in Christ, through which we are justified, is not just belief in Christ, or more exactly in the person of Christ, but belief in that [which] is Christ's...." "We must believe in him and in what is his." To the question, "What is his then?" Luther refers to the Church and to her authentic teaching. If the difficulties that exist between us were only a question of "ecclesiastical structures set up by human beings" (cf. *Confessio augustana*, 8), we could and should eliminate them immediately. According to the conviction of Catholics, disagreement revolves around "what is Christ's," around "what is his": his Church and her mission, her message, her sacraments, and the ministries placed in the service of the Word and the Sacrament. The dialogue established since the Council has brought us a good way further in this respect.

We must remain in dialogue and in contact. The questions to be faced together demand by their nature a more comprehensive treatment than is possible here and today. I hope that we will find together the way to continue our dialogue. Certainly the German bishops and the collaborators of the Secretariat for Christian Unity will give their help in this matter. We must leave no stone unturned.[9]

Unity through the Cross

We often hear it said today that the ecumenical movement of the Churches is at a standstill....I cannot agree with this judgment. Unity, which comes from God, is given to us at the Cross. We must not want to avoid the Cross, passing to rapid attempts at harmonizing differences, excluding the question of truth. But neither must we abandon one another, and go on our separate ways, because drawing closer calls for the patient and suffering love of Christ crucified. Let us not be diverted from the laborious way in order to remain where we are or to choose ways that are apparently shorter and lead astray.[10]

Unity between the Catholic and the Orthodox Sister Churches

Hence with these Churches relations are to be fostered as between sister Churches, to use the expression of Pope Paul VI in his letter to the Patriarch of Constantinople Athenagoras I (cf. *Anno ineunte*, 1967). The unity with these Churches which is sought (and must be sought) is full communion in one faith, in the sacraments and in ecclesial government (cf. *Lumen gentium*, 14), with full respect for legitimate liturgical, disciplinary and theological diversity, as I explained in my Apostolic Epistle [of 1988] *Euntes in mundum universum*, on the occasion of the millennium of the baptism of Kievan Rus.[11]

Practical Consequences of This Ecumenical Vision

From this there follow immediate and practical consequences [for Catholics and Orthodox in post-Communist Europe]. The first of these was stated by Pope Paul VI in the address which he gave in the Cathedral of the Ecumenical Patriarchate on the occasion of his visit [in 1967], and it retains all of its validity today: "We see more clearly thus that it belongs to the leaders of the Churches, to their hierarchy, to guide the Churches on the path which leads to recovering full communion. They must do so recognizing each other and respecting each other as shepherds of that part of the flock of Christ which has been entrusted to them, caring for the cohesion and faith of the people of God and avoiding all that could divide it or bring confusion into its ranks" (*Anno ineunte*, 1967).

A second consequence is the rejection of all undue forms of proselytism, with the avoidance in the most absolute way in pastoral action of any temptation to violence and any form of pressure. At the same time, pastoral action will not fail to respect the freedom of conscience and the right which each individual has to join, if he wishes, the Catholic Church. In brief, it is a matter of respecting the action of the Holy Spirit, who is the Spirit of truth (cf. John 16:13). The Council's Decree on Ecumenism stated this and gave the reason thus: "it is evident that the work of preparing and reconciling those individuals who wish for full Catholic communion is of its nature distinct from ecumenical action. But there is no opposition between the two, since both proceed from the wonderful providence of God" (*Unitatis redintegratio*, 4).

The third consequence is that it is obviously not enough just to avoid mistakes: it is also necessary to promote positively coexistence with mutual and harmonious respect. This attitude has certainly been proposed and reaffirmed as the rule of conduct in relations between Catholics and Orthodox, as was stated by Pope Paul VI and the Patriarch Athenagoras I in their joint declaration: "The dialogue of charity among their Churches must bear fruits of disinterested collaboration on the common plan of action at the pastoral, social and intellectual level, in mutual respect for the faithfulness that both must have for their own Churches" (*Joint declaration*, 1967). As I had occasion to state in my encyclical *Slavorum apostoli* [1985], all this will help the mutual enrichment of the two great traditions, the Eastern and the Western, and the path toward full unity.[12]

Ecumenical Initiatives at the End of the Second Millennium

Among the sins which require a greater commitment to repentance and conversion should certainly be counted those which *have been detrimental to the unity willed by God for his people*. In the course of the thousand years now drawing to a close, even more than in the first millennium, ecclesial communion has been painfully wounded, a fact "for which, at times, men of both sides were to blame" (*Unitatis redintegratio*, 3). Such wounds openly contradict the will of Christ and are a cause of scandal to the world (*Unitatis redintegratio*, 1)....

In these last years of the millennium, the Church should invoke the Holy Spirit with ever greater insistence, imploring from him the grace of *Christian unity*. This is a crucial matter for our testimony to the Gospel before the world. Especially since the Second Vatican Council many ecumenical initiatives have been undertaken with generosity and commitment: it can be said that the whole activity of the local Churches and of the Apostolic See has taken on an ecumenical dimension in recent years....

We are all, however, aware that the attainment of this goal cannot be the fruit of human efforts alone, vital though they are. *Unity, after all, is a gift of the Holy Spirit*. We are asked to respond to this gift responsibly, without compromise in our witness to the truth, generously implementing the guidelines laid down by the Council and in subsequent documents of the Holy See, which are also highly regarded by many Christians not in full communion with the Catholic Church.

This then is one of the tasks of Christians as we make our way to the Year 2000. The approaching end of the second millennium demands of everyone an *examination of conscience* and the promotion of fitting ecumenical initiatives, so that we can celebrate the Great Jubilee, if not completely united, *at least much closer to overcoming the divisions of the second millennium.* As everyone recognizes, an enormous effort is needed in this regard. It is essential not only to continue along the path of dialogue on doctrinal matters, but above all to be more committed to *prayer for Christian unity.* Such prayer has become much more intense after the Council, but it must increase still more, involving an ever greater number of Christians, in unison with the great petition of Christ before his Passion: "Father…that they also may all be one in us" (John 17:21).[13]

Common Declaration on Environmental Ethics

We are gathered here today in the spirit of peace for the good of all human beings and for the care of creation. At this moment in history, at the beginning of the third millennium, we are saddened to see the daily suffering of a great number of people from violence, starvation, poverty and disease. We are also concerned about the negative consequences for humanity and for all creation resulting from the degradation of some basic natural resources such as water, air and land, brought about by an economic and technological progress which does not recognize and take into account its limits. Almighty God envisioned a world of beauty and harmony, and he created it, making every part an expression of his freedom, wisdom and love (Gen 1:1–25).

At the center of the whole of creation, he placed us, human beings, with our inalienable human dignity. Although we share many features with the rest of the living beings, Almighty God went further with us and gave us an immortal soul, the source of self-awareness and freedom, endowments that make us in his image and likeness (cf. Gen 1:26–31; 2:7). Marked with that resemblance, we have been placed by God in the world in order to cooperate with him in realizing more and more fully the divine purpose for creation.

At the beginning of history, man and woman sinned by disobeying God and rejecting his design for creation. Among the results of this

135

first sin was the destruction of the original harmony of creation. If we examine carefully the social and environmental crisis which the world community is facing, we must conclude that we are still betraying the mandate God has given us: to be stewards called to collaborate with God in watching over creation in holiness and wisdom.

God has not abandoned the world. It is his will that his design and our hope for it will be realized through our cooperation in restoring its original harmony. In our own time we are witnessing a growth of an *ecological awareness* which needs to be encouraged, so that it will lead to practical programs and initiatives. An awareness of the relationship between God and humankind brings a fuller sense of the importance of the relationship between human beings and the natural environment, which is God's creation and which God entrusted to us to guard with wisdom and love (cf. Gen 1:28).

Respect for creation stems from respect for human life and dignity. It is on the basis of our recognition that the world is created by God that we can discern an objective moral order within which to articulate a code of environmental ethics. In this perspective, Christians and all other believers have a specific role to play in proclaiming moral values and in educating people in *ecological awareness*, which is none other than responsibility towards self, towards others, towards creation.

What is required is an act of repentance on our part and a renewed attempt to view ourselves, one another, and the world around us within the perspective of the divine design for creation. The problem is not simply economic and technological; it is moral and spiritual. A solution at the economic and technological level can be found only if we undergo, in the most radical way, an inner change of heart, which can lead to a change in lifestyle and of unsustainable patterns of consumption and production. A genuine *conversion* in Christ will enable us to change the way we think and act.

Firstly, we must regain humility and recognize the limits of our powers, and most importantly, the limits of our knowledge and judgment. We have been making decisions, taking actions and assigning values that are leading us away from the world as it should be, away from the design of God for creation, away from all that is essential for a healthy planet and a healthy commonwealth of people. A new approach and a new culture are needed, based on the centrality of the human person within creation and inspired by environmentally ethical behavior stemming from our triple relationship to God, to self and to creation. Such an ethics fosters interdependence and stresses the principles of universal solidarity, social justice and responsibility, in order to promote a true culture of life.

Secondly, we must frankly admit that humankind is entitled to something better than what we see around us. We and, much more, our children and future generations are entitled to a better world, a world free from degradation, violence and bloodshed, a world of generosity and love. Thirdly, aware of the value of prayer, we must implore God the Creator to enlighten people everywhere regarding the duty to respect and carefully guard creation.

We therefore invite all men and women of good will to ponder the importance of the following ethical goals:

1. To think of the world's children when we reflect on and evaluate our options for action;
2. To be open to study the true values based on the natural law that sustain every human culture;
3. To use science and technology in a full and constructive way, while recognizing that the findings of science have always to be evaluated in the light of the centrality of the human person, of the common good and of the inner purpose of creation. Science may help us to correct the mistakes of the past, in order to enhance the spiritual and material well-being of the present and future generations. It is love for our children that will show us the path that we must follow into the future;
4. To be humble regarding the idea of ownership and to be open to the demands of solidarity. Our mortality and our weakness of judgment together warn us not to take irreversible actions with what we choose to regard as our property during our brief stay on this earth. We have not been entrusted with unlimited power over creation, we are only stewards of the common heritage;
5. To acknowledge the diversity of situations and responsibilities in the work for a better world environment. We do not expect every person and every institution to assume the same burden. Everyone has a part to play, but for the demands of

137

justice and charity to be respected the most affluent societies must carry the greater burden, and from them is demanded a sacrifice greater than can be offered by the poor. Religions, governments and institutions are faced by many different situations; but on the basis of the principle of subsidiarity all of them can take on some tasks, some part of the shared effort;

6. To promote a peaceful approach to disagreement about how to live on this earth, about how to share it and use it, about what to change and what to leave unchanged. It is not our desire to evade controversy about the environment, for we trust in the capacity of human reason and the path of dialogue to reach agreement. We commit ourselves to respect the views of all who disagree with us, seeking solutions through open exchange, without resorting to oppression and domination.

It is not too late. God's world has incredible healing powers. Within a single generation, we could steer the earth toward our children's future. Let that generation start now, with God's help and blessing.[14]

8.2 *Ut unum sint* (That They May Be One), the outstanding 1995 encyclical on ecumenism, embraced Vatican II's fundamental convictions, affirming that the church "subsists" in the Catholic Church and recognizing the various ecclesial elements of churches and church communities not in full communion with the Catholic Church. "Ecumenism," it declared, "is directed precisely at making the partial communion existing between Christians grow toward full communion in truth and love" (no. 14). The encyclical catalogued the notable progress in various sectors made since the council ended in 1965, and insisted on the need for "ecumenical prayer" as a primary means for healing divisions. The encyclical reiterated what Paul VI had said about the Churches of the East and the West being "Sister Churches" (nos. 55–58).

Unity Essential to the Church

Jesus himself, at the hour of his Passion, prayed "that they may all be one" (John 17:21). This unity, which the Lord has bestowed on his Church and in which he wishes to embrace all people, is not something added on, but stands at the very heart of Christ's mission. Nor is it some secondary attribute of the community of his disciples. Rather, it belongs to the very essence of this community. God wills the Church, because he wills unity, and unity is an expression of the whole depth of his *agape*.

In effect, this unity bestowed by the Holy Spirit does not merely consist in the gathering of people as a collection of individuals. It is a unity constituted by the bonds of the profession of faith, the sacraments and hierarchical communion (cf. *Lumen gentium*, 14). The faithful are *one* because, in the Spirit, they are in *communion* with the Son and, in him, share in his *communion* with the Father: "Our *fellowship* is with the Father and with his Son Jesus Christ" (1 John 1:3). For the Catholic Church, then, the *communion* of Christians is none other than the manifestation in them of the grace by which God makes them sharers in his own *communion*, which is his eternal life. Christ's words "that they may be one" are thus his prayer to the Father that the Father's plan may be fully accomplished, in such a way that everyone may clearly see "what is the plan of the mystery hidden for ages in God who created all things" (Eph 3:9). To believe in Christ means to desire unity; to desire unity means to desire the Church; to desire the Church means to desire the communion of grace which corresponds to the Father's plan from all eternity. Such is the meaning of Christ's prayer: "*Ut unum sint.*"[15]

Unity in Faith Adheres to the Whole of Revelation

The unity willed by God can be attained only by the adherence of all to the content of revealed faith in its entirety. In matters of faith, compromise is in contradiction with God who is Truth. In the Body of Christ, "the way, and the truth, and the life" (John 14:6), who could consider legitimate a reconciliation brought about at the expense of the truth? The Council's Declaration on Religious Freedom, *Dignitatis humanae*, attributes to human dignity the quest for truth, "especially in what concerns God and his Church" (*Dignitatis humanae*, 1), and adherence to truth's demands. A "being together" which betrayed the truth would thus be opposed both to the nature of God who offers his communion and to the need for truth found in the depths of every human heart....

Love for the truth is the deepest dimension of any authentic quest for full communion between Christians....There must be charity towards one's partner in dialogue, and humility with regard to the truth which comes to light and which might require a review of assertions and attitudes....Full communion of course will have to come about through the acceptance of the whole truth into which the Holy Spirit guides Christ's disciples. Hence all forms of reductionism or facile "agreement" must be absolutely avoided. Serious questions must be resolved, for if not, they will reappear at another time, either in the same terms or in a different guise....

To uphold a vision of unity which takes account of all the demands of revealed truth does not mean to put a brake on the ecumenical movement. On the contrary, it means preventing it from settling for apparent solutions which would lead to no firm and solid results (cf. *Address to the Cardinals and the Roman Curia, June 28, 1985*).[16]

Differing Forms in Expressing Truth

Because by its nature the content of faith is meant for all humanity, it must be translated into all cultures. Indeed, the element which determines communion in truth is *the meaning of truth*. The expression of truth can take different forms. The renewal of these forms of expression becomes necessary for the sake of transmitting to the people of today the Gospel message in its unchanging meaning (cf. St. Vincent of Lerins, *Commonitorium primum*, 23)....

Ecumenical dialogue, which prompts the parties involved to question each other, to understand each other and to explain their positions to each other, makes surprising discoveries possible. Intolerant polemics and controversies have made incompatible assertions out of what was really the result of two different ways of looking at the same reality. Nowadays we need to find the formula which, by capturing the reality in its entirety, will enable us to move beyond partial readings and eliminate false interpretations.

One of the advantages of ecumenism is that it helps Christian Communities to discover the unfathomable riches of the truth. Here too, everything that the Spirit brings about in "others" can serve for the building up of all Communities (*Unitatis redintegratio*, 4) and in a certain sense instruct them in the mystery of Christ. Authentic ecumenism is a gift at the service of truth.[17]

Sharing Sacramental Life

It is a source of joy to note that Catholic ministers are able, in certain particular cases, to administer the Sacraments of the Eucharist, Penance and Anointing of the Sick to Christians who are not in full communion with the Catholic Church but who greatly desire to receive these sacraments, freely request them and manifest the faith which the Catholic Church professes with regard to these sacraments. Conversely, in specific cases and in particular circumstances, Catholics too can request these same sacraments from ministers of Churches in which these sacraments are valid. The conditions for such reciprocal reception have been laid down in specific norms; for the sake of furthering ecumenism these norms must be respected (cf. *Unitatis redintegratio*, 8 and 15; *Code of Canon Law*, Canon 844).[18]

The Importance of Constant Reform

Only the act of placing ourselves before God can offer a solid basis for that conversion of individual Christians and for that constant reform of the Church, insofar as she is also a human and earthly institution (*Unitatis redintegratio*, 6), which represent the preconditions for all ecumenical commitment. One of the first steps in ecumenical dialogue is the effort to draw the Christian Communities into this completely interior spiritual space in which Christ, by the power of the Spirit, leads them all, without exception, to examine themselves before the Father and to ask themselves whether they have been faithful to his plan for the Church.[19]

Christian Communities United by Their Martyrs and Saints

In a theocentric vision, we Christians already have a common *Martyrology*. This also includes the martyrs of our own century, more numerous than one might think, and it shows how, at a profound level, God preserves communion among the baptized in the supreme demand of faith, manifested in the sacrifice of life itself (cf. *Tertio millennio adveniente*, 37). The fact that one can die for the faith shows that other demands of the faith can also be met. I have already remarked, and with deep joy, how an imperfect but real communion is preserved and is growing at many levels of ecclesial life. I now add that this communion is already perfect in what we all consider the highest point of the life of grace, *martyria* unto death, the truest communion possible with Christ who shed his Blood, and by that sacrifice brings near those who once were far off (Eph. 2:13).

While for all Christian communities the martyrs are the proof of the power of grace, they are not the only ones to bear witness to that power. Albeit in an invisible way, the communion between our Communities, even if still incomplete, is truly and solidly grounded in the full communion of the Saints—those who, at the end of a life faithful to grace, are in communion with Christ in glory. These *Saints* come from all the Churches and Ecclesial Communities which gave them entrance into the communion of salvation.

When we speak of a common heritage, we must acknowledge as part of it not only the institutions, rites, means of salvation and the traditions which all the communities have preserved and by which they have been shaped, but first and foremost this reality of holiness (cf. Pope Paul VI, *Address at the Shrine in Namugengo, Uganda*, 1969).[20]

Positive Outcome of Divisions

Since God in his infinite mercy can always bring good even out of situations which are an offense to his plan, we can discover that the Spirit has allowed conflicts to serve in some circumstances to make explicit certain aspects of the Christian vocation, as happens in the lives of the Saints. In spite of fragmentation, which is an evil from which we need to be healed, there has resulted a kind of rich bestowal of grace which is meant to embellish the *koinonia*. God's grace will be with all those who, following the example of the Saints, commit themselves to meeting its demands. How can we hesitate to be converted to the Father's expectations? He is with us.[21]

Papal Primacy as Service: A Request for Forgiveness

In the beautiful expression of Pope Saint Gregory the Great, my ministry is that of *servus servorum Dei*. This designation is the best possible safeguard against the risk of separating power (and in particular the primacy) from ministry. Such a separation would contradict the very meaning of power according to the Gospel: "I am among you as one who serves" (Luke 22:27), says our Lord Jesus Christ, the Head of the Church. On the other hand, as I acknowledged on the important occasion of a visit to the World Council of Churches in Geneva on June 12, 1984, the Catholic Church's conviction that in the ministry of the Bishop of Rome she has preserved, in fidelity to the Apostolic Tradition and the faith of the Fathers, the visible sign and guarantor of unity, constitutes a difficulty for most other Christians, whose memory is marked by certain painful recollections. To the extent that we are responsible for these, I join my Predecessor Paul VI in asking forgiveness (cf. *Address at the World Council of Churches, Geneva, 1984*).[22]

Papal Primacy: Service of Unity, in Communion with Other Bishops

This service of unity, rooted in the action of divine mercy, is entrusted within the College of Bishops to one among those who have received from the Spirit the task, not of exercising power over the people—as the rulers of the Gentiles and their great men do (cf. Matt 20:25; Mark 10:42)—but of leading them towards peaceful pastures.... The mission of the Bishop of Rome within the College of all the Pastors consists precisely in "keeping watch" (*episkopein*), like a sentinel, so that, through the efforts of the Pastors, the true voice of Christ the Shepherd may be heard in all the particular Churches.... With the power and the authority without which such an office would be illusory, the Bishop of Rome must ensure the communion of all the Churches. For this reason, he is the first servant of unity. This primacy is exercised on various levels, including vigilance over the handing down of the Word, the celebration of the liturgy and the Sacraments, the Church's mission, discipline and the Christian life. It is the responsibility of the Successor of Peter to recall the requirements of the common good of the Church, should anyone be tempted to overlook it in the pursuit of personal interests. He has the duty to admonish, to caution and to declare at times that this or that opinion being circulated is irreconcilable with the unity of faith. When circumstances require it, he speaks in the name of all the Pastors in communion with him. He can also, under very specific conditions clearly laid down by the First Vatican Council, declare *ex cathedra* that a certain doctrine belongs to the deposit of faith (*Pastor aeternus*, 4.9). All this however must always be done in communion. When the Catholic Church affirms that the office of the Bishop of Rome corresponds to the will of Christ, she does not separate this office from the mission entrusted to the whole body of Bishops, who are also "vicars and ambassadors of Christ" (*Lumen gentium*, 27). The Bishop of Rome is a member of the "College," and the Bishops are his brothers in the ministry.[23]

Discerning Forms for
the Petrine Ministry

Christ ardently desires the full and visible communion of all those Communities in which, by virtue of God's faithfulness, his Spirit dwells. I am convinced that I have a particular responsibility in this regard, above all in acknowledging the ecumenical aspirations of the majority of the Christian Communities and in heeding the request made of me to find a way of exercising the primacy which, while in no way renouncing what is essential to its mission, is nonetheless open to a new situation. For a whole millennium Christians were united in "a brotherly fraternal communion of faith and sacramental life.... If disagreements in belief and discipline arose among them, the Roman See acted by common consent as moderator" (*Unitatis redintegratio*, 14). In this way the primacy exercised its office of unity. When addressing the Ecumenical Patriarch, His Holiness Dimitrios I, I acknowledged my awareness that "for a great variety of reasons, and against the will of all concerned, what should have been a service sometimes manifested itself in a very different light. But...it is out of a desire to obey the will of Christ truly that I recognize that as Bishop of Rome I am called to exercise that ministry.... I insistently pray the Holy Spirit to shine his light upon us, enlightening all the pastors and theologians of our Churches, that we may seek, together, of course, the forms in which this ministry may accomplish a service of love recognized by all concerned" (cf. *Homily in St. Peter's Basilica in the Presence of Dimitrios I, Archbishop of Constantinople and Ecumenical Patriarch, 1987*).

This is an immense task, which we cannot refuse and which I cannot carry out by myself. Could not the real but imperfect communion existing between us persuade Church leaders and their theologians to engage with me in a patient and fraternal dialogue on this subject, a dialogue in which, leaving useless controversies behind, we could listen to one another, keeping before us only the will of Christ for his Church and allowing ourselves to be deeply moved by his plea "that they may all be one...so that the world may believe that you have sent me" (John 17:21)?[24]

8.3 Constantly reaching out to Jews, Muslims, and those of other religions also characterized the work of John Paul II. Along with his speeches and writings, his gestures played a major and often unprecedented role. On August 19, 1985, at the invitation of King Hassan II of Morocco, he spoke in Casablanca to over 100,000 young Muslims on the religious and moral values common to Islam and Christianity. (Below we quote the address in full.) On April 13, 1986, John Paul II visited the main synagogue in Rome. He was most probably the first pope to visit and pray in a synagogue since the early days of Christianity. That same year, on October 27, he went with the Dalai Lama and other heads or representatives of the world's religions to pray for peace in Assisi. On April 7, 1994, he hosted a Holocaust memorial concert in the Vatican. The Royal Philharmonic Orchestra came from London and was conducted by Gilbert Levine, an American Jew who had served as conductor of the Krakow Philharmonic. John Paul II sat in the Paul VI Audience Hall alongside the chief rabbi of Rome, Elio Toaff, who attended with his congregation and with two hundred other Holocaust survivors from twelve different countries. For the Jubilee Year of 2000, the Pope wanted to make a pilgrimage not only to Jerusalem (see chapter 12), but also to Ur (now in Iraq) and Mount Sinai (now in Egypt) to honor, respectively, Abraham and Moses. The government of Egypt welcomed him to Mount Sinai, but the government of Iraq refused the permission. (John Paul II, during a ceremony in the Vatican, made a "virtual" visit to the home of Abraham and Sarah.) On May 6, 2001, on a visit to Syria John Paul II prayed in a mosque in Damascus, and so became the first pope ever to visit and pray in a mosque.

Along with his extraordinarily significant actions, the teaching of John Paul II remains enduringly important. In his very first encyclical, *Redemptor hominis* (The Redeemer of the Human Person) of March 1979, John Paul encouraged interreligious dialogue. He did the same on a February 1981 visit to several Asian countries, and praised the fruits of such dialogue on a visit to Madras (India) in February 1986.

Fostering Interreligious Dialogue

It is obvious that this new stage in the Church's life demands of us a faith that is particularly aware, profound and responsible. True ecumenical activity means openness, drawing closer, availability for dialogue, and a shared investigation of the truth in the full evangelical and Christian sense; but in no way does it or can it mean giving up or in any way diminishing the treasures of divine truth that the Church has constantly confessed and taught.... What we have just said must also be applied, although in another way and with the due differences, to activity for coming closer together with the representatives of the non-Christian religions, an activity expressed through dialogue, contacts, prayer in common, investigation of the treasures of human spirituality, in which, as we know well, the members of these religions also are not lacking. Does it not sometimes happen that the firm belief of the followers of the non-Christian religions, a belief that is also an effect of the Spirit of truth operating outside the visible confines of the Mystical Body, can make Christians ashamed at being often themselves so disposed to doubt concerning the truths revealed by God and proclaimed by the Church and so prone to relax moral principles and open the way to ethical permissiveness? It is a noble thing to have a predisposition for understanding every person, analyzing every system and recognizing what is right; this does not at all mean losing certitude about one's own faith (cf. *Dei Filius*, 3.6) or weakening the principles of morality....[25]

Different Routes, One Goal

The Council document on non-Christian religions, in particular, is filled with deep esteem for the great spiritual values, indeed for the primacy of the spiritual, which in the life of humankind finds expression in religion and then in morality, with direct effects on the whole of culture. The Fathers of the Church rightly saw in the various religions as it were so many reflections of the one truth, "seeds of the Word" (cf. St. Justin, *1 Apologia*, 46:1-4; *2 Apologia*, 7), attesting that, though the routes taken may be different, there is but a single goal to which is directed the deepest aspiration of the human spirit as expressed in its quest for God and also in its quest, through its tending towards God, for the full dimension of its humanity, or in other words for the full meaning of human life.[26]

Missionary Attitude Should Never Be Destructive

Thanks to this unity we can together come close to the magnificent heritage of the human spirit that has been manifested in all religions, as the Second Vatican Council's Declaration *Nostra aetate* says. It also enables us to approach all cultures, all ideological concepts, all people of good will. We approach them with the esteem, respect and discernment that since the time of the Apostles have marked the *missionary* attitude, the attitude *of the missionary*. Suffice it to mention Saint Paul and, for instance, his address in the Areopagus at Athens (Acts 17:22–31). The *missionary* attitude always begins with a feeling of deep esteem for "what is in the human being" (John 2:26), for what one has worked out in the depths of one's spirit concerning the most profound and important problems. It is a question of respecting everything that has been brought about in him by the Spirit, which "blows where it wills" (John 3:8). The mission is never destruction, but instead is a taking up and fresh building, even if in practice there has not always been full correspondence with this high ideal. And we know well that the conversion that is begun by the mission is a work of grace, in which men and women must fully find themselves again.[27]

Address to Young Muslims

(1) God Invites Change

I give thanks and glory to God, who permitted me to be with you today. His Majesty the king did me the honor of visiting me in Rome some years ago, and he had the courtesy to invite me to visit your country and to meet you. I joyfully accepted the invitation of the sovereign of this country to come and speak to you, in this year of youth. I salute you, young people of Morocco and young people from various Arab lands, who are guests in Morocco for the Pan-Arab Games.

I often meet young people, and generally they are Catholics. This is the first time I have found myself with young Muslims.

Christians and Muslims: we have many things in common as believers and as human beings. We live in the same world. It is marked by numerous signs of hope, but also by many signs of anguish. Abraham is the model for us all of faith in God, submission to his will and trust in his goodness. We believe in the same God, the one and only God, the living God, the God who creates worlds and brings creatures to their perfection. So it is to God that my thought goes and my heart is raised. It is of this same God that I want to speak to you above all; of him, because it is in him that we, Muslims and Catholics, believe. And I would also speak to you of the human values which have their basis in God, those values which concern the development of our persons, as well as of our families, of our societies and the international community too. The mystery of God: Is it not the highest reality on which depends the very meaning people give to their lives? And is it not the first problem presenting itself to young persons when they reflect on the mystery of their existence and the values which they intend to choose in order to construct their growing personalities?

For my part, in the Catholic Church, I hold the office of successor of Peter, the apostle whom Jesus chose to strengthen his brothers in the faith. Continuing the line of popes who have succeeded each other without interruption, I today am Bishop of Rome, called to be the witness of the faith among his brothers and sisters in the world and the guarantor of the unity of all members of the Church.

So it is as a believer that I come to you today, simply to give witness to what I believe, what I wish for the well being of my brothers and sisters, humankind, and what, through experience, I consider to be useful for all.

(2) *To Believe in God*

I first call upon the Most High, the almighty God who is our creator. He is at the origin of all life, as he is the source of all that is good, of all that is beautiful, of all that is holy. He divided the light from the darkness. He caused the whole of the universe to develop according to a marvelous order. He willed that plants should grow and bear their fruits, as he willed that the birds of the air, the beasts of the earth and the fish of the sea should multiply.

He made us and we are his. His holy law guides our lives. It is God's light which guides our fate and enlightens our conscience. He makes us capable of loving and transmitting life. He requires every human being to respect all human creatures and love them as friends, companions, brothers and sisters. He calls upon us to go to the aid of others when they are hurt, when they are abandoned, when they are hungry and thirsty, in short, when they no longer know how to find their way along the paths of life. Yes, God asks us to listen to his voice. He expects obedience from us to his holy will in free adherence of the mind and heart.

That is why we are responsible to him. It is he, God, who is our judge, he alone who is truly just. We know, however, that his mercy is inseparable from his justice. When someone comes back to him repentant and contrite after having gone astray in sin and the works of death, God then reveals himself as the one who pardons and gives mercy. So our love and adoration go out to him. For his benefits and his mercy we give him thanks at all times and everywhere.

This meeting is in the spirit of Vatican Council II, of the declaration on the Church's dialogue with non-Christian religions.

In a world which desires unity and peace but which experiences a thousand tensions and conflicts, should not believers foster friendship and union among humankind and the peoples who comprise a single community on earth? We know that all persons have the same origin and also the same end: the God who made them and who awaits them, because he will bring them together.

For its part during the Vatican Council II 20 years ago, the Catholic Church committed itself in the persons of its bishops, that is to say, its religious leaders, to seek collaboration among believers. It published a document on dialogue among religions (*Nostra aetate*). The Church affirms that all people, especially those of living faith, ought to respect one another, get over all discrimination, live together and serve universal brotherhood (cf. *ibid.*, 5). The Church shows particular concern for Muslim believers, in view of their faith in the one God, their sense of prayer and their esteem for an upright life (cf. *ibid,*. 3). The Church wishes "for the benefit of all men and women...(to) together preserve and promote peace, liberty, social justice and moral values" (*ibid.*).

(3) Call for Common Witness on the Meaning of God

The dialogue between Christians and Muslims is more necessary than ever today. It flows from our fidelity to God and supposes that we know how to recognize God through faith and to give witness to him through prayer and action in a world which is becoming more and more secularized and at times even atheistic.

The youth can build a better future if they first of all put their faith in God and commit themselves to building up this new world according to God's plan, with wisdom and confidence. Today we must give witness to the spiritual values which the world needs. First of all comes our faith in God. Is not faith the first big question facing young people when they reflect on the meaning of their lives and the orientations to follow in order to know happiness?

God is the source of all joy. So we have to give witness to our worship of God, to our adoration, to our prayer of praise and supplication. People cannot live without praying, any more than they can live without breathing. We have to give witness to our humble search for his will. It is he who ought to inspire all our commitment for a more just and more united world. The ways of God are not always our ways. They transcend our actions, which are always incomplete, and the intentions of our hearts, which are always imperfect. God may never be used for our purposes, for he is beyond all.

(4) Appeal for Common Witness to Human Dignity

This witness of faith is vital for us and should not have to suffer either infidelity to God or indifference to truth. It is given in respect for other religious traditions. All people expect to be respected for what they are, in fact, and for what they believe in conscience, free of external constraints unworthy of the free homage of reason and of the heart characteristic of human dignity. That is the true meaning of religious liberty, which respects both God and humans. It is from such worshipers that God expects sincere adoration, that of the adorers in spirit and in truth.

Our conviction is that "we cannot pray to God the Father of all if we treat people in other than brotherly fashion, for all men and women are created in God's image" (*Nostra aetate*, 5). We must therefore also respect, love and help all human beings because they are creatures of God and, in a certain sense, his image and representative, because they are the way leading to God and because they do not fully realize themselves unless they know God and accept him with all their heart and obey him even to the ways of perfection.

Thus, this obedience to God and this love for others ought to lead us to respect human rights, those rights which are the expression of God's will and the demand of human nature as God created it. Respect and dialogue therefore call for reciprocity in all fields, above all in what concerns fundamental liberties, more particularly religious liberty. They favor peace and understanding among peoples. They help to find solutions together to the problems of men and women of today, especially those of the young.

(5) Responsibilities and Joint Work of the Young for a More Humane World

The young normally look toward the future; they aspire to a world which is more just and humane. God has made the young like that, precisely so that they will help transform the world according to his plan for life. But, to the young as well, the situation often seems very shadowy.

In this world there are boundaries and divisions among peoples, as well as a lack of understanding between generations. There are also racism, wars and injustice, as well as hunger, disasters, a lack of work. These are dramatic ills which affect us all, more particularly the young of the whole world. Some are in danger of becoming discouraged, others are in danger of being resigned, others of wishing to change everything through violence or extremist solutions. Wisdom teaches us that self-discipline and love are then the only instruments of the desired renewal.

God does not wish humans to remain passive. He entrusted the earth to them for them to master it, cultivate it and make it bear fruit. You are responsible for the world of tomorrow. By fully accepting your responsibilities and doing so with courage, you will be able to overcome the present difficulties. So it is up to you to take initiatives and not expect everything from older people and those who are already established. It is up to you to construct the world, not only to dream about it.

People can be effective through working together. Work, well understood, is a service to others. It creates bonds of solidarity. The experience of working together enables us to purify ourselves and to discover the riches of others. That is how an atmosphere of confidence can arise, little by little, enabling each one to grow, to expand, and "to become something more." Do not fail, dear young people, to collaborate with adults, especially your parents and teachers, as well as with the leaders of society and of the state. The young should not isolate themselves from others. The young have need of adults, as adults have need of the young. The human person, man or woman, must never be sacrificed in this joint endeavor. Each person is unique in God's eyes and is irreplaceable in this work of development. All ought to be recognized for what they are, consequently respected as such. No one should use others. No one should exploit equals. No one should despise his or her brother or sister.

It is under these conditions that a more humane world can arise, a world which is more just and fraternal, where all may find their place in dignity and liberty. It is the world of the 21st century, which is in your hands. It will be what you make it.

(6) A Pluralist and Jointly Responsible World

This world to come depends on all the young of all countries in the world. Our world is divided; it has even exploded. It knows many conflicts and grave injustices. There is no real North-South solidarity, no mutual aid among the nations of the South. There are cultures and races in the world which are not respected. Why is all that so? It is because people do not accept their differences; they do not know each other well. They reject those who do not have the same civilization. They refuse to help one another. They do not know how to free themselves from selfishness and sufficiency.

Well, God created all men and women equal in dignity, but different as regards gifts and talents. Humankind is a single whole where each group has its part to play. We must acknowledge the values of the various peoples and cultures. The world is like a living organism: each one has something to receive from others and something to give them.

I am glad to meet you here in Morocco. Morocco has a tradition of openness. Your learned men and women have traveled and you have received scholars from other countries. Morocco has been a meeting place of civilizations: it has enabled exchanges to take place with the East, with Spain and with Africa. Morocco has a tradition of tolerance: in this Muslim country there have always been Jews and almost always Christians. This has taken place in respect, in a positive manner. You have been and you remain a hospitable country. So, young Moroccans, you are prepared to become citizens of the world of tomorrow, of that fraternal world to which you aspire together with the youth of the entire world.

I am sure that all of you, young people, are capable of this dialogue. You do not wish to be conditioned by prejudices. You are ready to build a civilization founded on love. You can work in order to tear down barriers which are sometimes caused by pride, more often by weakness and fear of people. You wish to love others without any limits whether they are national, racial or religious.

You therefore wish for justice and peace. "Peace and young walk together," I said in my message for this year's World Day of Peace. You do not want war or violence. You know the price they extract from the innocent. Nor do you want arms escalation. That does not mean you want peace at any price, but peace together with justice. You do not want anyone oppressed. You want peace in justice.

(7) Suitable Living Conditions for All

You first of all want people to have what they need to live. Young people with the opportunity to pursue their studies have a right to be concerned with their self-advancement. But they must also be concerned with the living conditions, which are often more difficult, of their brothers and sisters who live in the same country and those in the rest of the world. How can one remain indifferent when other human beings are dying of hunger in great numbers, when they are dying of undernourishment and lack of medical care, when they are suffering cruelly from drought, when they are reduced to joblessness, forced to emigrate by economic laws which are beyond them, when they suffer the precarious condition of the refugee, enclosed in camps because of conflicts among peoples. God gave the earth to the whole human race, so that men and women could draw their living from it in solidarity and each people might have the means to feed itself, take care of itself and live in peace.

(8) A Long Tradition of Study

But however important economic problems are, we do not live by bread alone. We need an intellectual and spiritual life. That is where the soul of that new world to which you aspire is to be found. One needs to develop one's spirit and one's conscience. That is what is lacking in people of today. The forgetting of values and the crisis of identity pervading our world oblige us to overcome these and to make a renewed effort at study and questioning. The inner light which will thus arise in our consciences will enable a meaning to be given to development that will orient it toward the good of each and every person, according to God's will.

The Arabs of the Machreq and of the Maghreb and Muslims in general have a long tradition of study and literary, scientific and philo-sophical knowledge.[28] You are the heirs of that tradition. You must study in order to get to know this world God has given to us, to understand it, to discover its meaning and to do so with a taste and respect for truth, in order that you may also get to know the peoples and those created and loved by God, so that you may better prepare yourselves to aid them.

(9) A Growth in the Spiritual Life

Even more, the search for truth will lead you beyond intellectual values to the spiritual dimension of the interior life. Humans are spiritual beings. We believers know that we are not living in a closed world. We believe in God. We are adorers of God. We are seekers of God. The Catholic Church respects and recognizes the quality of your religious approach, the richness of your spiritual tradition. We Christians are also proud of our religious tradition. I believe that we Christians and Muslims ought to acknowledge with joy the religious values we have in common and give God thanks for them. We and you believe in one God, the unique God, who is all justice and all mercy. We believe in the importance of prayer, of fasting and of almsgiving, of penitence and of pardon. We believe that God will be a merciful judge to us at the end of time and that after the resurrection he will be happy with us and we shall be happy with him.

Sincerity also requires that we recognize and respect our differences. The most fundamental is clearly the regard which we have for the person and work of Jesus of Nazareth. You know that, for Christians, Jesus provides an intimate knowledge of the mystery of God and provides filial communion of his gifts, if they acknowledge him and proclaim him Lord and Savior.

These are important differences, and we can accept them with humility and respect, in mutual tolerance. There is a mystery there, and God will enlighten us about it one day, I am sure.

Christians and Muslims, generally we have understood each other badly. Sometimes in the past we have opposed each other and even exhausted ourselves in polemics and wars. I believe God is calling us today to change our old habits. We have to respect each other and stimulate each other in good works upon the path of God.

You know, together with me, what the price of spiritual values is. Ideologies and slogans cannot satisfy you or resolve the problems of your lives. Only moral and spiritual values can do so, and they have God as their foundation.

(10) Thanks and Prayer

I hope, dear young people, that you will be able to contribute in that way to building a world where God shall have first place in order to aid and save humankind. Along the way, you may be sure of the esteem and collaboration of your Catholic brothers and sisters who I represent among you this evening. I would now like to thank His Majesty the king for having invited me, and to thank you too, dear young people of Morocco and of numerous other countries, for having come here and having trustingly listened to my testimony.

But even more, I want to thank God for permitting this meeting. We are all under his gaze. He is the prime witness of our meeting today. It is he who puts sentiments of mercy and understanding, of pardon and reconciliation, of service and collaboration, in our hearts. Isn't it necessary for believers, which we are, to reproduce in their lives and their social order the Three Good Names our religious traditions attribute to him [unknowable, creator, revealer]? Let us then be at his disposal and submissive to his will, to the appeals he directs to us! Our lives will thus find a renewed dynamism. Then, I am convinced, a world will be born in which men and women of living and effective faith will sing the glory of God and seek to build a human society according to God's will.

I will conclude by invoking him personally before you.

O God, you are our Creator, you are good, and your mercy is without bounds. To you goes the praise of every creature.

O God, you have given humans, which we are, an interior law by which we must live. Doing your will means doing our duty. Following your ways means knowing peace of soul. We offer our obedience to you. Lead us in all the initiatives which we undertake on earth. Free us from bad inclinations which turn our hearts from your will. Do not permit that, as we invoke your will, we should come to justify human disorders.

O God, you are the only one. To you goes our adoration, do not let us draw away from you, O God, judge of all, aid us to form part of your elect on the last day. O God, author of justice and peace, grant us true peace and authentic love, as well as lasting fraternity among peoples. Fill us with your gifts forever. Amen![29]

Encouraging Interreligious Dialogue

The Church of Jesus Christ in this age experiences a profound need *to enter into contact and dialogue with all these religions*. She pays homage to the many moral values contained in these religions, as well as to the potential for spiritual living which so deeply marks the traditions and the cultures of whole societies. What seems to bring together and unite, in a particular way, Christians and the believers of other religions is an acknowledgment of *the need for prayer* as an expression of human spirituality directed towards the Absolute. Even when, for some, he is the great Unknown, he nevertheless remains always in reality the same living God. We trust that wherever the human spirit opens itself in prayer to this Unknown God, an echo will be heard of the same Spirit who, knowing the limits and weakness of the human person, himself prays in us and on our behalf, "expressing our plea in a way that could never be put into words" (Rom 8:26). The intercession of the Spirit of God who prays in us and for us is the fruit of the mystery of the redemption of Christ, in which the all-embracing love of the Father has been shown to the world.

All Christians must therefore be committed to dialogue with the believers of all religions, so that mutual understanding and collaboration may grow; so that moral values may be strengthened; so that God may be praised in all creation. Ways must be developed to make this dialogue become a reality everywhere, but especially in Asia, the continent that is the cradle of ancient cultures and religions. Likewise the Catholics and the Christians of other Churches must join together in the search for full unity, in order that Christ may become ever more manifest in the love of his followers. The divisions that still exist between those who profess the name of Jesus Christ must be felt as an incentive to fervent prayer and to conversion of heart, so that a more perfect witness to the Gospel may be given. Christians will, moreover, join hands with all men and women of good will who share a belief in the inestimable dignity of each human person. They will work together in order to bring about a more just and perfect society in which the poor will be the first to be served. Asia is the continent where the spiritual is held in high esteem and where the religious sense is deep and innate; the preservation of this precious heritage must be the common task of all.[30]

Fruits of Interreligious Dialogue

Dialogue between members of different religions increases and deepens mutual respect and paves the way for relationships that are crucial in solving the problems of human suffering. Dialogue that is respectful and open to the opinions of others can promote union and a commitment to this noble cause. Besides, the experience of dialogue gives a sense of solidarity and courage for overcoming barriers and difficulties in the task of nation building. For without dialogue the barriers of prejudice, suspicion and misunderstanding cannot be effectively removed. With dialogue, each partner makes an honest attempt to deal with the common problems of life and receives courage to accept the challenge of pursuing truth and achieving good. The experience of suffering, disappointment, disillusionment and conflict are changed from signs of failure and doom to occasions for progress in friendship and trust.

Again, dialogue is *a means of seeking after truth* and of *sharing it* with others. For truth is light, newness and strength. The Catholic Church holds that "the search for truth, however, must be carried out in a manner that is appropriate to the dignity of human persons and their social nature, namely by free enquiry with the help of teaching or instruction, communication and dialogue. It is by these means that *human beings share with each other the truth they have discovered*, or are convinced they have discovered, in such a way that they help one another in the search for truth" (*Dignitatis humanae*, 3). Modern men and women seek dialogue as an apt means of establishing and developing mutual understanding, esteem and love, whether between individuals or groups. In this spirit of understanding, the Second Vatican Council urges Christians to acknowledge, preserve and promote the spiritual and moral values found among non-Christians, as well as their social and cultural values (cf. *Nostra aetate*, 2).

The fruit of dialogue is union between people and union of people with God, who is the source and revealer of all truth and whose Spirit guides people in freedom only when they meet one another in all honesty and love. By dialogue we let God be present in our midst; for as we open ourselves in dialogue to one another, we also open ourselves to God. We should use the legitimate means of human friendliness, mutual understanding and interior persuasion. We should respect the personal and civic rights of the individual. As followers of different religions we should join together in promoting and defending common ideals in the spheres of religious liberty, human brotherhood, education, culture, social welfare and civic order. Dialogue and collaboration are possible in all these great projects.

In the context of religious pluralism, the spirit of tolerance, which has always been part of the Indian heritage, is not only desirable but imperative and must be implemented in a framework of practical means of support. It is the teaching of the Church that *the human person has a right to religious freedom*. This freedom means that all men and women are to be immune from coercion on the part of individuals or social groups or any human power, so that none are forced to act against their convictions or are prevented from acting in accordance with their convictions in religious matters, whether privately or publicly, whether alone or in association with others, within due limits (cf. *Dignitatis humanae*, 2).[31]

8.4 Perhaps the most valuable way in which John Paul II pushed forward the doctrine on dialogue with other religions came through his vivid sense of the Holy Spirit present in every human heart and prompting authentic prayer wherever it goes up to God. In his 1986 encyclical *Dominum et vivificantem* (The Lord and Giver of Life) he expounded the universal activity of the Holy Spirit, a theme to which he returned at the end of the year when defending the World Day of Peace held at Assisi with leaders of different religious traditions and four years later in the encyclical *Redemptoris missio* (The Mission of the Redeemer).

The Universal Presence
of the Holy Spirit

We cannot limit ourselves to the two thousand years which have passed since the birth of Christ. We need to go further back, to embrace the whole of the action of the Holy Spirit even before Christ—from the beginning, throughout the world, and especially in the economy of the Old Covenant. For this action has been exercised, in every place and at every time, indeed in every individual, according to the eternal plan of salvation, whereby this action was to be closely linked with the mystery of the Incarnation and Redemption, which in its turn exercised its influence on those who believed in the future coming of Christ....Grace, therefore, bears within itself both a Christological aspect and a pneumatological one, which becomes evident above all in those who expressly accept Christ....

But...we need to look further and go further afield, knowing that "the wind blows where it wills..." (cf. John 3:8). The Second Vatican Council, centered primarily on the theme of the Church, reminds us of the Holy Spirit's activity also "outside the visible body of the Church." The Council speaks precisely of "all people of good will in whose hearts grace works in an unseen way. For, since Christ died for all, and since the ultimate vocation of all persons is in fact one and divine, we ought to believe that the Holy Spirit in a manner known to God offers to everyone the possibility of being associated with this Paschal Mystery" (*Gaudium et spes*, 22).[32]

Unity of Human Beings in Creation

More than once the Council established a relationship between the very identity and the mission of the Church on the one hand, and the unity of the human race on the other, especially when it chose to define the Church "as a Sacrament, i.e., a sign and instrument of intimate union with God and of the unity of all the human race" (*Lumen gentium*, 1:9; cf. *Gaudium et spes*, 42).

This radical unity, which belongs to the very identity of the human being, is based on the mystery of the divine creation. The one

161

God in whom we believe, Father, Son and Holy Spirit, the most Holy Trinity, created man and woman with a particular attention, according to the narrative in Genesis (cf. Gen 1:26ff., 2:7, 18–24). This affirmation contains and communicates a profound truth: the unity of the divine origin of all the human family, of every man and woman, which is reflected in the unity of the divine image which all bear in themselves (cf. Gen 1:26) and *per se* gives the orientation to a common goal (cf. *Nostra aetate*, 1). "You have made us for yourself, O Lord," exclaims St. Augustine, in the fullness of his maturity as a thinker, "and our heart has no rest until it rests in you" (*Confessions*, 1). The dogmatic constitution *Dei Verbum* declares that "God, who creates and conserves all things by his word, provides men and women with constant evidence of himself....And he has never ceased to take care of the human race, for he wishes to give eternal life to all who seek salvation through perseverance in doing good" (*Dei Verbum*, 3).

Accordingly, there is only one divine plan for all human beings who come into this world (cf. John 1:9), one single origin and goal, whatever may be the color of their skin, the historical and geographical framework within which they happen to live and act, or the culture in which they grow up and express themselves. The differences are a less important element when confronted with the unity which is radical, fundamental and decisive.[33]

Common Origin and Destiny

In the light of this mystery [the unity of the human race through creation and the salvific work of Christ] it becomes clear that the differences of every type, and first of all the religious differences, belong to another order to the extent that they derive from the design of God. If it is the order of unity that goes back to creation and redemption and is therefore, in this sense, "divine," such differences (and even religious differences) go back rather to a "human fact," and must be overcome in progress toward the realization of the mighty plan of unity which dominates the creation. There are undeniably differences that reflect the genius and the spiritual "riches" which God has given to the peoples (cf. *Ad gentes*, 11). I am not referring to these divergences. I intend here to speak of the differences in which are revealed the limitations, the evolutions and the falls of the human spirit, which is undermined by the spirit of evil in history (*Lumen gentium*, 16).

It may be the case that persons are often unaware of this radical unity of their origin and destination, and their place in one and the same divine plan; and when they profess religions which are diverse and mutually incompatible, they can also feel that their divisions are insuperable. Yet despite these divisions, they are included in the great and unique design of God, in Jesus Christ, who "has united himself in a certain manner to every person" (*Gaudium et spes*, 22), even if the person in question is not aware of this.[34]

The Day at Assisi

The day of Assisi, showing the Catholic Church holding the hands of brother Christians, and showing all these joining hands with the brothers and sisters of other religions, was a visible expression of these statements of the Second Vatican Council. With this day and by means of it, we have succeeded, by the grace of God, in realizing this conviction of ours, inculcated by the Council, about the unity of the origin and goal of the human family, and about the meaning and value of the non-Christian religions, without the least shadow of confusion or syncretism.

Has not the day taught us to read afresh, in our turn, with eyes more open and penetrating, the rich teaching of the Council about the salvific plan of God, about the centrality of this plan in Jesus Christ and about the profound unity which is the starting point and the goal of the Church's ministry? The Catholic Church is revealed to her children and to the world in the exercise of her function of "promoting unity and charity among human persons, indeed among the peoples" (*Nostra aetate*, 1).

In this sense, one must say also that the very identity of the Catholic Church and her self-awareness have been reinforced at Assisi. For the Church, that is, we ourselves, has understood better, in the light of this event, what the true sense is of the mystery of unity and reconciliation which the Lord has entrusted to us, and which he himself carried out first when he offered his life "not for the people only, but also to unite the children of God who had been scattered abroad" (John 11:52).[35]

The Holy Spirit in Every Heart

Every authentic prayer is under the influence of the Spirit "who intercedes insistently for us…because we do not even know how to pray as we ought," but he prays in us "with unutterable groanings" and "the one who searches hearts knows the desires of the Spirit" (cf. Rom 8:26-27). We can indeed maintain that every authentic prayer is called forth by the Holy Spirit, who is mysteriously present in the heart of every person. This too was seen at Assisi: the unity that comes from the fact that every man and woman is capable of praying, that is, of submitting oneself totally to God and of recognizing oneself to be poor in front of him. Prayer is one of the means of realizing the plan of God among human beings (cf. *Ad gentes*, 3).[36]

Christ's Mediation Allows for Participated Mediations

Christ is the one mediator between God and humankind: "For there is one God, and there is one mediator between God and humanity, the man Christ Jesus, who gave himself as a ransom for all, the testimony to which was borne at the proper time. For this I was appointed a preacher and apostle (I am telling the truth, I am not lying), a teacher of the Gentiles in faith and truth" (1 Tim 2:5–7; cf. Heb 4:14–16). No one, therefore, can enter into communion with God except through Christ, by the working of the Holy Spirit. Christ's one, universal mediation, far from being an obstacle on the journey toward God, is the way established by God himself…. Although participated forms of mediation of different kinds and degrees are not excluded, they acquire meaning and value *only* from Christ's own mediation, and they cannot be understood as parallel or complementary to his.[37]

Salvation for Nonmembers of the Church

The universality of salvation means that it is granted not only to those who explicitly believe in Christ and have entered the Church. Since salvation is offered to all, it must be made concretely available to all....For...people [outside the Church] salvation in Christ is accessible by virtue of a grace which, while having a mysterious relationship to the Church, does not make them formally part of the Church but enlightens them in a way which is accommodated to their spiritual and material situation. This grace comes from Christ; it is the result of his Sacrifice and is communicated by the Holy Spirit. It enables each person to attain salvation through his or her free cooperation.[38]

Universal Presence of the Spirit

The Spirit manifests itself in a special way in the Church and in her members. Nevertheless, his presence and activity are universal, limited neither by space nor time....The Spirit's presence and activity affect not only the individuals but also society and history, peoples, cultures and religions. Indeed, the Spirit is at the origin of the noble ideals and undertakings which benefit humanity on its journey through history...(cf. *Gaudium et spes*, 26, 38). Again, it is the Spirit who sows the "seeds of the Word" present in various customs and cultures, preparing them for full maturity in Christ (cf. *Lumen gentium*, 17).[39]

Interreligious Dialogue and Mission

Inter-religious dialogue is a part of the Church's evangelizing mission. Understood as a method and means of mutual knowledge and enrichment, dialogue is not in opposition to the mission *ad gentes*; indeed, it has special links with that mission and is one of its expressions. This mission, in fact, is addressed to those who do not know Christ and his Gospel, and who belong for the most part to other religions. In Christ, God calls all peoples to himself and he wishes to share with them the fullness of his revelation and love. He does not fail to make himself present in many ways, not only to individuals but also to entire peoples through their spiritual riches, of which their religions are the main and essential expression, even when they contain "gaps, insufficiencies and errors...."

In the light of the economy of salvation, the Church sees no conflict between proclaiming Christ and engaging in inter-religious dialogue. Instead, she feels the need to link the two in the context of her mission *ad gentes*. These two elements must maintain both their intimate connection and their distinctiveness; therefore they should not be confused, manipulated or regarded as identical, as though they were interchangeable.[40]

Principles and Fruits of Dialogue

Dialogue does not originate from tactical concerns or self-interest, but is an activity with its own guiding principles, requirements and dignity. It is demanded by deep respect for everything that has been brought about in human beings by the Spirit who blows where he wills. Through dialogue, the Church seeks to uncover the "seeds of the Word," a "ray of that truth which enlightens all people"; these are found in individuals and in the religious traditions of humankind. Dialogue is based on hope and love, and will bear fruit in the Spirit.

Those engaged in this dialogue must be consistent with their own religious traditions and convictions, and be open to understanding those of the other party without pretense or closed-mindedness, but with truth, humility and frankness, knowing that dialogue can enrich each side. There must be no abandonment of principles nor false irenicism, but instead a witness given and received for mutual advancement on the road of religious inquiry and experience, and at the same time for the elimination of prejudice, intolerance and misunderstandings. Dialogue leads to inner purification and conversion which, if pursued with docility to the Holy Spirit, will be spiritually fruitful....Many missionaries and Christian communities find in the difficult and often misunderstood path of dialogue their only way of bearing sincere witness to Christ and offering generous service to others....Dialogue is a path toward the kingdom and will certainly bear fruit, even if the times and seasons are known only to the Father (cf. Acts 1:7).[41]

NOTES

1. On that occasion John Paul II also wrote to Cardinal Willebrands, president of the Secretariat for Promoting Christian Unity: "A twofold effort is necessary, both in regard to Martin Luther and also for the reestablishment of unity. In the first place it is necessary to continue an accurate historical work. By means of an investigation without preconceived ideas, motivated only by a search for the truth, one must arrive at a true image of the reformer, of the whole period of the Reformation, and of the persons involved in it. Fault, where it exists, must be recognized, wherever it may lie. Where controversy has beclouded one's view, that view must be corrected independently of either party. Besides, we must now allow ourselves to be guided by the intention of setting ourselves up as judges of history, but solely by the motive of understanding better what happened and of becoming messengers of the truth" (cf. *AAS* 77 [1985], 717; *ND*, 928; *Origins* 13:29 [1983], 495–96). He also invited the new archbishop of Canterbury (George Carey) and a representative of Bartholomew I (the new ecumenical patriarch in Istanbul) to join him in January 2000 when opening the Holy Door in St. Paul's Outside the Walls; he also invited Patriarch Bartholomew I to preach at an evening Mass in St. Peter's Square on the Feast of Sts. Peter and Paul (June 29, 2004).

2. *Address in Istanbul, November 30, 1979*, in *AAS* 71 (1979), 1600; *ND*, 916; *OREnglish* 50 (December 10, 1979), 5; *Origins* 9:26 (1979), 415.

3. Ibid., in *AAS* 71 (1979), 1600–1601; *ND*, 917; *OREnglish* 50 (December 10, 1979), 5; *Origins* 9:26 (1979), 415.

4. Ibid., in *AAS* 71 (1979), 1601; *ND*, 918; *OREnglish* 50 (December 10, 1979), 5; *Origins* 9:26 (1979), 415.

5. Ibid., in *AAS* 71 (1979), 1602; *ND*, 920; *OREnglish* 50 (December 10, 1979), 5; *Origins* 9:26 (1979), 416.

6. Ibid., in *AAS* 71 (1979), 1602–3; *ND*, 921; *OREnglish* 50 (December 10, 1979), 5; *Origins* 9:26 (1979), 416.

7. *Homily to the Catholics at Osnabrück, November 16, 1980*, in *AAS* 73 (1981), 68–69; *ND*, 922; *OREnglish* 48 (December 1, 1980), 5.

8. *Address in Mainz to the Evangelical (Lutheran) Church Council of Germany, November 17, 1980*, in *AAS* 73 (1981), 74; *ND*, 923–24; *OREnglish* 49 (December 9, 1980), 3; *Origins* 10:25 (1980), 399.

9. Ibid., in *AAS* 73 (1981), 74; *ND*, 925–26; *OREnglish* 49 (December 9, 1980), 3; *Origins* 10:25 (1980), 399.

10. *Address to the German Episcopal Conference, November 18, 1980*, in *AAS* 73 (1981), 85; *ND*, 927; *Origins* 10:25 (1980), 387–88.

11. *Letter to Bishops of Europe, May 31, 1991*, in *AAS* 84 (1992), 167; *ND*, 930a; *Origins* 21:7 (1991), 119.

12. Ibid., in *AAS* 84 (1992), 167–68; *ND*, 930b; *Origins* 21:7 (1991), 119.
13. *Tertio millennio adveniente*, 34, in *AAS* 87 (1995), 26–27; *ND*, 933a, b, and c; *Origins* 24:24 (1994), 410–11; *Pope Speaks* 40:2 (1995), 101–2.
14. *Common Declaration on Environmental Ethics*, in *AAS* 94 (2002), 656–59; *Pope Speaks* 47:6 (2002), 375–77.
15. *Ut unum sint*, 9, in *AAS* 87 (1995), 926; *EncMiller*, 786; *ND*, 935a; *Origins* 25:4 (1995), 52–53; *Pope Speaks* 40:5 (1995), 299.
16. Ibid., 18, 36, 79, in *AAS* 87 (1995), 932, 942, 969; *EncMiller*, 791, 799, 820; *ND*, 935b; *Origins* 25:4 (1995), 54, 58, 67; *Pope Speaks* 303, 311, 330.
17. Ibid., 19, 38, in *AAS* 87 (1995), 933, 943–44; *EncMiller*, 791–92, 800; *ND*, 935c and d; *Origins* 25:4 (1995), 55, 58; *Pope Speaks* 304, 311–12.
18. Ibid., 46, in *AAS* 87 (1995), 948; *EncMiller*, 804; *ND*, 935e; *Origins* 25:4 (1995), 60; *Pope Speaks* 40:5 (1995), 315.
19. Ibid., 82, in *AAS* 87 (1995), 970–71; *EncMiller*, 821–22 *ND*, 936a; *Origins* 25:4 (1995), 67; *Pope Speaks* 40:5 (1995), 315.
20. Ibid., 84, in *AAS* 87 (1995), 971–72; *EncMiller*, 822; *ND*, 936b; *Origins* 25:4 (1995), 67–68; *Pope Speaks* 40:5 (1991), 331–32.
21. Ibid., 85, in *AAS* 87 (1995), 972; *EncMiller*, 823; *ND*, 936c; *Origins* 25:4 (1995), 68; *Pope Speaks* 40:5 (1991), 332.
22. Ibid., 88, in *AAS* 85 (1995), 974; *EncMiller*, 824; *ND*, 837a; *Origins* 25:4 (1995), 68; *Pope Speaks* 40:5 (1991), 333.
23. Ibid., 94–95, in *AAS* 85 (1995), 976–77; *EncMiller*, 826–27; *ND*, 937b; *Origins* 25:4 (1995), 69; *Pope Speaks* 40:5 (1991), 335–36.
24. Ibid., 95–96, in *AAS* 85 (1995), 977–78; *EncMiller*, 827–28; *ND*, 937c; *Origins* 25:4 (1995), 69–70; *Pope Speaks* 40:5 (1991), 336–37.
25. *Redemptor hominis*, 6, in *AAS* 71 (1979), 267–68; *EncMiller*, 53–54; *ND*, 1037; *Origins* 8:40 (1979), 629–30; *Pope Speaks* 24:2 (1979), 104–5.
26. Ibid., 11, in *AAS* 71 (1979), 276; *EncMiller*, 60; *ND*, 1038; *Origins* 8:40 (1979), 632; *Pope Speaks* 24:2 (1979), 111–12.
27. Ibid., 12 in *AAS* 71 (1979), 278–79; *EncMiller*, 61; *ND*, 1039; *Origins* 8:40 (1979), 632; *Pope Speaks* 24:2 (1979), 113–14.
28. These names refer to the Arab countries of the Middle East (Machreq) and of North Africa (Maghreb).
29. *Address to Young Muslims in Morocco, August 19, 1985*, in *AAS* 78 (1986), 95–104; *Origins* 15:11 (1985), 174–76; *Pope Speaks* 30 (1985), 311–18.
30. *Address to the People of Asia, February 21, 1981*, 4–5, in *AAS* 73 (1981), 393–94; *ND*, 1040; *OREnglish* 9 (March 2, 1981), 13–14.
31. *Address to the Leaders of Other Religions in Madras, February 5, 1985*, in *AAS* 78 (1986), 769–70; *Origins* 15:36 (1986), 597–98.

32. *Dominum et vivificantem*, 53, in *AAS* 78 (1986), 874–75; *EncMiller*, 285–86; *ND*, 1048; *Origins* 16:4 (1986), 94; *Pope Speaks* 31:2 (1986), 244–45.

33. *Address to the Roman Curia, December 22, 1986*, 3, in *AAS* 79 (1987), 1083–84; *ND*, 1048; *Origins* 16:31 (1987), 561.

34. Ibid., 5, in *AAS* 79, (1987), 1085; *ND*, 1050; *Origins* 16:31 (1987), 562.

35. Ibid., 9, in *AAS* 79 (1987), 1088; *ND*, 1052; *Origins* 16:31 (1987), 563.

36. Ibid., 11, in *AAS* 79 (1987), 1089; *Origins* 16:31 (1987), 563.

37. *Redemptoris missio*, 5, in *AAS* 83 (1991), 254; *EncMiller*, 439–40; *ND*, 1166; *Origins* 20:34 (1991), 544; *Pope Speaks* 36:3 (1991), 141.

38. Ibid., 10, in *AAS* 83 (1991), 258; *EncMiller*, 442; *ND*, 1168; *Origins* 20:34 (1990), 545; *Pope Speaks* 36:3 (1991), 143.

39. Ibid., 28, in *AAS* 83 (1991), 274–74; *EncMiller*, 453; *ND*, 1172; *Origins* 20:34 (1991), 549–50; *Pope Speaks* 36:3 (1991), 151.

40. Ibid., 55, in *AAS* 83 (1991), 302–3; *EncMiller*, 472–73; *ND*, 1054–55; *Origins* 20:34 (1991), 557; *Pope Speaks* 36:3 (1991), 165–66.

41. Ibid., 56–57, in *AAS* 83 (11991), 304–5; *EncMiller*, 473–74; *ND*, 1056–58; *Origins* 20:34 (1991), 557; *Pope Speaks* 36:3 (1991), 166–67.

CHAPTER NINE

Principles for Human and Christian Life

9.1 Beginning with his first encyclical, *Redemptor hominis* (The Redeemer of the Human Person) of 1979, John Paul II consistently highlighted the primacy of truth in approaching general moral principles. He derived freedom from truth, the freedom coming from Christ, the bearer of truth. In 1993 the title and content of the encyclical *Veritatis splendor* (The Splendor of Truth) was to emphasize the centrality of truth for human life and rights. *Redemptor hominis* also introduced a theme to which John Paul II returned in his 1981 encyclical *Laborem exercens* (Performing Work): the primacy of persons over things.

Freedom Founded on Truth

Jesus Christ meets the human person of every age, including our own, with the same words: "You will know the truth, and the truth will make you free" (John 8:32). These words contain both a fundamental requirement and a warning: the requirement of an honest relationship with regard to truth as a condition for authentic freedom, and the warning to avoid every kind of illusory freedom, every superficial unilateral freedom, every freedom that fails to enter into the whole truth about human beings and the world. Today also, even after two thousand years, we see Christ as the one who brings people freedom based on truth, frees them from what curtails, diminishes and, as it were, breaks off this freedom at its root, in their soul, their heart and their conscience.[1]

Truth Grounds Human Rights

Only God, the Supreme Good, constitutes the unshakable foundation and essential condition of morality, and thus of the commandments, particularly those negative commandments which always and in every case prohibit behavior and actions incompatible with the personal dignity of every person. The Supreme Good and the moral good meet in truth: the truth of God, the Creator and Redeemer, and the truth of human beings, created and redeemed by him. Only upon this truth is it possible to construct a renewed society and to solve the complex and weighty problems affecting it, above all the problem of overcoming the various forms of totalitarianism, so as to make way for the authentic freedom of the person.

[As I wrote in *Centesimus annus* (The Hundredth Year)], "totalitarianism arises out of a denial of truth in the objective sense. If there is no transcendent truth, in obedience to which human beings achieve their full identity, then there is no sure principle for guaranteeing just relations between people. Their self-interest as a class, group or nation would inevitably set them in opposition to one another. If one does not acknowledge transcendent truth, then the force of power takes over, and each person tends to make full use of the means at his or her disposal in order to impose his or her own interests or opinion, with no regard for the rights of others.... Thus, the root of modern totalitarianism is to be found in the denial of the transcendent dignity of human persons who, as the visible images of the invisible God, are therefore by their very nature the subject of rights which no one may violate—no individual, group, class, nation or state. Not even the majority of a social body may violate these rights, by going against the minority, by isolating, oppressing or exploiting it, or by attempting to annihilate it."

Consequently, the inseparable connection between truth and freedom, which expresses the essential bond between God's wisdom and will, is extremely significant for the life of persons in the socio-economic and socio-political sphere. This is clearly seen in the

Church's social teaching, which belongs to the field of theology and particularly of moral theology, and from her presentation of commandments governing social, economic and political life, not only with regard to general attitudes but also to precise and specific kinds of behavior and concrete acts.[2]

No less critical in the formation of conscience is the recovery of the necessary link between freedom and truth. As I have frequently stated, when freedom is detached from objective truth it becomes impossible to establish personal rights on a firm rational basis; and the ground is laid for society to be at the mercy of the unrestrained will of individuals or the oppressive totalitarianism of public authority.[3]

Reading the encyclical [*Rerum novarum* (Of New Things)] within the context of Pope Leo's whole magisterium, we see how it points essentially to the socio-economic consequences of an error which has even greater implications. As has been mentioned, this error consists in an understanding of human freedom which detaches it from obedience to the truth, and consequently from the duty to respect the rights of others. The essence of freedom then becomes self-love carried to the point of contempt for God and neighbor, a self-love which leads to an unbridled affirmation of self-interest and which refuses to be limited by any demand of justice.[4]

This is why the Church has something to say today, just as twenty years ago, and also in the future, about the nature, conditions, requirements and aims of authentic development, and also about the obstacles which stand in its way. In doing so the Church fulfills her mission to evangelize, for she offers her first contribution to the solution of the urgent problem of development when she proclaims the truth about Christ, about herself and about the human person, applying this truth to a concrete situation.[5]

The Primacy of Persons over Things

The essential meaning of this *kingship* and *dominion* of human beings over the visible world, which the Creator himself gave them for their task, consists in the priority of ethics over technology, in the primacy of the person over things, and in the superiority of spirit over matter.

This is why all phases of present-day progress must be followed attentively. Each stage of that progress must, so to speak, be x-rayed from this point of view. What is in question is the advancement of persons, not just the multiplying of things that people can use. It is a matter, as a contemporary philosopher has said and as the Council has stated, not so much of *having more* as of *being more*.[6] Indeed there is already a real perceptible danger that, while the dominion of human beings over the world of things is making enormous advances, they should lose the essential threads of their dominion, and in various ways let their humanity be subjected to the world and become themselves something subject to manipulation in many ways (even if the manipulation is often not perceptible directly) through the whole of the organization of community life, through the production system and through pressure from the means of social communication. Human beings cannot relinquish themselves or the place in the visible world that belongs to them; they cannot become the slave of things, the slave of economic systems, the slave of production, the slave of their own products.[7]

Human Beings Are Never Means

Obviously, the antinomy between labor and capital under consideration here—*the antinomy* in which *labor was separated from capital and set up in opposition to it*...as if it were just an element like any other in the economic process—did not originate merely in the philosophy and economic theories of the eighteenth century. Rather it originated in the whole *economic and social practice* of that time, the time of the birth and rapid development of industrialization, in which what was mainly seen was the possibility of vastly increasing material wealth, means, while the end, that is to say, the human person, who should be served by the means, was ignored. It was this practical error that *struck a blow* first and foremost against human labor, against *the working person*, and caused the ethically just social reaction already spoken of above. The same error, which is now part of history, and which was connected with the period of primitive capitalism and liberalism, can nevertheless be repeated in other circumstances of time and place, if people's thinking starts from the same theoretical or practical premises. The only chance there seems to be for radically overcoming this error is through adequate changes both in theory and in practice, changes *in line with* the definite *conviction of the primacy* of the person over things, and of human *labor over capital* as a whole collection of means of production.[8]

Being More

Speaking of the protection of the just rights of workers according to their individual professions, we must of course always keep in mind that which determines the subjective character of work in each profession. But at the same time, indeed before all else, we must keep in mind that which conditions the specific dignity of the subject of the work. The activity of union organizations opens up many possibilities in this respect, including their efforts to instruct and educate the workers and to foster their self-education. Praise is due to the work of the schools, what are known as workers' or people's universities, and the training programs and courses which have developed and are still developing this field of activity. It is always to be hoped that, thanks to the work of their unions, workers will not only *have* more, but above all *be* more: in other words, that they will realize their humanity more fully in every respect.[9]

Against War

"I was hungry and you gave me no food...naked and you did not clothe me...in prison and you did not visit me" (cf. Matt 25:42–43). These words become charged with even stronger warning, when we think that, instead of bread and cultural aid, the new states and nations awakening to independent life are being offered, sometimes in abundance, modern weapons and means of destruction placed at the service of armed conflicts and wars that are not so much a requirement for defending their just rights and their sovereignty but rather a form of chauvinism, imperialism, and neocolonialism of one kind or another. We all know well that the areas of misery and hunger on our globe could have been made fertile in a short time, if the gigantic investments for armaments at the service of war and destruction had been changed into investments for food at the service of life. This consideration will perhaps remain in part an abstract one. It will perhaps offer both sides an occasion for mutual accusation, each forgetting its own faults. It will perhaps provoke new accusations against the Church. The Church, however, who has no weapons at her disposal apart from those of the spirit, of the word and of love, cannot renounce her proclamation of "the word...in season and out of season" (cf. 2 Tim 4:2). For this reason she does not cease to implore both sides and to beg everybody in the name of God and in the name of the human person: Do not kill! Do not prepare destruction and extermination for human beings! Think of your brothers and sisters who are suffering hunger and misery! Respect each one's dignity and freedom![10]

9.2 Even before publishing *Redemptor hominis* (The Redeemer of the Human Person), John Paul II had insisted on the truth of human beings made in the divine image as the ground for basic human rights. In an address to the Third General Assembly of Latin American Bishops in Puebla (January 28, 1979), he developed this theme. In that same address he also drew attention to the incomparable dignity of the human person, a theme to which he would return: for instance, in the 1990 encyclical *Redemptoris missio* (The Mission of the Redeemer) and in the 1991 encyclical *Centesimus annus* (The Hundredth Year), which commemorated Leo XIII's 1891 encyclical *Rerum novarum* (Of New Things).

The Human Person in God's Image

Thanks to the Gospel, the Church possesses the truth about the human being. It is found in an anthropology that the Church never ceases to explore more deeply and to share. The primordial assertion of this anthropology is that the human being is the image of God and cannot be reduced to a mere fragment of nature or to an anonymous element in the human city (*Gaudium et spes*, 12, 14). This is the sense intended by St. Irenaeus when he wrote: "The glory of the human being is God; but the receptacle of all God's activity, wisdom, and power is the human being" (*Adversus haereses*, III, 20.2–3).[11]

Basic Rights

On the level of the individual, this dignity is crushed underfoot when due regard is not maintained for such values as freedom, the right to profess one's religion, physical and psychic integrity, the right to life's necessities, and the right to life itself. On the social and political level it is crushed when human beings cannot exercise their right to participate, when they are subjected to unjust and illegitimate forms of coercion, when they are subjected to physical and psychic torture, and so forth.[12]

In the light of what has been said above, the Church is profoundly grieved to see "the sometimes massive increase in violations of human rights in many parts of the world....Who can deny that today there are individual persons and civil authorities who are violating fundamental rights of the human person with impunity? I refer to such rights as the right to be born; the right to life; the right to responsible procreation; the right to work; the right to peace, freedom, and social justice; and the right to participate in making decisions that affect peoples and nations. And what are we to say when we run up against various forms of collective violence, such as racial discrimination against individuals and groups and the physical and psychological torturing of prisoners and political dissidents? The list grows when we add examples of abduction and of kidnapping for the sake of material gain, which represent such a traumatic attack on family life and the social fabric" (John Paul II, *Message to the United Nations*, December 2, 1978). We cry out once more: Respect the human being, who is the image of God! Evangelize so that this may become a reality, so that the Lord may transform hearts and humanize political and economic systems, with the responsible commitment of human beings as the starting point![13]

The Dignity of the Human Person

The Church and her missionaries also promote development through schools, hospitals, printing presses, universities and experimental farms. But a people's development does not derive primarily from money, material assistance or technological means, but from the formation of consciences and the gradual maturing of ways of thinking and patterns of behavior. *The person is the principal agent of development*, not money or technology. The Church forms consciences by revealing to peoples the God whom they seek and do not yet know, the grandeur of the human being created in God's image and loved by him, the equality of all men and women as God's sons and daughters, the mastery of human beings over nature created by God and placed at their service, and the obligation to work for the development of the whole person and all humankind.[14]

From this point forward it will be necessary to keep in mind that the main thread and, in a certain sense, the guiding principle of Pope Leo's encyclical [*Rerum novarum*], and of all the Church's social doctrine, is a *correct view of the human person* and of his or her unique value, inasmuch as "the human person...is the only creature on earth which God willed for itself." God has imprinted his own image and likeness on human beings (cf. Gen 1:26), conferring upon them an incomparable dignity, as the encyclical frequently insists. In effect, beyond the rights which human beings acquire by their own work, there exist rights which do not correspond to any work they perform, but which flow from their essential dignity as persons.[15]

9.3 In his 1984 apostolic exhortation *Reconciliatio et paenitentia* (Reconciliation and Penance), John Paul II expounded the nature of sin—not only in its personal sense but also in its various "social" meanings. In a 1986 address to a congress of moral theologians, he spoke of unchanging norms and intrinsically evil acts.

Sin as Rupture with God, within Oneself, and in Relationships with Others

As a rupture with God, sin is an act of disobedience by creatures who reject, at least implicitly, the very one from whom they came and who sustains them in life. It is therefore a suicidal act. Since by sinning human beings refuse to submit to God, their internal balance is also destroyed and it is precisely within themselves that contradictions and conflicts arise. Wounded in this way, they almost inevitably cause damage to the fabric of their relationship with others and with the created world. This is an objective law and an objective reality, verified in so many ways in the human psyche and in the spiritual life as well as in society, where it is easy to see the signs and effects of internal disorder.[16]

Personal Sin

Sin, in the proper sense, is always a personal act, since it is an act of freedom on the part of an individual person and not properly of a group or community. This individual may be conditioned, incited and influenced by numerous and powerful external factors. He or she may also be subjected to tendencies, defects and habits linked with his or her personal condition. In not a few cases such external and internal factors may attenuate, to a greater or lesser degree, the person's freedom and therefore his or her responsibility and guilt. But it is a truth of faith, also confirmed by our experience and reason, that the human person is free. This truth cannot be disregarded in order to place the blame for individuals' sins on external factors such as structures, systems or other people. Above all, this would be to deny the person's dignity and freedom, which are manifested—even though in a negative and disastrous way—also in this responsibility for sin committed. Hence there is nothing so personal and untransferable in each individual as merit for virtue or responsibility for sin.[17]

179

Social Sin

To speak of social sin means in the first place to recognize that, by virtue of human solidarity which is as mysterious and intangible as it is real and concrete, each individual's sin in some way affects others. This is the other aspect of that solidarity which on the religious level is developed in the profound and magnificent mystery of the communion of saints.... To this law of ascent there unfortunately corresponds the law of descent. Consequently one can speak of a communion of sin, whereby a soul that lowers itself through sin drags down with itself the Church and, in some way, the whole world. In other words, there is no sin, not even the most intimate and secret one, the one, the most strictly individual one, that exclusively concerns the person committing it.

Some sins, however, by their very matter constitute a direct attack on one's neighbor and more exactly, in the language of the Gospel, against one's brother or sister. They are an offense against God because they are offenses against one's neighbor. These sins are usually called social sins, and this is the second meaning of the term....

The third meaning of social sin refers to the relationships between the various human communities. These relationships are not always in accordance with the plan of God, who intends that there be justice in the world and freedom and peace between individuals, groups and peoples....

Having said this in the clearest and most unequivocal way, one must add at once that there is one meaning sometimes given to social sin that is not legitimate or acceptable even though it is very common in certain quarters today. This usage contrasts social sin and personal sin, not without ambiguity, in a way that leads more or less unconsciously to the watering down and almost the abolition of personal sin, with the recognition only of social guilt and responsibilities....

Whenever the Church speaks of situations of sin or when she condemns as social sins certain situations or the collective behavior of certain social groups, big or small, or even of whole nations and blocs of nations, she knows and she proclaims that such cases of social sin are the result of the accumulation and concentration of many personal sins. It is a case of the very personal sins of those who cause or support evil or who exploit it; of those who are in a position to avoid, eliminate or at least limit certain social evils but who fail to do so out of laziness, fear or the conspiracy of silence, through secret complicity or indifference; of those who take refuge in the supposed impossibility of changing the world and also of those who sidestep the effort and sacrifice required, producing specious reasons of higher order. The real responsibility, then, lies with individuals.[18]

Mortal Sin and Venial Sin

Now sin is a disorder perpetrated by the human being against this life-principle. And when "through sin, the soul commits a disorder that reaches the point of turning away from its ultimate end God to which it is bound by charity, then the sin is mortal; on the other hand, whenever the disorder does not reach the point of a turning away from God, the sin is venial." For this reason venial sin does not deprive the sinner of sanctifying grace, friendship with God, charity and therefore eternal happiness, whereas just such a deprivation is precisely the consequence of mortal sin....

Considering sin from the point of view of its matter, the ideas of death, of radical rupture with God, the supreme good, of deviation from the path that leads to God or interruption of the journey toward him (which are all ways of defining mortal sin) are linked with the idea of the gravity of sin's objective content. Hence, in the Church's doctrine and pastoral action, grave sin is in practice identified with mortal sin....

It must be added...that some sins are intrinsically grave and mortal by reason of their matter. That is, there exist acts which, *per se* and in themselves, independently of circumstances, are always seriously wrong by reason of their object. These acts, if carried out with sufficient awareness and freedom, are always gravely sinful.[19]

Loss of the Sense of Sin

This sense is rooted in the human person's moral conscience and is as it were its thermometer. It is linked to the sense of God, since it derives from the human being's conscious relationship with

God as Creator, Lord and Father. Hence, just as it is impossible to eradicate completely the sense of God or to silence the conscience completely, so the sense of sin is never completely eliminated.

Nevertheless, it happens not infrequently in history, for more or less lengthy periods and under the influence of many different factors, that the moral conscience of many people becomes seriously clouded. "Have we the right idea of conscience?"—I asked two years ago in an address to the faithful. "Is it not true that modern man is threatened by an eclipse of conscience? By a deformation of conscience? By a numbness or deadening of conscience" (*Angelus Message* of March 14, 1982)? Too many signs indicate that such an eclipse exists in our time. This is all the more disturbing in that conscience, defined by the Council as "the most secret core and sanctuary of a human being (*Gaudium et spes*, 16)," is "strictly related to human freedom.... For this reason conscience, to a great extent, constitutes the basis of human persons' interior dignity and, at the same time, of their relationship to God" (*Angelus Message* of March 14, 1982). It is inevitable therefore that in this situation there is an obscuring also of the sense of sin, which is closely connected with the moral conscience, the search for truth and the desire to make a responsible use of freedom. When the conscience is weakened the sense of God is also obscured, and as a result, with the loss of this decisive inner point of reference, the sense of sin is lost. This explains why my predecessor, Pius XII, one day declared, in words that have almost become proverbial, that "the sin of the century is the loss of the sense of sin" (Pope Pius XII, *Radio Message to the U.S. National Catechetical Congress in Boston*, October 26, 1946).

Why has this happened in our time? A glance at certain aspects of contemporary culture can help us to understand the progressive weakening of the sense of sin, precisely because of the crisis of conscience and crisis of the sense of God already mentioned.

"Secularism" is by nature and definition a movement of ideas and behavior which advocates a humanism totally without God, completely centered upon the cult of action and production and caught up in the heady enthusiasm of consumerism and pleasure seeking, unconcerned with the danger of "losing one's soul." This secularism cannot but undermine the sense of sin. At the very most, sin will be reduced to what offends the human person. But it is precisely here that we are faced with the bitter experience which I already alluded to in my first encyclical: namely, that human beings can build a world without God, but this world will end by turning against them (*Redemptor hominis*, 15). In fact, God is the origin and the supreme end of human beings, and they carry in themselves a divine seed (*Gaudium et spes*, 3; cf. 1 John 3:9.). Hence it is the reality of God that reveals and illustrates the mystery of the human being. It is therefore vain to hope that there will take root a sense of sin against human beings and against human values, if there is no sense of offense against God, namely the true sense of sin.

Another reason for the disappearance of the sense of sin in contemporary society is to be found in the errors made in evaluating certain findings of the human sciences. Thus on the basis of certain affirmations of psychology, concern to avoid creating feelings of guilt or to place limits on freedom leads to a refusal ever to admit any shortcoming. Through an undue extrapolation of the criteria of the science of sociology, it finally happens, as I have already said, that all failings are blamed upon society, and the individual is declared innocent of them. Again, a certain cultural anthropology so emphasizes the undeniable environmental and historical conditioning and influences which act upon human beings, that it reduces their responsibility to the point of not acknowledging their ability to perform truly human acts and therefore their ability to sin.

The sense of sin also easily declines as a result of a system of ethics deriving from a certain historical relativism. This may take the form of an ethical system which relativizes the moral norm, denying its absolute and unconditional value, and as a consequence denying that there can be intrinsically illicit acts independent of the circumstances in which they are performed by the subject. Herein lies a real "overthrowing and downfall of moral values," and "the problem is not so much one of ignorance of Christian ethics," but ignorance "rather of the meaning, foundations and criteria of the moral attitude" (John Paul II, *Address to the Bishops of the Eastern Region of France*, April 1, 1982). Another effect of this ethical turning upside down is always such an attenuation of the notion of sin as almost to reach the point of saying that sin does exist, but no one knows who commits it.

Finally the sense of sin disappears when (as can happen in the education of youth, in the mass media and even in education within the family) it is wrongly identified with a morbid feeling of guilt or with the mere transgression of legal norms and precepts.

The loss of the sense of sin is thus a form or consequence of the denial of God: not only in the form of atheism but also in the form of secularism. If sin is the breaking off of one's filial relationship to God in order to situate one's life outside of obedience to him, then to sin is not merely to deny God. To sin is also to live as if he did not exist, to eliminate him from one's daily life. A model of society which is mutilated or distorted in one sense or another, as is often encouraged by the mass media, greatly favors the gradual loss of the sense of sin. In such a situation the obscuring or weakening of the sense of sin comes from several sources: from a rejection of any reference to the transcendent in the name of the individual's aspiration to personal independence; from acceptance of ethical models imposed by general consensus and behavior, even when condemned by the individual conscience; from the tragic social and economic conditions that oppress a great part of humanity, causing a tendency to see errors and faults only in the context of society; finally and especially, from the obscuring of the notion of God's fatherhood and dominion over human life.

Even in the field of the thought and life of the Church, certain trends inevitably favor the decline of the sense of sin. For example, some are inclined to replace exaggerated attitudes of the past with other exaggerations: from seeing sin everywhere they pass to not recognizing it anywhere; from too much emphasis on the fear of eternal punishment they pass to preaching a love of God that excludes any punishment deserved by sin; from severity in trying to correct erroneous consciences they pass to a kind of respect for conscience which excludes the duty of telling the truth. And should it not be added that the confusion caused in the consciences of many of the faithful by differences of opinions and teachings in theology, preaching, catechesis and spiritual direction on serious and delicate questions of Christian morals ends by diminishing the true sense of sin almost to the point of eliminating it altogether? Nor can certain deficiencies in the practice of sacramental penance be overlooked. These include the tendency to obscure the ecclesial significance of sin and of conversion and to reduce them to merely personal matters; or vice versa, the tendency to nullify the personal value of good and evil and to consider only their community dimension. There also exists the danger, never totally eliminated, of routine ritualism that deprives the sacrament of its full significance and formative effectiveness.

The restoration of a proper sense of sin is the first way of facing the grave spiritual crisis looming over human beings today. But the sense of sin can only be restored through a clear reminder of the unchangeable principles of reason and faith which the moral teaching of the Church has always upheld.[20]

Intrinsically Evil Acts

To reduce the moral quality of our actions regarding creatures, to attempt to improve reality in its non-ethical content would be equivalent, in the last analysis, to destroying the very concept of morality. The first consequence, indeed, of this reduction is the denial that, in the context of such actions, there exist acts which are always and everywhere in themselves illicit.[21]

Unchanging Norms

Called, as persons, to immediate communion with God, the object, as persons, of an entirely singular providence, human beings bear a law written in their heart that they do not give to themselves but which expresses the immutable demands of their personal *being* created by God, granted a finality by God; and in itself endowed with a dignity that is infinitely superior to that of things. This law is not merely made up of general guidelines, whose specific extent is in their respective context conditioned by different and changeable historical situations. There are moral norms that have a precise context which is immutable and unconditioned. You are undertaking a rigorous reflection on some of these in the course of this congress: for example, the norm that prohibits contraception or that which forbids the direct killing of an innocent person. To deny the existence of norms having such a value can be done only by one who denies the existence of a *truth* above the person, of an immutable nature in human beings based ultimately on the creative Wisdom which is the measure of all reality. It is necessary, therefore, that ethical reflection be founded and rooted even more deeply in true anthropology, and this, ultimately on the metaphysics of creation which is at the center of all Christian thinking.[22]

9.4 In his 1993 encyclical *Veritatis splendor* (The Splendor of Truth), John Paul II broke new ground by elaborating the foundations and principles of Catholic moral doctrine. Vatican II's Pastoral Constitution on the Church in the Modern World, *Gaudium et spes* (Joy and Hope), did contain a considerable amount of ethical teaching. John Paul II drew on that document to develop in detail Christian moral teaching in a way that went beyond any earlier pope or council. The following extracts illustrate some of the major themes of the encyclical.

Development within the Tradition

Within Tradition, *the authentic interpretation* of the Lord's law develops, with the help of the Holy Spirit. The same Spirit who is at the origin of the revelation of Jesus' commandments and teachings guarantees that they will be reverently preserved, faithfully expounded and correctly applied in different times and places. This constant "putting into practice" of the commandments is the sign and fruit of a deeper insight into revelation and of an understanding in the light of faith of new historical and cultural situations. Nevertheless, it can only confirm the permanent validity of revelation and follow in the line of the interpretation given to it by the great tradition of the Church's teaching and life, as witnessed by the teaching of the Fathers, the lives of the saints, the Church's liturgy and the teaching of the Magisterium.[23]

Freedom and Law

God's law does not reduce, much less do away with human freedom; rather, it protects and promotes that freedom. In contrast, however, some present-day cultural tendencies have given rise to several currents of thought in ethics which center upon *an alleged conflict between freedom and law*. These doctrines would grant to individuals or social groups the right *to determine what is good or evil*.[24]

The Nature of the Human Person as Norm

At this point the true meaning of the natural law can be understood: it refers to the human being's proper and primordial nature, the "nature of the human person" (*Gaudium et spes*, 51), which is *the person himself or herself in the unity of soul and body*, in the unity of his or her spiritual and biological inclinations and of all the other specific characteristics necessary for the pursuit of their end. "The natural moral law expresses and lays down the purposes, rights and duties which are based upon the bodily and spiritual nature of the human person. Therefore this law cannot be thought of as simply a set of norms on the biological level; rather it must be defined as the rational order whereby the human person is called by the Creator to direct and regulate his or her life and actions and in particular to make use of their own body" (Congregation for the Doctrine of the Faith, *Instruction on Respect for Human Life in Its Origin and on the Dignity of Procreation*, "*Donum vitae*" [February 22, 1987], Introduction, 3). To give an example, the origin and the foundation of the duty of absolute respect for human life are to be found in the dignity proper to the person and not simply in the natural inclination to preserve one's own physical life. Human life, even though it is a fundamental good of human beings, thus acquires a moral significance in reference to the good of the person, who must always be affirmed for his or her own sake. While it is always morally illicit to kill an innocent human being, it can be licit, praiseworthy or even imperative to give up one's own life (cf. John 15:13) out of love of neighbor or as a witness to the truth. Only in reference to the human person in his or her "unified totality," that is, as "a soul which expresses itself in a body and a body informed by an immortal spirit" (*Familiaris consortio* [November 22,

187

1981], 11) can the specifically human meaning of the body be grasped. Indeed, natural inclinations take on moral relevance only insofar as they refer to human persons and their authentic fulfillment, a fulfillment which for that matter can take place always and only in human nature. By rejecting all manipulations of corporeity which alter its human meaning, the Church serves human beings and shows them the path of true love, the only path on which they can find the true God.[25]

The Judgment of Conscience and Erroneous Conscience

Saint Bonaventure teaches that "conscience is like God's herald and messenger; it does not command things on its own authority, but commands them as coming from God's authority, like a herald when he proclaims the edict of the king. This is why conscience has binding force" (*In II Librum Sentent.*, dist. 39, a. 1, q. 3). Thus it can be said that conscience bears witness to the human person's own rectitude or iniquity [and does so] to human beings themselves. But, together with this and indeed even beforehand, conscience is *the witness of God himself*, whose voice and judgment penetrate the depths of the soul of human beings, calling them strongly and sweetly to obedience. "Moral conscience does not close human beings within an insurmountable and impenetrable solitude, but opens them to the call, to the voice of God. In this, and not in anything else, lies the entire mystery and the dignity of the moral conscience: in being the place, the sacred place where God speaks to human beings" (General Audience, *Address*, August 17, 1983, 2).[26]

The judgment of conscience is a *practical judgment*, a judgment which makes known what human beings must do or not do, or which assesses an act already performed by them. It is a judgment which applies to a concrete situation the rational conviction that one must love and do good and avoid evil. This first principle of practical reason is part of the natural law; indeed it constitutes the very foundation of the natural law, inasmuch as it expresses that primordial insight about good and evil, that reflection of God's creative wisdom which, like an imperishable spark...shines in the heart of every person. But whereas the natural law discloses the objective and universal demands of the moral good, conscience is the application of the law to a particular case; this application of the law thus becomes an inner dictate for the individual, a summons to do what is good in this particular situation. Conscience thus formulates *moral obligation* in the light of the natural law: it is the obligation to do what individuals, through the workings of their conscience, *know* to be a good they are called to do *here and now*. The universality of the law and its obligation are acknowledged, not suppressed, once reason has established the law's application in concrete present circumstances. The judgment of conscience states "in an ultimate way" whether a certain particular kind of behavior is in conformity with the law; it formulates the proximate norm of the morality of a voluntary act, "applying the objective law to a particular case" (Supreme Sacred Congregation of the Holy Office, *Instruction on "Situation Ethics, Contra Doctrinam"* [February 2, 1956]).[27]

Conscience, as the judgment of an act, is not exempt from the possibility of error. As the Council puts it, "not infrequently conscience can be mistaken as a result of invincible ignorance, although it does not on that account forfeit its dignity; but this cannot be said when a person shows little concern for seeking what is true and good, and conscience gradually becomes almost blind from being accustomed to sin" (*Gaudium et spes*, 16). In these brief words the Council sums up the doctrine which the Church down the centuries has developed with regard to the *erroneous conscience*.[28]

Fundamental Option

There is no doubt that Christian moral teaching, even in its biblical roots, acknowledges the specific importance of a fundamental choice which qualifies the moral life and engages freedom on a radical level before God. It is a question of the decision of faith, of the *obedience of faith* (cf. Rom 16:26) "by which the human person makes a total and free self-commitment to God, offering the full submission of intellect and will to God as he reveals" (*Dei Verbum*, 5).[29]

To separate the fundamental option from concrete kinds of behavior means to contradict the substantial integrity or personal unity of the moral agent in his body and in his soul.[30]

Intrinsically Evil Acts

Reason attests that there are objects of the human act which are by their nature "incapable of being ordered" to God, because they radically contradict the good of the person made in his image. These are the acts which, in the Church's moral tradition, have been termed "intrinsically evil" (*intrinsece malum*): they are such *always and per se*, in other words, on account of their very object, and quite apart from the ulterior intentions of the one acting and the circumstances.[31]

Moral Norms Are Not Decided by Surveys and Votes

Moreover, the fact that some believers act without following the teachings of the Magisterium, or erroneously consider as morally correct a kind of behavior declared by their pastors as contrary to the law of God, cannot be a valid argument for rejecting the truth of the moral norms taught by the Church. The affirmation of moral principles is not within the competence of formal empirical methods. While not denying the validity of such methods, but at the same time not restricting its viewpoint to them, moral theology, faithful to the supernatural sense of the faith, takes into account first and foremost *the spiritual dimension of the human heart and its vocation to divine love.…*

While exchanges and conflicts of opinion may constitute normal expressions of public life in a representative democracy, moral teaching certainly cannot depend simply upon respect for a process: indeed, it is in no way established by following the rules and deliberative procedures typical of a democracy.[32]

9.5 In his 1998 encyclical *Fides et ratio* (Faith and Reason), John Paul II dealt with the role of philosophy in theology.

Moral Theology Needs Philosophy and Philosophical Ethics

Moral theology has perhaps an even greater need of philosophy's contribution. In the New Testament, human life is much less governed by prescriptions than in the Old Testament. Life in the Spirit leads believers to a freedom and responsibility which surpass the Law. Yet the Gospel and the Apostolic writings still set forth both general principles of Christian conduct and specific teachings and precepts. In order to apply these to the particular circumstances of individual and communal life, Christians must be able fully to engage their conscience and the power of their reason. In other words, moral theology requires a sound philosophical vision of human nature and society, as well as of the general principles of ethical decision-making....

Throughout the encyclical [*Veritatis splendor*] I underscored clearly the fundamental role of truth in the moral field. In the case of the more pressing ethical problems, this truth demands of moral theology a careful enquiry rooted unambiguously in the word of God. In order to fulfill its mission, moral theology must turn to a philosophical ethics which looks to the truth of the good, to an ethics which is neither subjectivist nor utilitarian. Such an ethics implies and presupposes a philosophical anthropology and a metaphysics of the good.[33]

NOTES

1. *Redemptor hominis*, 12, in *AAS* 71 (1979), 280–81; *EncMiller*, 62; *ND*, 2064; *Origins* 8:40 (1979), 632; *Pope Speaks*, 24:2 (1979), 114–15.

2. *Veritatis splendor*, 99, in *AAS* 85 (1993), 1210–11; *EncMiller*, 647; *Origins* 23:18 (1993), 326; *Pope Speaks* 39:1 (1994), 50–51. The section in *Centesimus annus* to which the pope refers is 24, in *AAS* 83 (1991), 821–22; *EncMiller*, 530–31; *Origins* 21:1 (1991), 10; *Pope Speaks* 36:5 (1991), 287–88.

3. *Evangelium vitae*, 96, in *AAS* 87 (1995), 510; *EncMiller*, 755; *Origins* 24:42 (1995), 722; *Pope Speaks* 40:4 (1995), 270.

4. *Centesimus annus*, 17, in *AAS* 83 (1991), 821–22; *EncMiller*, 525–26; *Origins* 21:1 (1991), 8; *Pope Speaks* 36:5 (1991), 284.

5. *Sollicitudo rei socialis*, 41, in *AAS* 80 (1988), 570–71; *EncMiller* 411; *Origins* 17:38 (1988), 655; *Pope Speaks* 33:1 (1988), 148.

6. Through Pope Paul VI, this saying from Gabriel Marcel (1889–1973) entered the text of Vatican II's *Gaudium et spes* (The Constitution on the Church in the Modern World), 35. John Paul II was to quote the saying again: for example, in *Laborem exercens*, 20, and *Centesimus annus*, 31.

7. *Redemptor hominis*, 16, in *AAS* 71 (1979), 289–90; *EncMiller*, 68; *ND*, 429; *Origins* 8:40 (1979), 635; *Pope Speaks* 24:2 (1979), 121–22.

8. *Laborem exercens*, 13, in *AAS* 73 (1981), 608–10; *EncMiller*, 172; *Origins* 11:14 (1981), 235; *Pope Speaks* 26:4 (1981), 311. In section two of his *Foundations of the Metaphysics of Morals*, Immanuel Kant (1724–1804) developed the notion of the human person being an end and never the means—a notion to which John Paul II was to return in 1993 in *Veritatis splendor*, 48, and in 1996 in his *Address to the Pontifical Academy of Sciences*, 5.

9. Ibid., 20, in *AAS* 73 (1981), 631–32; *EncMiller* 183; *Origins* 11:14 (1981), 240; *Pope Speaks* 26:4 (1981) 324–25.

10. *Redemptor hominis*, 16, in *AAS* 71 (1979), 295; *EncMiller*, 71; *Origins* 8:37 (1979), 636; *Pope Speaks* 24:2 (1979), 125–26.

11. *Address to the Third General Assembly of Latin American Bishops* (Puebla, January 28, 1979), 1.9, in *AAS* 71 (1979), 195–96; *ND*, 425; *Origins* 8:33 (1979), 534; *Pope Speaks* 24:1 (1979), 58. The creation of the human person in the image of God forms the basis for the highest and most important goods; see the 1987 encyclical *Sollicitudo rei socialis* (Concern for Social Matters), 27–34.

12. Ibid., 3.1, in *AAS* 71 (1979), 198; *ND*, 426; *Origins* 8:33 (1979), 536; *Pope Speaks* 24:1 (1979), 60–61.

13. Ibid., 3.5, in *AAS* 71 (1979), 201; *ND*, 426; *Origins* 833 (1979), 537; *Pope Speaks* 24:1 (1979), 63–64. John Paul II was well aware of an eloquent passage in Vatican II's Constitution on the Church in the Modern World, *Gaudium et spes* 26, on the sublime dignity of human persons and their rights. In a New Year address (On the Dignity of the Human Person as the Basis for Justice and Peace) to the 34th General Assembly of the United Nations (October 2, 1979), he would provide a full list of human rights (cf. *AAS* 71 [1979], 1143–60; *Origins* 9:17 [1979], 257–66; *Pope Speaks* 24:4 [1979], 297–311).

14. *Redemptoris missio*, 58, in *AAS* 83 (1991), 306–7; *EncMiller*, 475; *Origins* 20:34 (1991), 558; *Pope Speaks* 36:3 (1991), 167.

15. *Centesimus annus*, 11, in *AAS* 83 (1991), 806–7; *EncMiller* 521; *Origins* 211 (1991), 6; *Pope Speaks* 36:5 (1991), 280. The quotation in this passage is taken from *Gaudium et spes*, 24. In *Veritatis splendor* (no. 90) John Paul II insisted on the "unconditional respect" due to the personal dignity of everyone.

16. *Reconciliatio et paenitentia*, 15, in *AAS* 77 (1985), 213; *ApExMiller*, 283; *ND*, 2067a; *Origins* 14:27 (1984), 440–41; *Pope Speaks* 30:1 (1985), 40.

17. Ibid., 16, in *AAS* 77 (1985), 213–14; *ApExMiller*, 283–84; *ND*, 2067b; *Origins* 14:27 (1984), 441; *Pope Speaks* 30:1 (1985), 40–41.

18. Ibid., 16, in *AAS* 77 (1985), 215–19; *ApExMiller*, 284–86; *ND*, 2067c; *Origins* 14:27 (1984), 441; *Pope Speaks* 30:1 (1985), 41–43. In his address at Puebla (January 28, 1979) John Paul II had clearly referred to "sinful structures" in our world.

19. Ibid., 17, in *AAS* 77 (1985), 220–22; *ApExMiller*, 289–90; *ND*, 2067d; *Origins* 14:27 (1984), 442; *Pope Speaks* 30:4 (1985), 45–46. The quotation in this passage is taken from St. Augustine. The pope is also referring to the teachings of the Council of Trent on this issue (cf. decree on justification, chapter 2, canons 23, 25, 27; also chapter 15).

20. Ibid., 18, in *AAS* 77 (1985), 224–26; *ApExMiller* 291–94; *ND*, 2067e; *Origins* 14:27 (1984), 443–44; *Pope Speaks* 30:4 (1985), 48–49.

21. *Address to Moral Theologians*, 3, in *AAS* 78 (1986), 1100; *ND*, 2068; *OREnglish* 17 (April 28, 1986), 12; *Pope Speaks* 31:1 (1986), 176–77.

22. Ibid., 4, in *AAS* 78 (1986), 1000–1001; *ND*, 2069; *OREnglish* 17 (April 28,1986), 12; *Pope Speaks* 31:1 (1986), 177.

23. *Veritatis splendor*, 27, in *AAS* 85 (1993), 1155; *EncMiller*, 601–2: *Origins* 23:18 (1993), 908; *Pope Speaks* 39:1 (1994), 9.

24. Ibid., 35, in *AAS* 85 (1993), 1162; *EncMiller*, 607; *Origins* 23:18 (1993), 309; *Pope Speaks* 39:1 (1994), 23.

25. Ibid., 50, in *AAS* 85 (1993), 1173–74; *EncMiller*, 616–17; *ND*, 2079; *Origins* 23:18 (1993), 313; *Pope Speaks* 39:1 (1994), 29–30.

26. Ibid., 58, in *AAS* 85 (1993), 1179–80; *EncMiller*, 622; *Origins* 23:18 (1993), 315; *Pope Speaks* 39:1 (1994), 33.
27. Ibid., 59, in *AAS* 85 (1993), 1180–81; *EncMiller*, 622–23; *ND*, 2080b; *Origins* 23:18 (1993), 315; *Pope Speaks* 39:1 (1994), 33.
28. Ibid., 62, in *AAS* 85 (1993), 1182; *EncMiller*, 624; *ND*, 2080d; *Origins* 23:18 (1993), 315; *Pope Speaks* 391 (1994), 34.
29. Ibid., 66, in *AAS* 85 (1993), 1185; *EncMiller*, 627; *ND*, 2081a; *Origins* 23:18 (1993), 317; *Pope Speaks* 39:1 (1994), 36–37.
30. Ibid., 67, in *AAS* 85 (1993), 1187; *EncMiller*, 628; *ND*, 2081b; *Origins* 23:18 (1993), 317; *Pope Speaks* 39:1 (1994), 37.
31. Ibid., 80, in *AAS* 85 (1993), 1197; *EncMiller*, 636; *ND*, 2082e; *Origins* 23:18 (1993), 321; *Pope Speaks* 39:1 (1994), 43.
32. Ibid., 112,113, in *AAS* 85 (1993), 1221–22; *EncMiller*, 655–56; *ND*, 2084a and b; *Origins* 23:18 (1993), 329–30; *Pope Speaks* 39:1 (1994), 56–57.
33. *Fides et ratio*, 68 and 98, in *AAS* 91 (1999), 57–58, 82; *EncMiller*, 890 and 908; *ND*, 2087, 2088; *Origins* 28:19 (1998), 335 and 343; *Pope Speaks* 44:1 (1999), 38 and 54.

CHAPTER TEN

The Social Doctrine
of the Church

10.1 In his first two encyclicals, *Redemptor hominis* (The Redeemer of the Human Person) of 1979 and *Dives in misericordia* (Rich in Mercy) of 1980, John Paul II expounded several themes that concern the social order. Technological and economic progress that ignore the demands of the proper social order become a threat (*Redemptor hominis*, 8). Respect for human rights and the dignity of labor promotes the common good. Justice without love is not enough.

Progress or Threat

Human beings of today seem to be ever under threat from what they produce, that is to say from the result of the work of their hands and, even more so, of the work of their intellect and the tendencies of their will. All too soon, and often in an unforeseeable way, what this manifold activity of human beings yields is not only subjected to "alienation," in the sense that it is simply taken away from the person who produces it, but rather it turns against human beings themselves, at least in part, through the indirect consequences of its effects returning on them. It is or can be directed against them. This seems to make up the main chapter of the drama of present-day human existence in its broadest and universal dimension. Human beings therefore live increasingly in fear. They are afraid that what they produce—not all of it, of course, or even most of it, but part of it and precisely that part that contains a special share of their genius and initiative—can radically turn against them; they are afraid that it can become the means and instrument for an unimaginable self-destruction, compared with which all the cataclysms and catastrophes of history known to us seem to fade away. This gives rise to a question: Why is it that the power given to human beings from the beginning by which they were to subdue the earth [Gen 1:28] turns against them, producing an understandable state of disquiet, of conscious or unconscious fear and of menace, which in various ways is being communicated to the whole of the present-day human family and is manifesting itself under various aspects?

This state of menace for human beings from what they produce shows itself in various directions and various degrees of intensity. We seem to be increasingly aware of the fact that the exploitation of the earth, the planet on which we are living, demands rational and honest planning. At the same time, exploitation of the earth not only for industrial but also for military purposes and the uncontrolled development of technology outside the framework of a long-range authentically humanistic plan often bring with them a threat to the natural environment of human beings, alienate them in their relations with nature and remove them from nature. They often seem to see no other meaning in their natural environment than what serves for immediate use and consumption. Yet it was the Creator's will that the human person should communicate with nature as an intelligent and noble "master" and "guardian," and not as a heedless "exploiter" and "destroyer."

The development of technology and the development of contemporary civilization, which is marked by the ascendancy of technology, demand a proportional development of morals and ethics.[1]

10.2 In various ways the 1981 encyclical *Laborem exercens* (Performing Work) developed the human aspect of work: for instance, the priority of labor over capital; just wages; the role of the State as the "indirect employer"; the spirituality of work. John Paul II also defended the rights of women, a theme to which he returned in the same year in his apostolic exhortation *Familiaris consortio* (The Family), 22–24.

The Personal Meaning of Work

The basis for determining the value of human work is not primarily the kind of work being done but the fact that the one who is doing it is a person. The sources of the dignity of work are to be sought primarily in the subjective dimension, not in the objective one.

Such a concept practically does away with the very basis of the ancient differentiation of people into classes according to the kind of work done. This does not mean that, from the objective point of view, human work cannot and must not be rated and qualified in any way. It only means that *the primary basis of the value of work is the human person*, who is its subject. This leads immediately to a very important conclusion of an ethical nature: however true it may be that human beings are destined for work and called to it, in the first place work is "for human beings" and not human beings "for work." Through this conclusion one rightly comes to recognize the pre-eminence of the subjective meaning of work over the objective one. Given this way of understanding things, and presupposing that different sorts of work that people do can have greater or lesser objective value, let us try nevertheless to show that each sort is judged above all by *the measure of the dignity* of the subject of work, that is to say the person, *the individual who carries it out*. On the other hand: independently of the work that every one does, and presupposing that this work constitutes a purpose, at times a very demanding one, of their activity, this purpose does not possess a definitive meaning in itself. In fact, in the final analysis it is always the human being who is *the purpose of the work*, whatever work it is that is done by a human being, even if the common scale of values rates it as the merest "service," as the most monotonous even the most alienating work.[2]

The Priority of Labor over Capital

The structure of the present-day situation is deeply marked by many conflicts caused by human beings, and the technological means produced by human work play a primary role in it. We should also consider here the prospect of worldwide catastrophe in the case of a nuclear war, which would have almost unimaginable possibilities of destruction. In view of this situation we must first of all recall a principle that has always been taught by the Church: *the principle of the priority of labor over capital*. This principle directly concerns the process of production: in this process labor is always a primary *efficient cause*, while capital, the whole collection of means of production, remains a mere *instrument* or instrumental cause. This principle is an evident truth that emerges from the whole of the historical experience of human beings....

Since the concept of capital includes not only the natural resources placed at the disposal of human beings but also the whole collection of means by which they appropriate natural resources and transforms them in accordance with their needs (and thus in a sense humanizes them), it must immediately be noted that *all these means are the result of the historical heritage of human labor.*[3]

Human Development in Relation to Nature

Working at any workbench, whether a relatively primitive or an ultramodern one, human beings can easily see that *through their work they enter into two inheritances*: the inheritance of what is given to the whole of humanity in the resources of nature, and the inheritance of what others have already developed on the basis of those resources, primarily by developing technology, that is to say, by producing a whole collection of increasingly perfect instruments for work. In working, the human person also "enters into the labor of others." Guided both by our intelligence and by the faith that draws light from the word of God, we have no difficulty in accepting this image of the sphere and process of human labor. It is *a consistent image, one that is humanistic as well as theological.* In it human beings are the masters of the creatures placed at their disposal in the visible world. If some dependence is discovered in the work process, it is dependence on the Giver of all the resources of creation, and also on other human beings, those to whose work and initiative we owe the perfected and increased possibilities of our own work. All that we can say of everything in the production process which constitutes a whole collection of "things," the instruments, the capital, is that it *conditions* human work; we cannot assert that it constitutes as it were an impersonal "subject" *putting* human beings and human work *into a position of dependence.*[4]

Workers Sharing Management and Ownership

While the position of "rigid" capitalism must undergo continual revision...it must be stated that, from the same point of view, these many deeply desired reforms cannot be achieved by an *a priori elimination of private ownership of the means of production....*

Merely converting the means of production into state property in the collectivist system is by no means equivalent to "socializing" that property. We can speak of socializing only when the subject character of society is ensured, that is to say, when on the basis of his work each person is fully entitled to consider himself a part-owner of the great workbench at which he or she is working with every one else.[5]

The Indirect Employer

The concept of indirect employer includes both persons and institutions of various kinds, and also collective labor contracts and the *principles* of conduct which are laid down by these persons and institutions and which determine the whole socioeconomic *system* or are its result. The concept of "indirect employer" thus refers to many different elements. The responsibility of the indirect employer differs from that of the direct employer (the term itself indicates that the responsibility is less direct) but it remains a true responsibility: the indirect employer substantially determines one or other facet of the labor relationship, thus conditioning the conduct of the direct employer when the latter determines in concrete terms the actual work contract and labor relations. This is not to absolve the direct employer from his own responsibility, but only to draw attention to the whole network of influences that condition his conduct. When it is a question of establishing an *ethically correct labor policy*, all these influences must be kept in mind. A policy is correct when the objective rights of the worker are fully respected.[6]

Just Wage as Criterion of Justice

It should also be noted that the justice of a socioeconomic system and, in each case, its just functioning, deserve in the final analysis to be evaluated by the way in which human work is properly remunerated in the system. Here we return once more to the first principle of the whole ethical and social order, namely, *the principle of the common use of goods*. In every system, regardless of the fundamental relationships within it between capital and labor, wages, that is to say *remuneration for work*, are still a *practical means* whereby the vast majority of people can have access to those goods which are intended for common use: both the goods of nature and manufactured goods.[7]

No Discrimination against Women

The whole labor process must be organized and adapted in such a way as to respect the requirements of the person and his or her forms of life, above all life in the home, taking into account the individual's age and sex. It is a fact that in many societies women work in nearly every sector of life. But it is fitting that they should be able to fulfill their tasks *in accordance with their own nature*, without being discriminated against and without being excluded from jobs for which they are capable, but also without lack of respect for their family aspirations and for their specific role in contributing, together with men, to the good of society. The *true advancement of women* requires that labor should be structured in such a way that women do not have to pay for their advancement by abandoning what is specific to them and at the expense of the family, in which women as mothers have an irreplaceable role.[8]

Through Labor, Humans Participate in the Projects of Creation and Redemption

The word of God's revelation is profoundly marked by the fundamental truth that *human beings*, created in the image of God, *share by their work in the activity of the Creator* and that, within the limits of their own human capabilities, they in a sense continue to develop that activity, and perfect it as they advance further and further in the discovery of the resources and values contained in the whole of creation....

The truth that by means of work human beings participate in the activity of God himself, their Creator, was *given particular prominence by Jesus Christ*....For Jesus not only proclaimed but first and foremost fulfilled by his deeds the "gospel," the word of eternal Wisdom, that had been entrusted to him. Therefore this was also "the gospel of work," because *he who proclaimed it was himself a man of work*, a craftsman like Joseph of Nazareth....It can indeed be said that *he looks with love upon human work* and the different forms that it takes, seeing in each one of these forms a particular facet of human likeness with God, the Creator and Father....

The Christian finds in human work a small part of the Cross of Christ and accepts it in the same spirit of redemption in which Christ accepted his Cross for us. In work, thanks to the light that penetrates us from the Resurrection of Christ, we always find a *glimmer* of new life, of the *new good*, as if it were an announcement of "the new heavens and the new earth" (cf. 2 Pet 3:13; Rev 21:1)....On the one hand, this confirms the indispensability of the Cross in the spirituality of human work; on the other hand, the Cross which this toil constitutes reveals a new good springing from work itself, from work understood in depth and in all its aspects and never apart from work.[9]

Dignity, Rights, and Responsibility of Women

Above all it is important to underline the equal dignity and responsibility of women with men. This equality is realized in a unique manner in that reciprocal self-giving by each one to the other and by both to the children which is proper to marriage and the family. What human reason intuitively perceives and acknowledges is fully revealed by the word of God: the history of salvation, in fact, is a continuous and luminous testimony to the dignity of women....

There is no doubt that the equal dignity and responsibility of men and women fully justify women's access to public functions. On the other hand, the true advancement of women requires that clear recognition be given to the value of their maternal and family role, by comparison with all other public roles and all other professions. Furthermore, these roles and professions should be harmoniously combined, if we wish the evolution of society and culture to be truly and fully human....With due respect to the different vocations of men and women, the Church must in her own life promote as far as possible their equality of rights and dignity: and this for the good of all, the family, the Church and society.

But clearly all of this does not mean for women a renunciation of their femininity or an imitation of the male role, but the fullness of true feminine humanity which should be expressed in their activity, whether in the family or outside of it, without disregarding the differences of customs and cultures in this sphere.[10]

(In the 1988 apostolic letter *Mulieris dignitatem* [The Dignity of a Woman], John Paul II was to argue that the true liberation of women "must not under any condition lead to the 'masculinization' of women." This would deform women who would *"lose what constitutes their essential richness."*[11])

10.3 Among the most important pieces of Catholic social teaching, the 1987 encyclical *Sollicitudo rei socialis* (Concern for Social Matters) took up issues connected with world development: the suffering of developing countries, the promotion of interdependence and total human development, respect for creation, social "structures of sin" (a phrase used nine times in nos. 36–39), and the duty of solidarity.

Human Underdevelopment

However, the picture just given would be incomplete if one failed to add to the "economic and social indices" of underdevelopment other indices which are equally negative and indeed even more disturbing, beginning with the cultural level. These are illiteracy, the difficulty or impossibility of obtaining higher education, the inability to share in the building of one's own nation, the various forms of exploitation and of economic, social, political and even religious oppression of the individual and his or her rights, discrimination of every type, especially the exceptionally odious form based on difference of race....In brief, modern underdevelopment is not only economic but also cultural, political and simply human, as was indicated twenty years ago by the Encyclical *Populorum progressio*. Hence at this point we have to ask ourselves if the sad reality of today might not be, at least in part, the result of a too narrow idea of development, that is, a mainly economic one.[12]

Developing Countries

Countries which have recently achieved independence, and which are trying to establish a cultural and political identity of their own, and need effective and impartial aid from all the richer and more developed countries, find themselves involved in, and sometimes overwhelmed by, ideological conflicts, which inevitably create internal divisions, to the extent in some cases of provoking full civil war. This is also because investments and aid for development are often diverted from their proper purpose and used to sustain conflicts, apart from and in opposition to the interests of the countries which ought to benefit from them.[13]

Growing Awareness of Interdependence

In a world divided and beset by every type of conflict, the conviction is growing of a radical interdependence and consequently of the need for a solidarity which will take up interdependence and transfer it to the moral plane. Today perhaps more than in the past, people are realizing that they are linked together by a common destiny, which is to be constructed together, if catastrophe for all is to be avoided. From the depth of anguish, fear and escapist phenomena like drugs, typical of the contemporary world, the idea is slowly emerging that the good to which we are all called and the happiness to which we aspire cannot be obtained without an effort and commitment on the part of all, nobody excluded, and the consequent renouncing of personal selfishness.[14]

Need for Integral Development

The "economic" concept itself, linked to the word development, has entered into crisis. In fact there is a better understanding today that the mere accumulation of goods and services, even for the benefit of the majority, is not enough for the realization of human happiness. Nor, in consequence, does the availability of the many real benefits provided in recent times by science and technology, including the computer sciences, bring freedom from every form of slavery. On the contrary, the experience of recent years shows that unless all the considerable body of resources and potential at human disposal is guided by a moral understanding and by an orientation towards the true good of the human race, it easily turns against human beings to oppress them.

A disconcerting conclusion about the most recent period should serve to enlighten us: side-by-side with the miseries of underdevelopment, themselves unacceptable, we find ourselves up against a form of super-development, equally inadmissible, because like the former it is contrary to what is good and to true happiness. This super-development, which consists in an excessive availability of every kind of material goods for the benefit of certain social groups, easily makes people slaves of "possession" and of immediate gratification, with no other horizon than the multiplication or continual replacement of the things already owned with others still better....

This then is the picture: there are some people—the few who possess much—who do not really succeed in "being" because, through a reversal of the hierarchy of values, they are hindered by the cult of "having"; and there are others—the many who have little or nothing—who do not succeed in realizing their basic human vocation because they are deprived of essential goods....

Peoples or nations too have a right to their own full development, which while including, as already said, the economic and social aspects, should also include individual cultural identity and openness to the transcendent. Not even the need for development can be used as an excuse for imposing on others one's own way of life or own religious belief.[15]

Respect for Creation

The moral character of development cannot exclude respect for the beings which constitute the natural world...called the "cosmos." Such realities also demand respect, by virtue of a threefold consideration which it is useful to reflect upon carefully. The first consideration is the appropriateness of acquiring a growing awareness of the fact that one cannot use with impunity the different categories of beings, whether living or inanimate—animals, plants, the natural elements—simply as one wishes, according to one's own economic needs. On the contrary, one must take into account the nature of each being and of its mutual connection in an ordered system, which is precisely the cosmos.

The second consideration is based on the realization...that natural resources are limited; some are not, as it is said, renewable. Using them as if they were inexhaustible, with absolute dominion, seriously endangers their availability not only for the present generation but above all for generations to come. The third consideration refers directly to the consequences of a certain type of development on the quality of life in the industrialized zones. We all know that the direct or indirect result of industrialization is, ever more frequently, the pollution of the environment, with serious consequences for the health of the population.

Once again it is evident that development, the planning which governs it, and the way in which resources are used must include respect for moral demands. One of the latter undoubtedly imposes limits on the use of the natural world…we are subject not only to biological laws but also to moral ones, which cannot be violated with impunity. A true concept of development cannot ignore the use of the elements of nature, the renewability of resources and the consequences of haphazard industrialization—three considerations which alert our consciences to the moral dimension of development.[16]

Sinful Structures

"Sin" and "structures of sin" are categories which are seldom applied to the situation of the contemporary world. However, one cannot easily gain a profound understanding of the reality that confronts us, unless we give a name to the root of the evils which afflict us. One can certainly speak of "selfishness," of "shortsightedness," of "mistaken political calculations," and of "imprudent economic decisions." And in each of these evaluations one hears an echo of an ethical and moral nature. The human condition is such that a more profound analysis of individuals' actions and omissions cannot be achieved without implying, in one way or another, judgments or references of an ethical nature….

The exercise of solidarity within each society is valid when its members recognize one another as persons. Those who are more influential, because they have a greater share of goods and common services, should feel responsible for the weaker and be ready to share with them all they possess. Those who are weaker, for their part, in the same spirit of solidarity, should not adopt a purely passive attitude or one that is destructive of the social fabric, but, while claiming their legitimate rights, should do what they can for the good of all. The intermediate groups, in their turn, should not selfishly insist on their particular interests, but respect the interests of others….

The "structures of sin" and the sins which they produce are likewise radically opposed to peace and development, for development, in the familiar expression of Pope Paul's encyclical [*Populorum progressio*], is "the new name for peace."[17]

Interdependence and Solidarity

It is above all a question of interdependence, sensed as a system determining relationships in the contemporary world, in its economic, cultural, political and religious elements, and accepted as a moral category. When interdependence becomes recognized in this way, the correlative response as a moral and social attitude, as a "virtue," is solidarity. This then is not a feeling of vague compassion or shallow distress at the misfortunes of so many people, both near and far. On the contrary, it is a firm and persevering determination to commit oneself to the common good; that is to say to the good of all and of each individual, because we are all really responsible for all. This determination is based on the solid conviction that what is hindering full development is that desire for profit and that thirst for power already mentioned. These attitudes and "structures of sin" are only conquered (presupposing the help of divine grace) by a diametrically opposed attitude: a commitment to the good of one's neighbor with the readiness, in the gospel sense, to "lose oneself" for the sake of the other instead of exploiting him, and to "serve him" instead of oppressing him for one's own advantage (cf. Matt 10:40–42; 20:25; Mark 10:42–45; Luke 22:25–27)....

Solidarity, therefore, must play its part in the realization of this divine plan, both on the level of individuals and on the level of national and international society. The "evil mechanisms" and "structures of sin" of which we have spoken can be overcome only through the exercise of the human and Christian solidarity to which the Church calls us and which she tirelessly promotes.[18]

Nature of the Church's Social Teaching

The Church's social doctrine is not a "third way" between liberal capitalism and Marxist collectivism, nor even a possible alternative to other solutions less radically opposed to one another: rather, it constitutes a category of its own. Nor is it an ideology, but rather the accurate formulation of the results of a careful reflection on the complex realities of human existence, in society and in the international order, in the light of faith and of the Church's tradition. Its main aim is to interpret these realities, determining their conformity with or divergence from the lines of the Gospel teaching on human beings and their vocation, a vocation which is at once earthly and transcendent; its aim is thus to guide Christian behavior. It therefore belongs to the field, not of ideology, but of theology and particularly of moral theology.[19]

Preferential Option for the Poor

Today, furthermore, given the worldwide dimension which the social question has assumed, this love of preference for the poor, and the decisions which it inspires in us, cannot but embrace the immense multitudes of the hungry, the needy, the homeless, those without medical care and, above all, those without hope of a better future. It is impossible not to take account of the existence of these realities. To ignore them would mean becoming like the "rich man" who pretended not to know the beggar Lazarus lying at his gate (cf. Luke 16:19–31).[20]

10.4 One hundred years after the landmark encyclical of Pope Leo XIII, *Rerum novarum* (Of New Things) and on the occasion of the collapse of European Communism, John Paul II issued his third great social encyclical, *Centesimus annus* (The Hundredth Year). It took up such themes as solidarity, peace, love and justice toward the poor, the free market economy, profit and human dignity, ecology, and democracy.

Solidarity

What we nowadays call the principle of solidarity…is clearly seen to be one of the fundamental principles of the Christian view of social and political organization. This principle is frequently stated by

Pope Leo XIII, who uses the term *friendship*, a concept already found in Greek philosophy. Pope Pius XI refers to it with the equally meaningful term *social charity*. Pope Paul VI, expanding the concept to cover the many modern aspects of the social question, speaks of a *civilization of love*.[21]

True Peace

It must be remembered that true peace is never simply the result of military victory, but rather implies both the removal of the causes of war and genuine reconciliation between peoples....I myself, on the occasion of the recent tragic war in the Persian Gulf, repeated the cry: "Never again war!" No, never again war, which destroys the lives of innocent people, teaches how to kill, throws into upheaval even the lives of those who do the killing and leaves behind a trail of resentment and hatred, thus making it all the more difficult to find a just solution of the very problems which provoked the war....

For this reason, another name for peace is *development*. Just as there is a collective responsibility for avoiding war, so too there is a collective responsibility for promoting development. Just as within individual societies it is possible and right to organize a solid economy which will direct the functioning of the market to the common good, so too there is a similar need for adequate interventions on the international level. For this to happen, *a great effort must be made to enhance mutual understanding and knowledge, and to increase the sensitivity of consciences*.[22]

The Marginalization of the Poor

It will be necessary above all to abandon a mentality in which the poor, as individuals and as peoples, are considered a burden, as irksome intruders trying to consume what others have produced.... The advancement of the poor constitutes a great opportunity for the moral, cultural and even economic growth of all humanity....

The risks and problems connected with this kind of process [modern business economy] should be pointed out....[For] many people...have no possibility of acquiring the basic knowledge which would enable them to express their creativity and develop their potential. They have no way of entering the network of knowledge and intercommunication which would enable them to see their qualities appreciated and utilized. Thus, if not actually exploited, they are to a great extent marginalized; economic development takes place over their heads, so to speak, when it does not actually reduce the already narrow scope of their old subsistence economies. They are unable to compete against the goods which are produced in ways which are new and which properly respond to needs, needs which they had previously been accustomed to meeting through traditional forms of organization. Allured by the dazzle of an opulence which is beyond their reach, and at the same time driven by necessity, these people crowd the cities of the Third World where they are often without cultural roots, and where they are exposed to situations of violent uncertainty, without the possibility of becoming integrated....

In spite of the great changes which have taken place in the more advanced societies, the human inadequacies of capitalism and the resulting domination of things over people are far from disappearing. In fact, for the poor, to the lack of material goods has been added a lack of knowledge and training which prevents them from escaping their state of humiliating subjection.... Unfortunately, the great majority of people in the Third World still live in such conditions. It would be a mistake, however, to understand this *"world"* in purely geographic terms.[23]

Free Market Economy, the Third World, and Profit

It would appear that, on the level of individual nations and of international relations, the *free market* is the most efficient instrument for utilizing resources and effectively responding to needs. But this is true only for those needs which are "solvent," insofar as they are endowed with purchasing power, and for those resources which are "marketable," insofar as they are capable of obtaining a satisfactory price. But there are many human needs which find no place on the market. It is a strict duty of justice and truth not to allow fundamental human needs to remain unsatisfied, and not to allow those burdened by such needs to perish. It is also necessary to help these needy people to acquire expertise, to enter the circle of exchange, and to develop their skills in order to make the best use of their capacities and resources....In Third World contexts, certain objectives stated by *Rerum novarum* [by Leo XIII] remain valid, and, in some cases, still constitute a goal yet to be reached, if human work and the very being of humans are not to be reduced to the level of a mere commodity. These objectives include a sufficient wage for the support of the family, social insurance for old age and unemployment, and adequate protection for the conditions of employment....

The Church acknowledges the legitimate *role of profit* as an indication that a business is functioning well....But profitability is not the only indicator of a firm's condition. It is possible for the financial accounts to be in order, and yet for the people, who make up the firm's most valuable asset, to be humiliated and their dignity offended....The purpose of a business firm is not simply to make a profit, but is to be found in its very existence as a *community of persons* who in various ways are endeavoring to satisfy their basic needs, and who form a particular group at the service of the whole of society. Profit is a regulator of the life of a business, but it is not the only one; *other human and moral factors* must also be considered....It is unacceptable to say that the defeat of so-called "Real Socialism" leaves capitalism as the only model of economic organization. It is necessary to break down the barriers and monopolies which leave so many countries on the margins of development, and to provide all individuals and nations with the basic conditions which will enable them to share in development.[24]

Natural and Human Ecology

At the root of the senseless destruction of the natural environment lies an anthropological error....Human beings, who discover their capacity to transform and in a certain sense create the world through their own work, forget that this is always based on God's prior and original gift of the things that are....Instead of carrying out their role as co-operators with God in the work of creation, they set themselves up in place of God and thus end up provoking a rebellion on the part of nature, which is more tyrannized than governed by them....

Too little effort is made to *safeguard the moral conditions for an authentic "human ecology."* Not only has God given the earth to human beings, who must use it with respect for the original good purpose for which it was given to them, but humanity too is God's gift to human beings. The first and fundamental structure for "human ecology" is the family, in which human beings receive their first formative ideas about truth and goodness, and learn what it means to love and to be loved, and thus what it actually means to be a person.[25]

The Social Teaching of the Church

The Church has no models to present; models that are real and truly effective can only arise within the framework of different historical situations, through the efforts of all those who responsibly confront concrete problems in all their social, economic, political and cultural aspects, as these interact with one another (*Gaudium et spes*, 36). For such a task the Church offers her social teaching as an *indispensable and ideal orientation*, a teaching which, as already mentioned, recognizes the positive value of the market and of enterprise, but which at the same time points out that these need to be oriented towards the common good.[26]

Democratic Systems

The Church values the democratic system inasmuch as it ensures the participation of citizens in making political choices, guarantees to the governed the possibility both of electing and holding accountable those who govern them, and of replacing them through peaceful means when appropriate....Nowadays there is a tendency to claim that agnosticism and skeptical relativism are the philosophy and the basic attitude which correspond to democratic forms of political life. Those who are convinced that they know the truth and firmly adhere to it are considered unreliable from a democratic point of view, since they do not accept that truth is determined by the majority, or that it is subject to variation according to different political trends. It must be observed in this regard that if there is no ultimate truth to guide and direct political activity, then ideas and convictions can easily be manipulated for reasons of power. As history demonstrates, a democracy without values easily turns into open or thinly disguised totalitarianism.

But freedom attains its full development only by accepting the truth. In a world without truth, freedom loses its foundation and human beings are exposed to the violence of passion and to manipulation, both open and hidden. Christians uphold freedom and serve it, constantly offering to others the truth which they have known (cf. John 8:31–32), in accordance with the missionary nature of their vocation.…The Church respects *the legitimate autonomy of the democratic order* and is not entitled to express preferences for this or that institutional or constitutional solution. Her contribution to the political order is precisely her vision of the dignity of the person revealed in all its fullness in the mystery of the Incarnate Word.[27]

Rights to Food, Clothing, Shelter, Family Life, and Health Care

Among the most important of these rights, mention must be made of the right to life, an integral part of which is the right of the child to develop in the mother's womb from the moment of conception; the right to live in a united family and in a moral environment conducive to the growth of the child's personality; the right to develop one's intelligence and freedom in seeking and knowing the truth; the right to share in the work which makes wise use of the earth's material resources, and to derive from that work the means to support oneself and one's dependents; and the right freely to establish a family, to have and to rear children through the responsible exercise of one's sexuality. In a certain sense, the source and synthesis of these rights is religious freedom, understood as the right to live in the truth of one's faith and in conformity with one's transcendent dignity as a person....

In order to overcome today's widespread individualistic mentality, what is required is *a concrete commitment to solidarity and charity*, beginning in the family with the mutual support of husband and wife and the care which the different generations give to one another. In this sense the family too can be called a community of work and solidarity....A great effort must be made to enhance mutual understanding and knowledge, and to increase the sensitivity of consciences. This is the culture which is hoped for, one which fosters trust in the human potential of the poor, and consequently in their ability to improve their condition through work or to make a positive contribution to economic prosperity.[28]

Justice and Love for the Poor

Love for others, and in the first place love for the poor, in whom the Church sees Christ himself, is made concrete in the *promotion of justice*. Justice will never be fully attained unless people see in the poor person, who is asking for help in order to survive, not an annoyance or a burden, but an opportunity for showing kindness and a chance for greater enrichment. Only such an awareness can give the courage needed to face the risk and the change involved in every authentic attempt to come to the aid of another. It is not merely a matter of "giving from one's surplus," but of helping entire peoples which are presently excluded or marginalized to enter into the sphere of economic and human development.[29]

10.5 In various addresses to diplomats, messages for World Peace Days, and in other texts, John Paul II constantly pleaded against the proliferation of nuclear weapons and for the cause of world peace. We take one example from an address to the diplomatic corps accredited to the Holy See (January 13, 1997).

Disarmament and Peace

Peace cannot be just nor can it long endure unless it rests upon sincere dialogue between equal partners, with respect for each other's identity and history, unless it rests on the right of peoples to the free determination of their own destiny, upon their independence and security. There can be no exception.

What the international community perhaps lacks most of all today is not written conventions or forums for self-expression—there is a profusion of these—but a moral law and the courage to abide by it. The community of nations, like every human society, cannot escape this basic principle. It must be regulated by a rule of law valid for all of them without exception. Every juridical system, as we know, has as its foundation and end the common good. And this applies to the international community as well: the good of all and the good of the whole. This is what makes possible equitable solutions in which gain is not made at the expense of the others, even when those who benefit are the majority. Justice is for all, without injustice being inflicted on anyone. The function of law is to give each person their due, to give what is owed to them in justice. Law therefore has a strong moral implication.[30]

10.6 Among other issues within the social teaching of the Catholic Church, John Paul II also addressed the themes of globalization and foreign debt in his apostolic exhortation *Ecclesia in America* (The Church in America) of January 22, 1999.

Cultural Globalization and External Debt

There is an economic globalization which brings some positive consequences....However, if globalization is ruled merely by the laws of the market applied to suit the powerful, the consequences cannot but be negative. While acknowledging the positive values which come with globalization, the Church considers with concern the negative aspects which follow in its wake. And what should we say about the cultural globalization produced by the power of the media? Everywhere the media impose new scales of values which are often arbitrary and basically materialistic, in the face of which it is difficult to maintain a lively commitment to the values of the Gospel....

Among the causes which have helped to create massive external debt are not only high interest rates, caused by speculative financial policies, but also the irresponsibility of people in government who, in incurring debt, have given too little thought to the real possibility of repaying it. This has been aggravated by the fact that huge sums obtained through international loans sometimes go to enrich individuals instead of being used to pay for the changes needed for the country's development. At the same time, it would be unjust to impose the burden resulting from these irresponsible decisions upon those who did not make them.[31]

NOTES

1. *Redemptor hominis*, 15, in *AAS* 71 (1979), 286–87; *EncMiller*, 66; *ND*, 2172; *Origins* 8:40 (1979), 634; *Pope Speaks* 24:2 (1979), 119–20.

2. *Laborem exercens*, 6, in *AAS* 73 (1981), 591–92; *EncMiller*, 161–62; *ND*, 2175; *Origins* 11:3 (1981), 230; *Pope Speaks*, 26:4 (1981), 298–99.

3. Ibid., 12, in *AAS* 73 (1981), 605–7; *EncMiller*, 169–70; *ND*, 2176; *Origins* 11:3 (1981), 233–34; *Pope Speaks*, 26:4 (1981), 307–8.

4. Ibid., 13, in *AAS* 73 (1981), 609–10; *EncMiller*, 171; *Origins* 11:3 (1981), 234; *Pope Speaks* 26:4 (1981), 309–10.

5. Ibid., 14, in *AAS* 73 (1981), 615–16; *EncMiller*, 174–75; *ND*, 2177; *Origins* 11:3 (1981), 236; *Pope Speaks* 26:4 (1981), 314.

6. Ibid., 17, in *AAS* 73 (1981), 620; *EncMiller*, 177; *Origins* 11:3 (1981), 237; *Pope Speaks* 26:4 (1981), 317.

7. Ibid., 19, in *AAS* 73 (1981), 626; *EncMiller*, 180; *ND*, 2178; *Origins* 11:3 (1981), 238; *Pope Speaks* 26:4 (1981), 321.

8. Ibid., 19, in *AAS* 73 (1981), 628; *EncMiller*, 181; *ND*, 2179: *Origins* 11:3 (1981), 239; *Pope Speaks* 26:4 (1981).

9. Ibid., 25–27, in *AAS* 73 (1981), 638–46; *EncMiller* 187, 192; *ND*, 2180; *Origins* 11:3 (1981), 241–43; *Pope Speaks* 26:4 (1981), 329–35.

10. *Familiaris consortio*, 22–23, in *AAS* 74 (1982), 107–9; *ApExMiller*, 168–70; *ND*, 2181; *Origins* 11:28–29 (1981), 445–46; *Pope Speaks* 27:1 (1982), 19–20.

11. *Mulieris dignitatem*, 10, in *AAS* 80 (1988), 1676; *Origins* 18:16 (1988), 269; *Pope Speaks* 34:1 (1989), 22.

12. *Sollicitudo rei socialis*, 15, in *AAS* 80 (1988), 528–30; *EncMiller*, 388–89; *Origins* 17:3 (1988), 646; *Pope Speaks* 33:2 (1988), 129–30.

13. Ibid., 21, in *AAS* 80 (1988), 538; *EncMiller*, 393; *ND*, 2188; *Origins* 17:3 (1988), 648; *Pope Speaks* 33:2 (1988), 133.

14. Ibid., 26, in *AAS* 80 (1988), 545; *EncMiller*, 397; *ND*, 2189; *Origins* 17:3 (1988), 649; *Pope Speaks* 33:2 (1988), 136.

15. Ibid., 28, 32, in *AAS* 80 (1988), 548–50, 557; *EncMiller* 398–99, 403; *ND*, 2189a and b; *Origins* 17:3 (1988), 650, 652; *Pope Speaks* 33:2 (1988), 137–38, 143.

16. Ibid., 34, in *AAS* 80 (1988), 559–60; *EncMiller*, 405; *ND*, 2189c; *Origins* 17:3 (1988), 653; *Pope Speaks* 33:2 (1988), 143.

17. Ibid., 36, 39, in *AAS* 80 (1988), 562, 566–67; *EncMiller*, 407, 409; *Origins* 17:3 (1988), 653, 654–55; *Pope Speaks* 33:2 (1988), 144, 146–47.

18. Ibid., 38, 40, in *AAS* 80 (1988), 565–66, 569; *EncMiller*, 408–9, 411; *Origins* 17:3 (1988), 654, 655; *Pope Speaks* 33:2 (1988), 146, 148. In his

1979 encyclical *Redemptor hominis*, John Paul II had already proposed "the principle of solidarity" (no. 16).

19. Ibid., 41, in *AAS* 80 (1988), 571; *EncMiller*, 412; *ND*, 2191; *Origins* 17:3 (1988), 655–56; *Pope Speaks* 33:2 (1988), 149.

20. Ibid., 42, in *AAS* 80 (1988), 572–73; *EncMiller*, 412; *Origins* 17:3 (1988), 656; *Pope Speaks* 33:2 (1988), 149.

21. *Centesimus annus*, 10, in *AAS* 83 (1991), 805–6; *EncMiller* 520; *ND*, 2193; *Origins* 21:1 (1991), 6; *Pope Speaks* 36:5 (1991), 279–80.

22. Ibid., 18, 52, in *AAS* 83 (1991), 815, 857–58; *EncMiller*, 526, 554–55; *Origins* 21:1 (1991), 8, 20; *Pope Speaks* 36:5 (1991), 284, 305–6.

23. Ibid., 28, 33, in *AAS* 83 (1991), 828, 834–35; *EncMiller*, 535, 538–39; *ND*, 2194b, 2194e, 2194f; *Origins* 21:1 (1991) 12, 13–14; *Pope Speaks* 36:5 (1991), 291, 293–94.

24. Ibid., 34–35, in *AAS* 83 (1991), 835–37; *EncMiller*, 540, 541; *ND*, 2194g, 2194h; *Origins* 21:1 (1991), 14; *Pope Speaks* 36:5 (1991), 194–95.

25. Ibid., 37–39, in *AAS* 83 (1991), 840–41; *EncMiller* 543–44; *ND*, 2195c; *Origins* 21:1 (1991), 15; *Pope Speaks* 36:5 (1991), 296–97.

26. Ibid., 43, in *AAS* 83 (1991), 846; *EncMiller*, 547; *ND*, 2196a; *Origins* 21:1 (1991), 17; *Pope Speaks* 36:5 (1991), 300.

27. Ibid., 46–47, in *AAS* 83 (1991), 850–51, 852; *EncMiller*, 549–51; *ND*, 2196b and c; *Origins* 21:1 (1991), 18; *Pope Speaks* 35:5 (1991), 301–3.

28. Ibid., 47, 49, 52, in *AAS* 83(1991), 851–52, 855, 858; *Origins* 21:1 (1991), 18–20; *EncMiller*, 550, 553, 555; *Pope Speaks* 36:5 (1991), 302, 304, 306.

29. Ibid., 58, in *AAS* 83 (1991), 863; *EncMiller*, 558; *ND*, 2197c; *Origins* 21:1 (1991), 21; *Pope Speaks* 36:5 (1991), 308.

30. *Address to the Diplomatic Corps*, in *AAS* 89 (1997), 471–73; *ND*, 2198 e and f; *Origins* 26:32 (1997), 521–23; *Pope Speaks* 42:5 (1997), 258–60.

31. *Ecclesia in America*, 20, 22, in *AAS* 91 (1999), 756, 758; *ND*, 2199d; *Origins* 28:33 (1999), 573; *Pope Speaks* 44:4 (1999), 216–17.

CHAPTER ELEVEN

Respect for Life

In his 1995 encyclical *Evangelium vitae* (The Gospel of Life), John Paul II championed the inviolability of human life and strongly rejected the "culture of death" (no. 12), manifested especially in euthanasia (no. 64) and in abortion, "a tyrannical decision with regard to the weakest and most defenseless of human beings" (no. 70). He took a more restrictive position on the death penalty than previous official teaching.

Crimes against Life

Decisions that go against life sometimes arise from difficult or even tragic situations of profound suffering, loneliness, a total lack of economic prospects, depression and anxiety about the future. Such circumstances can mitigate even to a notable degree subjective responsibility and the consequent culpability of those who make these choices which in themselves are evil. But today the problem goes far beyond the necessary recognition of these personal situations. It is a problem which exists at the cultural, social and political level, where it reveals its more sinister and disturbing aspect in the tendency, ever more widely shared, to interpret the above crimes against life as legitimate expressions of individual freedom, to be acknowledged and protected as actual rights.

In this way, and with tragic consequences, a long historical process is reaching a turning-point. The process which once led to discovering the idea of "human rights," rights inherent in every person and prior to any Constitution and State legislation, is today marked by a surprising contradiction. Precisely in an age when the inviolable rights of the person are solemnly proclaimed and the value of life is publicly affirmed, the very right to life is being denied or trampled upon, especially at the more significant moments of existence: the moment of birth and the moment of death.[1]

War and the Death Penalty

Among the signs of hope we should also count the spread, at many levels of public opinion, of a new sensitivity ever more opposed to war as an instrument for the resolution of conflicts between peoples, and increasingly oriented to finding effective but "non-violent" means to counter the armed aggressor. In the same perspective there is evidence of a growing public opposition to the death penalty, even when such a penalty is seen as a kind of "legitimate defense" on the part of society. Modern society in fact has the means of effectively suppressing crime by rendering criminals harmless without definitively denying them the chance to reform....

Public authority must redress the violation of personal and social rights by imposing on the offender an adequate punishment for the crime, as a condition for the offender to regain the exercise of his or her freedom. In this way authority also fulfills the purpose of defending public order and ensuring people's safety, while at the same time offering the offender an incentive and help to change his or her behavior and be rehabilitated (cf. *Catechism of the Catholic Church*, no. 2266).

It is clear that, for these purposes to be achieved, the nature and extent of the punishment must be carefully evaluated and decided upon, and ought not go to the extreme of executing the offender except in cases of absolute necessity: in other words, when it would not be possible otherwise to defend society. Today, however, as a result of steady improvements in the organization of the penal system, such cases are very rare, if not practically non-existent.[2]

Authoritative Rejection of Abortion

By the authority which Christ conferred upon Peter and his successors, in communion with the Bishops—who on various occasions have condemned abortion and who in the aforementioned consultation, albeit dispersed throughout the world, have shown unanimous agreement concerning this doctrine—I declare that direct abortion, that is, abortion willed as an end or as a means, always constitutes a grave moral disorder, since it is the deliberate killing of an innocent human being. This doctrine is based upon the natural law and upon the written Word of God, transmitted by the Church's Tradition and taught by the ordinary and universal Magisterium (*Lumen gentium*, 25).[3]

Human Embryos Not to Be Objects of Experimentation

The use of human embryos or fetuses as an object of experimentation constitutes a crime against their dignity as human beings who have a right to the same respect owed to a child once born, just as to every person.[4]

Euthanasia Differs from Disproportionate Means of Prolonging Life

The temptation grows to have recourse to euthanasia, that is, to take control of death and bring it about before its time, "gently" ending one's own life or the life of others. In reality, what might seem logical and humane, when looked at more closely is seen to be senseless and inhumane. Here we are faced with one of the more alarming symptoms of the "culture of death," which is advancing above all in prosperous societies, marked by an attitude of excessive preoccupation with efficiency and which sees the growing number of elderly and disabled people as intolerable and too burdensome. These people are very often isolated by their families and by society, which are organized almost exclusively on the basis of criteria of productive efficiency, according to which a hopelessly impaired life no longer has any value.

For a correct moral judgment on euthanasia, in the first place a clear definition is required. Euthanasia in the strict sense is understood to be an action or omission which of itself and by intention causes death, with the purpose of eliminating all suffering. "Euthanasia's terms of reference, therefore, are to be found in the intention of the will and in the methods used" (Congregation for the Doctrine of the Faith, Declaration on Euthanasia *Iura et Bona* [May 5, 1980]).

Euthanasia must be distinguished from the decision to forego so-called "aggressive medical treatment," in other words, medical procedures which no longer correspond to the real situation of the patient, either because they are by now disproportionate to any expected results or because they impose an excessive burden on the patient and his family. In such situations, when death is clearly imminent and inevitable, one can in conscience "refuse forms of treatment that would only secure a precarious and burdensome prolongation of life, so long as the normal care due to the sick person in similar cases is not interrupted" (*ibid.*). Certainly there is a moral obligation to care for oneself and to allow oneself to be cared for, but this duty must take account of concrete circumstances. It needs to be determined whether the means of treatment available are objectively proportionate to the prospects for improvement. To forego extraordinary or disproportionate means is not the equivalent of suicide or euthanasia; it rather expresses acceptance of the human condition in the face of death (*ibid.*).[5]

Unjust Laws and Conscience

Abortion and euthanasia are thus crimes which no human law can claim to legitimize. There is no obligation in conscience to obey such laws; instead there is a grave and clear obligation to oppose them by conscientious objection....In the case of an intrinsically unjust law, such as a law permitting abortion or euthanasia, it is therefore never licit to obey it, or to "take part in a propaganda campaign in favor of such a law, or vote for it...." (Congregation for the

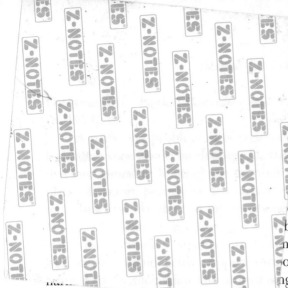

...can arise in cases where a ...passage of a more restric- ...of authorized abortions, in ...passed or ready to be voted ...d, when it is not possible to ...bortion law, an elected offi- ...n to procured abortion was ...osals aimed at limiting the ...ng its negative consequences at the level of general opinion and public morality. This does not in fact represent an illicit cooperation with an unjust law, but rather a legitimate and proper attempt to limit its evil aspects.[6]

Democratic Principles and the Promotion of Life

All have a responsibility for shaping society and developing cultural, economic, political and legislative projects which, with respect for all and in keeping with democratic principles, will contribute to the building of a society in which the dignity of each person is recognized and protected and the lives of all are defended and enhanced....The Church encourages political leaders, starting with those who are Christians, not to give in, but to make those choices which, taking into account what is realistically attainable, will lead to the re-establishment of a just order in the defense and promotion of the value of life.[7]

To Women Who Have Had an Abortion

The Church is aware of the many factors which may have influenced your decision, and she does not doubt that in many cases it was a painful and even shattering decision. The wound in your heart may not yet have healed. Certainly what happened was and remains terribly wrong. But do not give in to discouragement and do not lose hope....You will come to understand that nothing is definitively lost and you will also be able to ask forgiveness from your child, who is now living in the Lord.[8]

NOTES

1. *Evangelium vitae*, 18, in *AAS* 87 (1995), 420; *EncMiller*, 693–94; *Origins* 24:42 (1995), 696; *Pope Speaks* 40:4 (1995), 211.
2. Ibid., 27, 56, in *AAS* 87 (1995), 432, 464; *EncMiller*, 702, 723; *Origins* 24:42 (1995), 699, 709; *Pope Speaks* 40:4 (1995), 219, 240–41.
3. Ibid., 62, in *AAS* 87 (1995), 472; *EncMiller*, 729; *ND*, 2257; *Origins* 24:42 (1995), 711; *Pope Speaks* 40:4 (1995), 245.
4. Ibid., 63, in *AAS* 87 (1995), 473; *EncMiller*, 730; *ND*, 2258; *Origins* 24:42 (1995), 711; *Pope Speaks* 40:4 (1995), 246.
5. Ibid., 64–65, in *AAS* 87 (1995), 475–76; *EncMiller*, 731; *Origins* 24:42 (1995), 712; *Pope Speaks* 40:4 (1995), 247–48.
6. Ibid., 73, in *AAS* 87 (1995), 486–87; *EncMiller*, 739; *ND*, 2261a, 2261b, 2262; *Origins* 24:42 (1995), 715; *Pope Speaks* 40:4 (1995), 254–55.
7. Ibid., 90, in *AAS* 87 (1995), 503–4; *EncMiller*, 750–51; *ND*, 2263; *Origins* 24:42 (1995), 720; *Pope Speaks* 40:4 (1995), 265–66.
8. Ibid., 99, in *AAS* 87 (1995), 515; *EncMiller*, 758; *ND*, 2265; *Origins* 24:42 (1995), 723; *Pope Speaks* 40:4 (1995), 273.

CHAPTER TWELVE

Christian Spirituality

12.1 Earlier chapters in this book have already included extracts from the writings of John Paul II that illustrate his teaching on the practice of Christian and Catholic spiritual life. Chapters 1 and 3, for instance, drew some passages from his first encyclical, *Redemptor hominis* (The Redeemer of the Human Person), that vividly reflect the Christ-centered kind of life he proclaimed and personally practiced. When providing passages from his teaching on the sacraments, chapter 6 recalled the intense devotion to the Eucharist that visibly marked the life of the late pope. The same chapter also included some teaching on the sacrament of reconciliation, a sacrament that John Paul II received every Saturday, right through to the day he died. On the morning of Saturday, April 2, 2005, his confessor came to give a final absolution to the dying pope. A deeply spiritual vision colored much of the papal teaching that we have already provided. As two other examples we can cite what he wrote on sin (chapter 9) and the spirituality of work (chapter 10).

Nevertheless, it is worth adding further passages that indicate some particulars about the Christian spirituality that John Paul II taught and practiced. The centrality of this personal union with Christ shone through his whole pontificate, right from the homily he preached at the Mass that inaugurated his papal ministry in 1978. Two years later, in a discourse to senior citizens in Munich, he linked the trials of the elderly and the dying with the crucified Christ. His words on that occasion proved to be a prophetic sketch of what he himself was to experience in the final stages of his own life. Then the attempt on his life on May 13, 1981, prompted both a remarkable broadcast from his hospital bed the following Sunday (when it was still not clear that he would survive) and, three years later, his apostolic letter, *Salvifici doloris* (Suffering That Saves). Never before had official teaching ever developed so much teaching on the theme of suffering—or, more accurately, suffering with Christ.

Among the strikingly new features John Paul II introduced into the Jubilee Year of 2000 was the ecumenical celebration of witnesses to the faith in the twentieth century, held on May 7 at the Coliseum, a place that vividly evokes the witness of faith given by early Christian martyrs. The ceremony brought together Anglicans, Catholics, Orthodox, and Protestants to acknowledge the heroic example of countless men and women who bore witness to Christ in all parts of the world and left an extraordinary example to the present and future generations of Christians. In his 1994 apostolic letter *Tertio millennio adveniente* (The Arrival of the Third Millennium), John Paul II prepared the way for this celebration: "In our own century the martyrs have returned, many of them nameless, 'unknown soldiers,' as it were, of God's great cause. As far as possible, their witness should not be lost to the Church....This gesture cannot fail to have an ecumenical character and expression. Perhaps the most convincing form of ecumenism is the ecumenism of saints and martyrs. The *communio sanctorum* [communion of saints] speaks louder than the things that divide us" (no. 37). A year later John Paul II reflected on the witness of martyrdom in the 1993 encyclical *Veritatis splendor* (The Splendor of Truth) (nos. 90–93). In the 1995 encyclical *Ut unum sint* (That They May Be One), he would take up the theme of martyrdom in an ecumenical context (nos. 1, 74).

Accept Christ

Brothers and sisters! Fear not to welcome Christ and accept his power.

Help the pope and all who wish to serve Christ and by his power, to serve all of humankind! Do not be afraid! Open the doors to Christ, open them wide! Open the frontiers of states to his saving power, open the economic systems and the political systems, the vast realms of culture, civilization and development! Do not be afraid! Christ knows "what is in humans." He alone knows!

So often today human beings do not know what lies within themselves in the depths of their souls and hearts. So often they are uncertain of the meaning of their lives on this earth. They are attacked by doubt and the doubt turns into despair. I ask you, I implore you humbly and confidently: allow Christ to speak to you. Only he has the words of life, yes, of life that is eternal! On this very day the Church is celebrating World Mission Day. I ask you, therefore, to meditate on it and to act so that Christ's words of life may reach every human being and be received as a message of hope, salvation, and complete liberation.[1]

Christ with the Elderly and Dying

What can the pope say to this? How shall I console you? I do not want to take it too easy. I do not want to belittle the anxieties of old age, your weaknesses and illnesses, your helplessness and loneliness. But I would like to see them in a reconciling light, in the light of our Savior "who for us did sweat blood, who for us was scourged at the pillar, who for us was crowned with thorns."

In the trials of old age he is the companion of your pain, and you are his companions on his way of the cross. There is no tear you have to shed alone, and none you shed in vain (cf. Ps 56:9). By this suffering he has redeemed suffering, and through your suffering you cooperate in his salvation (cf. Col 1:24). Accept your suffering as his embrace and turn it into a blessing by accepting it from the hand of the Father. In his inscrutable, yet unquestionable wisdom and love he is using this to bring about your perfection. It is in the furnace that ore turns into gold (cf. 1 Pet 1:7); it is in the press that the grape becomes wine.

In this spirit, which God alone can give us, it becomes also easier to be understanding with those, who through negligence, carelessness, or heedlessness, add to our need, and it becomes possible for us to forgive also those who knowingly and even intentionally make us suffer without conceiving fully, however, how much pain they cause us. "Father, forgive them, for they do not know what they are doing"

(Luke 23:34). Also with regard to us was this word, which alone brings salvation, spoken....

The last consolation we are seeking together, my dear fellow pilgrims "in this vale of tears" (cf. Acts 20:35), is consolation in the face of death. Since our birth we have been going to meet it, but in old age we become more conscious of its approach from year to year, if only we do not drive it forcefully from our thoughts and feelings. The Creator has arranged it so that in old age accepting and standing the test of death is prepared for, made easier and learned in an almost natural manner. Hence becoming old, as we have seen, means a slow taking leave of the unbroken fullness of life, of unimpeded contact with the world.

The great school of living and dying then brings us to many an open grave; it makes us stand at many a deathbed before we are the ones around whom other people will be standing in prayer—so God grant. An old person has experienced such lessons of life in greater number than the young do. These people see them with increasing frequency. That is their great advantage on the way to that great threshold which we often in a biased way conceive of as being an abyss of night. The view across the threshold is dark from outside, but God in his love will allow those who have gone before us to accompany our lives and surround us with care more often than we think. The conviction of deep and living faith gave to a church in this city [Munich] the name of "All Souls' Church." Then two German churches in Rome are called: "St. Mary of the Cemetery"—*in Campo Santo*—and "St. Mary of the Holy Souls"—*Dell'anima*.

The more the fellow beings of our visible world reach the limits of their ability to help, the more we should see the messengers of the love of God in those who already have passed the test of death and who now wait for us over there: the saints, especially our personal patrons, and our deceased relatives and friends who we hope are at home in God's mercy. Many of you, my dear sisters and brothers, have lost the visible presence of partners. To you I direct my pastoral admonition: allow God ever more to be the partner of your lives; then you will also be united to the one whom he gave you as a companion once upon a time and who now himself has found his center in God.

Without familiarity with God there is in the very end no consolation on earth. For that is exactly what God intends with death! That at least in this one sublime hour of our life we allow ourselves to fall into his love without any other security than just this love of his. How could we show him our faith, our hopes, our love in a more lucid manner?

One last consideration in this context. I am sure it echoes the conviction of many a heart. Death itself is a consolation. Life on this earth, even if there were no "vale of tears," could not offer a home to us forever. It would turn more and more into prison, an "exile" (cf. *Salve Regina*). "For all that passes is just a likeness" (Goethe, *Faust*, *II*, final chorus); and so the words of St. Augustine, which never lose their color, come to our lips: "You have created us for you, Lord, and our heart is restless until it rests in you" (*Confessions*, 1.1.1). And so there are not these who are destined to die and those who remain in so-called life. What is awaiting all of us is a birth, a transformation. We fear the pains with Jesus on the Mount of Olives, but its radiant end we already carry within ourselves, since at our baptism we have been submerged in the death and victory of Jesus (cf. Rom 6:3; Col 2:12).[2]

After Being Shot (May 1981)

Praised be Jesus Christ! Beloved brothers and sisters, I know that during these days and especially in this hour of the *Regina Coeli* you are united with me. With deep emotion I thank you for your prayers and I bless you all. I am particularly close to the two persons wounded together with me. I pray for that brother of ours who shot me and whom I have sincerely pardoned. United with Christ, priest and victim, I offer my sufferings for the Church and for the world. To you, Mary, I repeat: *"Totus tuus ego sum"* (I belong entirely to you).[3]

Christ-Centered Prayer

All of her [St. Teresa of Avila's] prayer strives to draw near to the mystery of God, to Jesus, "having Jesus present" (*Life*, 4, 8). This consists of a personal encounter with him who is the only way that leads to the Father (*Interior Castle*, 6.7.6). Teresa reacted against the books which proposed contemplation as a vague assimilation into divinity (*Life*, 22, 1) or as a "thinking about nothing" (*Interior Castle*, 6.3.6), seeing in it a danger of folding in upon oneself, of separation from Jesus from whom we receive "all good things" (*Life*, 22, 4). Hence her exclamation: "to be separated from Christ...I cannot bear it" (*ibid.*, 22, 1). This exclamation applies also in our days against some methods of prayer which do not draw their inspiration from the Gospel and which practically tend to prescind from Christ, in favor of an empty mental state which has no meaning in Christianity. All means of prayer are valid inasmuch as they inspire us to know Christ, the Way, the Truth and the Life (cf. John 14:6).

It is true that the Christ of Teresian prayer goes beyond all corporeal imagination and all figurative representation (cf. *Life*, 9, 6). It is Christ resurrected, living and present, who goes beyond the limits of space and time, being at the same time human and divine (cf. *ibid.*, 27, 7–8). At the same time it is Jesus Christ son of the Virgin who accompanies us and helps us (*ibid.*, 27, 4).

Christ bridges the entire path of Teresian prayer from the first steps to the summit of perfect communion with God; Christ is the door through which the soul reaches the mystical state (cf. *ibid.*, 10, 1). Christ introduces us to the mystery of the Trinity (cf. *ibid.*, 27, 2–9). His presence in the unfolding of this "relationship of friendship," which is prayer, is required and necessary; he engenders it and makes it real. He also is the object of the same. He is the "living book," the Word of the Father (*ibid.*, 25, 5). We learn to remain in profound silence when Christ teaches us interiorly, "without noise or words" (cf. *Way of Perfection*, 25, 2); he empties himself in us when we are "gazing at the Crucified One" (cf. *Interior Castle*, 7.4.9). Teresian contemplation is not a search for subjective and hidden possibilities through technical methods which are without interior purification, but a means to open oneself in humility to Christ and to his mystical body which is the Church.[4]

Sharing in Christ's Suffering

While the first great chapter of the Gospel of suffering is written down, as the generations pass, by those who suffer persecutions for Christ's sake, simultaneously another great chapter of this Gospel unfolds through the course of history. This chapter is written by all those who suffer together with Christ, uniting their human sufferings to his salvific suffering. In these people there is fulfilled what the first witnesses of the Passion and Resurrection said and wrote about sharing in the sufferings of Christ. Therefore in those people there is fulfilled the Gospel of suffering, and, at the same time, each of them continues in a certain sense to write it: they write it and proclaim it to the world, they announce it to the world in which they live and to the people of their time.

Down through the centuries and generations it has been seen that in suffering there is concealed a particular power that draws a person interiorly close to Christ, a special grace. To this grace many saints, such as Saint Francis of Assisi, Saint Ignatius of Loyola and others, owe their profound conversion. A result of such a conversion is not only that the individual discovers the salvific meaning of suffering but above all that he becomes a completely new person. He discovers a new dimension, as it were, of his entire life and vocation. This discovery is a particular confirmation of the spiritual greatness which in human beings surpasses the body in a way that is completely beyond compare. When this body is gravely ill, totally incapacitated, and the person is almost incapable of living and acting, all the more do interior maturity and spiritual greatness become evident, constituting a touching lesson to those who are healthy and normal.

This interior maturity and spiritual greatness in suffering are certainly the *result* of a particular *conversion* and cooperation with the grace of the Crucified Redeemer. It is he himself who acts at the heart of human sufferings through his Spirit of truth, through the consoling Spirit. It is he who transforms, in a certain sense, the very substance of the spiritual life, indicating for the person who suffers a place close to himself. *It is he*, as the interior Master and Guide, *who reveals* to the suffering brother and sister this wonderful interchange, situated at the very heart of the mystery of the Redemption. Suffering is, in itself, an experience of evil. But Christ has made suffering the firmest basis of the definitive good, namely the good of eternal salvation. By his suffering on the Cross, Christ reached the very roots of evil, of sin and death. He conquered the author of evil, Satan, and his permanent rebellion against the Creator. To the suffering brother or sister Christ discloses and gradually reveals the horizons of the Kingdom of God: the horizons of a world converted to the Creator, of a world free from sin, a world being built on the saving power of love. And slowly but effectively, Christ leads into this world, into this Kingdom of the Father, suffering people, in a certain sense through the very heart of his suffering. For suffering cannot be transformed and changed by a grace from outside, but *from within*. And Christ through his own salvific suffering is very much present in every human suffering, and can act from within that suffering by the power of his Spirit of truth, his consoling Spirit.

This is not all: the Divine Redeemer wishes to penetrate the soul of every sufferer through the heart of his holy Mother, the first and the most exalted of all the redeemed. As though by a continuation of that motherhood which by the power of the Holy Spirit had given him life, the dying Christ conferred upon the ever Virgin Mary a *new kind of motherhood*, spiritual and universal, towards all human beings, so that every individual, during the pilgrimage of faith, might remain, together with her, closely united to him unto the Cross, and so that every form of suffering, given fresh life by the power of this Cross, should become no longer the weakness of humankind but the power of God.[5]

The Message of the Cross

Although you rightly look forward to the full recovery of your health, I would like however to invite you, dear sick people, not to undervalue the period you are going through right now. It too forms part of the design of Providence. We all know through direct experience, that suffering and illness belong to the condition of human beings, fragile and limited creatures that they are. It happens quite often that those who are afflicted by these things yield to the temptation of viewing them as a "chastisement" of God and, in consequence, begin to doubt the goodness of God whom Jesus has revealed to us as a "father" who *always* and *in spite of everything* loves his children.

In a society like today's, then, which claims to thrive on wellbeing and on consumerism and where everything is valued on the basis of efficiency and profit, the problem of sickness and of suffering, which cannot be denied, is either "removed" or people think it can be solved by relying exclusively on the means offered by advanced modern technology. All of this constitutes a veritable "challenge" for those who prove to be believers and who have from revelation, and above all from the Gospel, *an answer* to welcome into their own lives and to offer to the world as a sign of hope and as a light which gives meaning to existence. This is the "word of the Cross," which all who work in the world of health and of sickness are called to make their own, to witness to, and to announce to others.

You sick, especially! The Pope, having come among you today, says to you then: *look to Christ crucified and learn from him!* Having taken on the human condition totally he freely willed to bear the burden of human sufferings and, by offering himself to the Father as an innocent victim for us and for our salvation "with loud cries and tears" (Heb 5:7), he redeemed suffering, transforming it into a gift of love for the redemption of all. Sickness and suffering certainly are a "limitation" and a "trial"; they can therefore constitute a stumbling-block on the path of life. In the perspective of the Cross, however, they become *a moment of growth in faith* and an invaluable instrument for our own *contribution*, in union with Christ to the *fulfillment of the divine plan of salvation.*

Dear Patients, Brothers and Sisters, live your experience in this marvelous way! The help of God and the strength that comes from the Spirit Consoler will not be lacking to you. The Pope is with you and prays for you every day. This Church of Rome, called to spiritual renewal in the *Diocesan Synod*, is counting on your invaluable contribution of offering and supplication, so that it can live its fellowship in a more intense way and devote itself with renewed commitment to a "new evangelization" of the City.

The "word of the Cross" has a meaning for you too, health-care workers, who, at various levels and with various responsibilities, perform your service in the hospital. It is actually Jesus Christ who is hidden and revealed in the face and in the flesh, in the hearts and in the minds of those whom you are called to help and care for. When anything is done to one of these least brothers and sisters, to the sick who are often lonely and rejected by society, he considers it done to himself (cf. Matt 25:40).

This requires that you have interior attitudes, word and deeds which are inspired not only by a profound and rich humanity, but by an authentic spirit of faith and of charity. I know that you are already committed to this delicate and difficult mission. I exhort you nevertheless to grow and progress even farther in this direction.

I ask of you and, through you, of all those who work in the City health-care structures to overcome the temptation of indifference and selfishness and to work above all to *humanize hospitals and make them more livable* so that the sick person may be cared for in the totality of body and spirit. Work to see that *the fundamental rights and values of the human person* are recognized and promoted, and above all that of life, from its beginning to its natural end. This requires you to pay attention to the different situations; it demands respectful and patient dialogue, generous love for every human being viewed as an image of God and for those who are believers, as an "icon" of the suffering Christ.

This requires not only striking human qualities, professional skill and a serious desire to cooperate, but also a *profound moral cohesion* and a *mature awareness of the ethical values* which are at stake when life is threatened by sickness and death. We must approach the human being who suffers, like "good Samaritans," as Jesus did and as he taught all those who wished to be his disciples to do. We must know how to "see" the sufferings of our own brothers and sisters, not "passing them by" in the haste of laziness, but making them "neighbors," standing near them to speak words of consolation and administer the necessary attentions with acts of service and of love directed to the integral health of the human person. This is particularly the task of the *health-care apostolate*, which endeavors to bring about an effective presence of the Church to carry the light of the Gospel and the Lord's grace, through the sacraments, to those who suffer and those who take care of them, most of all to the family of the sick who are often more exposed to the consequences which suffering entails in human existence.[6]

Witnesses to Christ

Dear Brothers and Sisters united by faith in Jesus Christ! I am especially happy today to offer you my brotherly embrace of peace, as we commemorate together the witnesses to the faith in the twentieth century. I warmly greet the representatives of the Ecumenical Patriarchate and of the other Orthodox Sister Churches, as well as those of the ancient Churches of the East. I likewise thank the representatives of the Anglican Communion, of the worldwide Christian Communities of the West, and of the Ecumenical Organizations for their fraternal presence.

Gathered as we are at the Coliseum for this meaningful jubilee celebration, our coming together this evening is for all of us a source of great emotion. The monuments and ruins of ancient Rome speak to humanity of the sufferings and persecutions endured with fortitude by our forebears in the faith, the Christians of the first generations. These ancient remains remind us how true are the words of Tertullian who wrote: *"sanguis martyrum semen christianorum"*— the blood of the martyrs is the seed of new Christians (*Apol.*, 50,13).

The experience of the martyrs and the witnesses to the faith is not a characteristic only of the Church's beginnings but marks every epoch of her history. In the twentieth century, and maybe even more than in the first period of Christianity, there has been a vast number of men and women who bore witness to the faith through sufferings that were often heroic. How many Christians in the course of the twentieth century, on every continent, showed their love of Christ by the shedding of blood! They underwent forms of persecution both old and new; they experienced hatred and exclusion, violence and murder. Many countries of ancient Christian tradition once more became lands where fidelity to the Gospel demanded a very high price. In our century "the witness to Christ" borne even to the shedding of blood has become a common inheritance of Catholics, Orthodox, Anglicans and Protestants (*Tertio millennio adveniente*, 37).

The generation to which I belong experienced the horror of war, the concentration camps, persecution. In my homeland, during the Second World War, priests and Christians were deported to extermination camps. In Dachau alone some three thousand priests were interned. Their sacrifice was joined to that of many Christians from other European countries, some of whom belonged to other Churches and Ecclesial Communities.

I myself am a witness of much pain and many trials, having seen these in the years of my youth. My priesthood, from its very beginning, was marked "by the great sacrifice of countless men and women of my generation" (*Gift and Mystery*, p. 39). The experience of the Second World War and of the years following brought me to consider carefully and with gratitude the shining example of those who, from the beginning of the twentieth century to its end, met persecution, violence, death, because of their faith and because their behavior was inspired by the truth of Christ.

And there are so many of them! They must not be forgotten, rather they must be remembered and their lives documented. The names of many are unknown; the names of some have been denigrated by their persecutors, who tried to add disgrace to martyrdom; the names of others have been concealed by their executioners. But Christians preserve the memory of a great number of them. This is shown by the numerous replies to the invitation not to forget, received by the "New Martyrs" Commission within the Committee for the Great Jubilee. The Commission has worked hard to enrich and update the Church's memory with the witness of all those people, even those who are unknown, who "risked their lives for the sake of our Lord Jesus Christ" (Acts 15:26).[7]

12.2 Along with his Christ-centered spirituality, John Paul II constantly showed an intense devotion to Mary, the Mother of the Savior. Before he joined the Latin American bishops for the Third General Assembly at Puebla (January 1979), he went to pray at the Sanctuary of Our Lady of Guadalupe (outside Mexico City). She had her place in his first encyclical, published a few weeks later, *Redemptor hominis* (The Redeemer of the Human Person). That same year he made his first visit as pope to the United States; en route he stopped to pray at the Shrine of Our Lady of Knock (Ireland). In May 1981, when John Paul II was almost killed in St. Peter's Square, he attributed his survival to the Virgin Mary and made a pilgrimage of thanksgiving to Fatima (Portugal). In 1987 he dedicated an encyclical letter to her, *Redemptoris mater* (The Mother of the Redeemer). Naturally she appeared in his 1988 apostolic letter, *Mulieris dignitatem* (The Dignity of a Woman).

The Motherhood and Mystery of Mary

Mary is Mother of the Church because, on account of the Eternal Father's ineffable choice (*Lumen gentium*, 56) and due to the Spirit of Love's special action (*Lumen gentium*, 56), she gave human life to the Son of God, for whom and by whom all things exist (cf. Heb 2:10) and from whom the whole of the People of God receives the grace and dignity of election. Her Son explicitly extended his Mother's maternity in a way that could easily be understood by every soul and every heart by designating, when he was raised on the Cross, his beloved disciple as her son (cf. John 19:26). The Holy Spirit inspired her to remain in the Upper Room, after our Lord's Ascension, recollected in prayer and expectation, together with the Apostles, until the day of Pentecost, when the Church was to be born in visible form, coming forth from darkness (cf. Acts 1:14; 2). Later, all the generations of disciples, of those who confess and love Christ, like the Apostle John, spiritually took this Mother to their own homes (cf. John 19:27), and she was thus included in the history of salvation and in the Church's mission from the very beginning, that is, from the moment of the Annunciation. Accordingly, we who form today's generation of disciples of Christ all wish to unite ourselves with her in a special way. We do so with all our attachment to our ancient tradition and also with full respect and love for the members of all the Christian Communities.

We do so at the urging of the deep need of faith, hope and charity. For if we feel a special need, in this difficult and responsible phase of the history of the Church and of humankind, to turn to Christ, who is Lord of the Church and Lord of human history on account of the mystery of the Redemption, we believe that nobody else can bring us as Mary can into the divine and human dimension of this mystery. Nobody has been brought into it by God himself as Mary has. It is in this that the exceptional character of the grace of the divine Motherhood consists. Not only is the dignity of this Motherhood unique and unrepeatable in the history of the human race, but Mary's participation, due to this Maternity, in God's plan for human salvation through the mystery of the Redemption is also unique in profundity and range of action.

We can say that the mystery of the Redemption took shape beneath the heart of the Virgin of Nazareth when she pronounced her "fiat." From then on, under the special influence of the Holy Spirit, this heart, the heart of both a virgin and a mother, has always followed the work of her Son and has gone out to all those whom Christ has embraced and continues to embrace with inexhaustible love. For that reason her heart must also have the inexhaustibility of a mother. The special characteristic of the motherly love that the Mother of God inserts in the mystery of the redemption and the life of the Church finds expression in its exceptional closeness to human beings and all that happens to them. It is in this that the mystery of the Mother consists. The Church, which looks to her with altogether special love and hope, wishes to make this mystery her own in an ever deeper manner. For in this the Church also recognizes the way for her daily life, which is each person.

The Father's eternal love, which has been manifested in the history of humankind through the Son whom the Father gave, "that whoever believes in him should not perish but have eternal life" (John 3:16), comes close to each of us through this Mother and thus takes on signs that are more understandable and accessible to each person. Consequently, Mary must be present on all the roads of the daily life for the Church. Through her maternal presence the Church acquires certainty that she is truly living the life of her Master and Lord and that she is living the mystery of the Redemption in all its life-giving profundity and fullness. Likewise the Church, which has struck root in many varied fields of the life of the whole of present-day humanity, also acquires the certainty and, one could say, the experience of being close to human beings, to each person, of being each person's Church, the Church of the People of God.[8]

Mary's Journey of Faith

In the expression "Blessed is she who believed," we can…rightly find a kind of "key" which unlocks for us the innermost reality of Mary, whom the angel hailed as "full of grace." If as "full of grace" she has been eternally present in the mystery of Christ, through faith she became a sharer in that mystery in every extension of her earthly journey....From [the moment of Pentecost] there...begins that journey of faith, the Church's pilgrimage through the history of individuals and peoples. We know that at the beginning of this journey Mary is present. We see her in the midst of the Apostles in the Upper Room, "prayerfully imploring the gift of the Spirit" (*Lumen gentium*, 59).

In a sense her journey of faith is longer. The Holy Spirit had already come down upon her, and she became his faithful spouse at the Annunciation, welcoming the Word of the true God, offering "the full submission of intellect and will...and freely assenting to the truth revealed by him," indeed abandoning herself totally to God through "the obedience of faith" (*Dei Verbum*, 5)....

The Mediation of Mary

In effect, Mary's mediation is intimately linked with her motherhood. It possesses a specifically maternal character, which distinguishes it from the mediation of the other creatures who in various and always subordinate ways share in the one mediation of Christ, although her own mediation is also a shared mediation. In fact, while it is true that "no creature could ever be classed with the Incarnate Word and Redeemer," at the same time "the unique mediation of the Redeemer does not exclude but rather gives rise among creatures to a manifold cooperation which is but a sharing in this unique source." And thus "the one goodness of God is in reality communicated diversely to his creatures" (*Lumen gentium,* 62).[9]

The Dignity and Vocation of Women

The reality [woman-mother of God] determines the essential horizon of reflection on the dignity and the vocation of women. In anything we think, say or do concerning the dignity and the vocation of women, our thoughts, hearts and actions must not become detached from this horizon. The dignity of every human being and the vocation corresponding to that dignity find their definitive measure in union with God. Mary, the woman of the Bible, is the most complete expression of this dignity and vocation. For no human being, male or female, created in the image and likeness of God, can in any way attain fulfillment apart from this image and likeness.[10]

Virginity and Motherhood

Virginity and motherhood [are] two particular dimensions of the fulfillment of the female personality. In the light of the Gospel, they acquire their full meaning and value in Mary, who as a Virgin became the Mother of the Son of God. These *two dimensions of the female vocation* were united in her in an exceptional manner, in such a way that one did not exclude the other but wonderfully complemented it....Virginity and motherhood coexist in her: they do not mutually exclude each other or place limits on each other. Indeed, the person of the Mother of God helps everyone, especially women, to see how these two dimensions, these two paths in the vocation of women as persons, explain and complete each other.[11]

12.3 *Incarnationis mysterium* (The Mystery of the Incarnation), the "bull of indiction" or document fixing the dates of the jubilee year of 2000, included two major features of the "spiritual" teaching and personal practice of John Paul II: constant pilgrimages and requests for forgiveness from those whom Catholics have harmed and offended. On ninety-four occasions, he acknowledged the grave sins committed by Catholics against others, and asked pardon of Jews and Muslims, as well as from Protestant and Orthodox Christians. He proved an outstanding role model in trying to reconcile people. An unprecedented moment in the history of Catholic-Jewish relations was John Paul II's prayer (March 16, 2000) at the Western Wall; on his Holy Year pilgrimage to Jerusalem, he prayed in front of all that remains from the Temple compound after the Romans destroyed the city in AD 70.

The Value of Pilgrimage

In the course of its history, the institution of the Jubilee has been enriched by signs which attest to the faith and foster the devotion of the Christian people. Among these, the first is the notion of *pilgrimage*, which is linked to the situation of human beings who readily describe their life as a journey. From birth to death, the condition of each individual is that of the *homo viator*. Sacred Scripture, for its part, often attests to the special significance of setting out to go to sacred places....

Pilgrimages have always been a significant part of the life of the faithful, assuming different cultural forms in different ages. A pilgrimage evokes the believer's personal journey in the footsteps of the Redeemer: it is an exercise of practical asceticism, of repentance for human weaknesses, of constant vigilance over one's own frailty, of interior preparation for a change of heart. Through vigils, fasting and prayer, the pilgrim progresses along the path of Christian perfection, striving to attain, with the support of God's grace, "the state of the perfect man, to the measure of the full maturity of Christ" (Eph 4:13).[12]

Asking Pardon

God of our fathers,
You chose Abraham and his descendants
to bring your Name to the Nations:
we are deeply saddened
by the behavior of those
who in the course of history
have caused these children of yours to suffer,
and asking your forgiveness
we wish to commit ourselves
to genuine brotherhood
with the people of the Covenant.[13]

NOTES

1. *Inaugural Homily of Pontificate (October 22, 1978)*, in *AAS* 70 (1978), 947; *Origins* 8:20 (1978), 307–8.

2. *Address to Senior Citizens in Munich (November 19, 1980)*, 4, 7, in *Pope Speaks* 26:3 (1981), 260–61, 262–3.

3. *Tape Recorded Message in St. Peter's Square (May 17, 1981)* in *Origins* 11:2 (1981), 17.

4. *Homily in Avila (November 1, 1982)*, in *AAS* 75 (1983), 256–57; *Origins* 12:22 (1982), 359–60; *Pope Speaks* 28:2 (1982), 114–15.

5. *Salvifici doloris*, 26, in *AAS* 76 (1984), 238–40; *Origins* 13:37 (1984), 621; *Pope Speaks* 29:2 (1984), 130–32.

6. *Address to the Sick and Staff in a Hospital in Rome (April 1, 1990)*, in *OREnglish*, 18 (April 30, 1990), 8.

7. *Address at the Coliseum (May 7, 2000)*, in *AAS* 92 (2000), 677–79; *Origins* 30:1 (2000), 4–5.

8. *Redemptor hominis*, 22, in *AAS* 71 (1979), 321–23; *EncMiller*, 87–89; *Origins* 8:40 (1979), 642–43; *Pope Speaks* 24:2 (1979), 145–46.

9. *Redemptoris mater*, 19, 26, 38, in *AAS* 79 (1987), 384, 394–95; 411; *EncMiller*, 333, 339, 350; *ND*, 721, a, b, c; *Origins* 16:43 (1987), 753, 755, 759; *Pope Speaks* 32:2 (1987), 171, 177, 186.

10. *Mulieris dignitatem*, 5, in *AAS* 80 1988), 1661–62; *ND*, 723; *Origins* 18:17 (1988), 265; *Pope Speaks* 34:1 (1989), 14–15.

11. Ibid., 17, in *AAS* 80 (1988), 1692–93; *ND*, 724; *Origins* 18:17 (1988), 273; *Pope Speaks* 34:1 (1989), 30.

12. *Incarnationis mysterium*, 7, in *AAS* 91 (1999), 135–36; *ND*, 1692/2; *Origins* 28:26 (1998), 449; *Pope Speaks* 44:3 (1999), 184–85.

13. For the history of this prayer at the Western Wall as well as its text see Edward I. Cassidy, *Ecumenism and Interreligious Dialogue* (New York: Paulist, 2005), 214–26.

Alphabetical List of Documents Quoted and Summary of the Contents of Each

Ad gentes (To The Nations)—Decree of Vatican II on Missionary Activity (1965).

Anno ineunte (The Beginning of the Year)—A 1967 brief of Pope Paul VI indicating his willingness to do everything possible to "re-establish full communion between the Church of the West and that of the East," the "sister Churches."

Apostolicam actuositatem (Apostolic Activity)—The 1965 Decree of Vatican II on the apostolate of the laity.

Catechesi tradendae (Handing on Catechesis)—A 1979 apostolic exhortation by Pope John Paul II on catechesis in our time.

CELAM (Conferencia General del Episcopado Latinoamericano y del Caribe)—The Bishops' Conference of Latin America and the Caribbean founded in 1955 by Pope Pius XII.

Centesimus annus (The Hundredth Year)—The 1991 encyclical of Pope John Paul II issued on the hundredth anniversary of Pope Leo XIII's encyclical on labor (*Rerum novarum*).

Christifideles laici (The Lay Faithful)—The apostolic exhortation of Pope John Paul II written after the 1987 Synod of Bishops on the vocation and mission of the lay faithful in the church and in the world.

Dei Filius (The Son of God)—Vatican I's 1870 dogmatic constitution on the Catholic faith.

Dei Verbum (The Word of God)—Vatican II's 1965 dogmatic constitution on divine revelation.

Dies Domini (The Day of the Lord)—The 1998 apostolic letter of Pope John Paul II on keeping the Lord's Day holy.

Dignitatis humanae (Human Dignity)—Vatican II's 1965 declaration on the right of persons and of communities to social and civil and religious freedom in matters religious.

Dives in misericordia (Rich in Mercy)—Pope John Paul II's 1980 encyclical on the mercy of God.

Divino afflante Spiritu (With the Breathing of the Divine Spirit)—The 1943 encyclical of Pope Pius XII on promoting biblical studies and commemorating the fiftieth anniversary of *Providentissimus Deus.*

Divinum illud (That Divine [Office])—The 1897 encyclical of Pope Leo XIII on the Holy Spirit.

Dominicae cenae (The Lord's Supper)—A Holy Thursday (1980) letter of Pope John Paul II on the mystery and worship of the Eucharist.

Dominum et vivificantem (The Lord and Giver of Life)—The 1986 encyclical of Pope John Paul II on the Holy Spirit in the life of the church and the world.

Donum vitae (The Gift of Life)—A 1987 instruction of the Congregation for the Doctrine of the Faith concerning respect for human life in its origin and on the dignity of procreation, replying to certain questions of the day.

Ecclesia de Eucharistia (The Church from the Eucharist)—The 2003 encyclical of Pope John Paul II on the Eucharist and on its relationship to the church.

Ecclesia in America (The Church in America)—Pope John Paul II's apostolic exhortation after the 1999 Synod of Bishops on the encounter with the living Jesus Christ, the way to conversion, communion, and solidarity in America.

Enchiridion Biblicum (cf. *EB* in abbreviations)—The standard collection of church documents on scripture.

Euntes in mundum universum (Going into the Whole World)—The 1988 apostolic letter of Pope John Paul II commemorating the millennium of the baptism of Rus of Kiev.

Evangelium nuntiandi (Proclaiming the Gospel)—The 1975 apostolic exhortation of Pope Paul VI on bringing the good news to all strata of humanity.

Evangelium vitae (The Gospel of Life)—The 1995 encyclical of Pope John Paul II on the value and inviolability of human life.

Familiaris consortio (The Family)—Pope John Paul II's 1981 apostolic exhortation on the role of the Christian family in the modern world.

Fides et ratio (Faith and Reason)—The 1998 encyclical of Pope John Paul II on the relationship between faith and reason.

Gaudium et spes (Joy and Hope)—Vatican II's 1965 pastoral constitution on the church in the modern world.

Humani generis (The Human Race)—The 1950 encyclical of Pope Pius XII concerning some false opinions threatening to undermine the foundations of Catholic doctrine.

Incarnationis mysterium (The Mystery of the Incarnation)—The 1998 "Bull of Indiction" issued by Pope John Paul II convoking the great jubilee of the year 2000.

Laborem exercens (Performing Work)—Pope John Paul II's 1981 encyclical on human work on the ninetieth anniversary of *Rerum novarum.*

Lumen gentium (The Light of Nations)—Vatican II's dogmatic constitution on the church promulgated in 1964.

Mulieris dignitatem (The Dignity of a Woman)—The 1998 apostolic letter of Pope John Paul II on the dignity and vocation of women on the occasion of the Marian year.

Mysterium fidei (Mystery of Faith)—Pope Paul VI's 1965 encyclical on the Eucharist.

Nostra aetate (In Our Age)—Vatican II's 1965 declaration on the relation of the church to non-Christian religions.

Novo millennio ineunte (The Beginning of the New Millennium)—The 2001 apostolic letter of Pope John Paul II issued at the close of the great jubilee of the year 2000.

Pastor aeternus (Eternal Shepherd)—Vatican I's 1870 dogmatic constitution on the church.

Pastores dabo vobis (I Will Give You Shepherds)—Pope John Paul II's apostolic exhortation after the 1992 Synod of Bishops on the formation of priests in the circumstances of the present day.

Pastores gregis (Shepherds of the Flock)—The apostolic exhortation published by Pope John Paul II after the 2003 Synod of Bishops on the bishop, servant of the gospel of Jesus Christ for the hope of the world.

Populorum progressio (The Development of Peoples)—A 1967 encyclical of Pope Paul VI on the development of peoples.

Presbyterorum ordinis (The Order of Priests)—The 1965 decree on the ministry and life of priests issued by Pope Paul VI.

Providentissimus Deus (The Most Provident God)—Pope Leo XIII's 1893 encyclical on the study of holy scripture.

Reconciliatio et paenitentia (Reconciliation and Penance)—The 1984 apostolic exhortation of Pope John Paul II following the Synod of Bishops on reconciliation and penance.

Redemptor hominis (The Redeemer of the Human Person)—The 1979 encyclical of Pope John Paul II on redemption and the dignity of the human race.

Redemptoris mater (The Mother of the Redeemer)—The 1987 encyclical of Pope John Paul II on the Blessed Virgin Mary in the life of the pilgrim church.

Redemptoris missio (The Mission of the Redeemer—Pope John Paul II's 1990 encyclical on the permanent validity of the church's missionary mandate.

Rerum novarum (Of New Things)—Pope Leo XIII's 1891 encyclical on capital and labor.

Sacrosanctum concilium (The Sacred Council)—Vatican II's 1963 constitution on the sacred liturgy.

Salvifici doloris (Suffering That Saves)—The 1984 apostolic letter of Pope John Paul II on the Christian meaning of human suffering.

Slavorum apostoli (The Apostles of the Slavs)—Pope John Paul II's 1985 encyclical commemorating the eleventh centenary of the evangelizing work of Sts. Cyril and Methodius.

Sollicitudo rei socialis (Concern for Social Matters)—The 1987 encyclical of Pope John Paul II commemorating the twentieth anniversary of *Populorum progressio*.

Tertio millennio adveniente (The Arrival of the Third Millennium)—The 1994 apostolic letter of Pope John Paul II on preparation for the jubilee of the year 2000.

Unitatis redintegratio (The Restoration of Unity)—Vatican II's 1964 decree on ecumenism.

Ut unum sint (That They May Be One)—Pope John Paul II's 1995 encyclical on commitment to ecumenism.

Veritatis splendor (The Splendor of Truth)—The 1993 encyclical of Pope John Paul II regarding certain fundamental questions of the church's moral teaching.

Vicesimus quintus annus (The Twenty-fifth Year)—The 1988 apostolic letter of Pope John Paul II on the twenty-fifth anniversary of the promulgation of the conciliar constitution *Sacrosanctum concilium* on the sacred liturgy.

Vigilantiae (Of Vigilance)—Pope Leo XIII's 1902 apostolic letter establishing the Pontifical Biblical Commission.

Vita consecrata (The Consecrated Life)—Pope John Paul II's 1996 apostolic exhortation following the Synod of Bishops' deliberations on the consecrated life and its mission in the church and in the world.

Chronological List of Documents Quoted

Dei Filius (1870)—Vatican I's dogmatic constitution of the Catholic faith.

Pastor aeternus (1870)—Vatican I's dogmatic constitution on the church.

Rerum novarum (1891)—Pope Leo XIII's encyclical on capital and labor.

Providentissimus Deus (1893)—Pope Leo XIII's encyclical on the study of holy scripture.

Divinum illud (1897)—Pope Leo XIII's encyclical on the Holy Spirit.

Vigilantiae (1902)—Pope Leo XIII's apostolic letter establishing the Pontifical Biblical Commission.

Divino afflante Spiritu (1943)—Pope Pius XII's encyclical on promoting biblical studies and commemorating the fiftieth anniversary of *Providentissimus Deus*.

Humani generis (1950)—Pope Pius XII's encyclical concerning some false opinions threatening to undermine the foundations of Catholic doctrine.

CELAM (1955)—The Bishops' Conference of Latin America and the Caribbean founded by Pope Pius XII.

Sacrosanctum concilium (1963)—Vatican II's constitution on the sacred liturgy.

Lumen gentium (1964)—Vatican II's dogmatic constitution on the church.

Unitatis redintegratio (1964)—Vatican II's decree on ecumenism.

Ad gentes (1965)—Decree of Vatican II on missionary activity.

Apostolicam actuositatem (1965)—Decree of Vatican II on the apostolate of the laity.

Dei Verbum (1965)—Vatican II's dogmatic constitution on divine revelation.

Dignitatis humanae (1965)—Vatican II's declaration on the right of persons and of communities to social and civil and religious freedom in matters religious.

Gaudium et spes (1965)—Vatican II's pastoral constitution on the church in the modern world.

Mysterium fidei (1965)—Pope Paul VI's encyclical on the eucharist.

Nostra aetate (1965)—Vatican II's declaration on the relation of the Church to non-Christian religions.

Presbyterorum ordinis (1965)—Pope Paul VI's decree on the ministry and life of priests.

Anno ineunte (1967)—A brief of Pope Paul VI indicating his willingness to do everything possible to "re-establish full communion between the Church of the West and that of the East," the "sister Churches."

Populorum progressio (1967)—Pope Paul VI's encyclical on the development of peoples.

Evangelium nuntiandi (1975)—The apostolic exhortation of Pope Paul VI on bringing the good news to all strata of humanity.

Catechesi tradendi (1979)—An apostolic exhortation by Pope John Paul II on catechesis in our time.

Redemptor hominis (1979)—Pope John Paul II's encyclical on redemption and the dignity of the human race.

Dives in misericordia (1980)—Pope John Paul II's encyclical on the mercy of God.

Dominicae cenae (1980)—A Holy Thursday letter of Pope John Paul II on the mystery and worship of the Eucharist.

Familiaris consortio (1981)—Pope John Paul II's apostolic exhortation on the role of the Christian family in the modern world.

Laborem exercens (1981)— Pope John Paul II's encyclical on human work on the ninetieth anniversary of *Rerum novarum*.

Reconciliatio et paenitentia (1984)—The apostolic exhortation of Pope John Paul II following the Synod of Bishops on reconciliation and penance.

Salvifici doloris (1984)—The apostolic letter of Pope John Paul II on the Christian meaning of human suffering.

Slavorum apostoli (1985)—Pope John Paul II's encyclical commemorating the eleventh centenary of the evangelizing work of Sts. Cyril and Methodius.

Dominum et vivificantem (1986)—The encyclical of Pope John Paul II on the Holy Spirit in the life of the church and the world.

Christifideles laici (1987)—The apostolic exhortation of Pope John Paul II written after the Synod of Bishops on the vocation and mission of the lay faithful in the church and in the world.

Donum vitae (1987)—An instruction of the Congregation for the Doctrine of the Faith concerning respect for human life in its origin and on the dignity of procreation, replying to certain questions of the day.

Redemptoris mater (1987)—Pope John Paul II's encyclical on the Blessed Virgin Mary in the life of the pilgrim church.

Sollicitudo rei socialis (1987)—Pope John Paul II's encyclical commemorating the twentieth anniversary of *Populorum progressio*.

Euntes in mundum universum (1988)—The apostolic letter of Pope John Paul II commemorating the millennium of the baptism of Rus of Kiev.

Vicesimus quintus annus (1988)—The apostolic letter of Pope John Paul II on the twenty-fifth anniversary of the promulgation of the conciliar constitution *Sacrosanctum concilium* on the sacred liturgy.

Redemptoris missio (1990)—Pope John Paul II's encyclical on the permanent validity of the church's missionary mandate.

Centesimus annus (1991)—The encyclical of Pope John Paul II issued on the hundredth anniversary of Pope Leo XIII's encyclical on labor and capital (*Rerum novarum*).

Pastores dabo vobis (1992)—Pope John Paul II's apostolic exhortation after the Synod of Bishops on the formation of priests in the circumstances of the present day.

Veritatis splendor (1993)—Pope John Paul II's encyclical regarding certain fundamental questions of the church's moral teaching.

Tertio millennio adveniente (1994)—The apostolic letter of Pope John Paul II on preparation for the jubilee of the year 2000.

Evangelium vitae (1995)—The encyclical of Pope John Paul II on the value and inviolability of human life.

Ut unum sint (1995)—Pope John Paul II's encyclical on commitment to ecumenism.

Vita consecrata (1996)—Pope John Paul II's apostolic exhortation following the Synod of Bishops' deliberations on the consecrated life and its mission in the church and in the world.

Dies Domini (1998)—The apostolic letter of Pope John Paul II on keeping the Lord's Day holy.

Fides et ratio (1998)—Pope John Paul II's encyclical on the relationship between faith and reason.

Incarnationis mysterium (1998)—The "Bull of Indiction" issued by Pope John Paul II convoking the great jubilee of the year 2000.

Mulieris dignitatem (1998)—The apostolic letter of Pope John Paul II on the dignity and vocation of women on the occasion of the Marian year.

Ecclesia in America (1999)—Pope John Paul II's apostolic exhortation after the Synod of Bishops on the encounter with the living Jesus Christ, the way to conversion, communion, and solidarity in America.

Novo millennio ineunte (2001)—The apostolic letter of Pope John Paul II issued at the close of the great jubilee of the year 2000.

Ecclesia de Eucharistia (2003)—The encyclical of Pope John Paul II on the Eucharist and in its relationship to the church.

Pastores gregis (2003)—The apostolic exhortation given by John Paul II after the Synod of Bishops on the bishop, servant of the gospel of Jesus Christ for the hope of the world.

Indexes

II. Documents, Names, and Subjects

Pope John Paul II: A Reader